Autobiographies
by
Americans of Color
1980-1994

Autobiographies
by
Americans of Color
1980-1994:

An Annotated Bibliography

by

Rebecca   Stuhr-Rommereim

The Whitston Publishing Company
Troy, New York
1997

Library of Congress Catalog Card Number 96-60510

ISBN 0-87875-466-0

Printed in the United States of America

To my husband John,
and to my children Martin and Helen.

CONTENTS

Acknowledgments

I am grateful for the assistance and help of many people. Working on a project such as this has made me fully aware of how interdependent we all are. I would like to thank first and foremost Deborah Stuhr Iwabuchi, who acted as editor and advisor from the early stages of my work on this book. Her assistance was invaluable and I am extremely grateful to her for her time and effort. I extend my most sincere thanks to Betty Moffett of the Grinnell College Writing Lab for taking the time to read through my completed manuscript. She showed an interest in, and enthusiasm for, my research which was encouraging. I can not show enough gratitude to my colleagues at the Grinnell College Libraries who consistently offered me support, encouragement, and patience, and to the director of the Library, Christopher McKee, who also provided me with time to complete this book. Shealey Sieck and Russ Motta, of the Grinnell College Libraries Interlibrary Loan department, cheerfully provided me with hundreds of the books I needed. I was never without a stack of books to read. I had assistance from three outstanding Grinnell College students, Emily Bogusch, Amy Goldmacher, and Darcie Rives. I thank all of my friends and family who listened to me talk about my work on this book and especially my good friend, Lisa Hughes, who provided me with the moral support and confidence I needed to pursue this project in the first place. And finally, my most sincere thanks to Grinnell College for its support in the form of a sabbatical leave and two faculty grants without which this book would never have been written.

R. S.
Grinnell College

Introduction

The past twenty-five years have seen a steady increase in the writing of autobiography. The number of autobiographies included in this bibliography which were published during the first five years of the 1990s is exactly twice the number of autobiographies included which were published during the first five years of the 1980s (220 vs. 110). This growing number of personal stories made public encompasses a rich diversity of cultures, personalities, motivations, and, of course, experiences. There has been some scholarly discussion of what constitutes autobiography, and I believe the definition is wide open. Philippe Lejeune writes in "The Autobiographical Contract" that a work can be called an autobiography if the author of the work, the narrator, and the subject of the work all have the same name, and if the author claims to be telling the truth. He defines autobiography to be "a retrospective prose narrative produced by a real person concerning his own existence, focusing on his individual life, in particular on the development of his personality" (p. 193). Lynn Z. Bloom includes partial and full-length self portraits, dual portraits, group histories, diaries, letters, oral histories, collections of personal narratives, slave narratives, accounts of particular events, and blends of fiction, myth, and personal narrative (p. 171) among the kinds of literature that she would categorize as autobiography in her article "American Autobiography: the Changing Critical Canon." James Olney, in his book *Metaphors of Self*, includes poetry as a permissible genre for autobiography, and presents an extensive discussion of the autobiographical nature of T. S. Eliot's *Four Quartets*.

I have not applied a strict definition of autobiography in this compilation, and the term may seem to have been liberally applied in some instances. I did not include autobiographical fiction, but some works border on the fictional, such as Ray Young

Bear's *Black Eagle Child*, Maxine Hong Kingston's *Warrior Woman*, and Oscar Zeta Acosta's *Autobiography of a Brown Buffalo* and *Revolt of the Cockroach People*. Some of the books included are non-autobiographical collections of essays critiquing some aspect of society, but they nonetheless provide insight into the workings of the mind of the author. Some examples of this type of book are Richard Rodriguez' *Days of Obligation: An Argument With My Mexican Father*, Pat Mora's *Nepantla: Essays From the Land in the Middle*, Nikki Giovanni's *Racism 101*, and Patricia Williams' *The Alchemy of Race and Rights*. A few of the works are family histories, focusing on parents, children, or siblings, but including the experiences, impressions, and feelings of the author. The works of internationally-recognized writers and unknown individuals whose autobiographies may be their first and perhaps their only written work, oral testimonies instigated by the subject or by a third party, and "as told to" or "written with" works by celebrities or other socially-prominent people are all included in this bibliography. I have excluded straight interviews, theses and dissertations, and unpublished materials such as typescripts. Also excluded are journal articles or isolated autobiographical chapters (the entries for Lucille Clifton and Haunani-Kay Trask might be considered exceptions to this policy). As one last detail, I will point out that there were 20 or so books that I was unable to locate, and these have been left unannotated.

Although this book aims at a comprehensive presentation of material published since 1980, I have, no doubt, overlooked some books. The autobiographies of sports stars and other high-profile celebrities are more difficult to track down because these individuals have transcended society's need (or perhaps merely that of the Library of Congress) to categorize citizens by race. There are a number of idiosyncrasies in this compilation surrounding the limitation of dates. It is easy enough to select a cut off date (although it is tempting to include the autobiographies published during 1995), but it is difficult to define a clear starting date. The overall goal of this bibliography is to serve as a practical tool: it should establish the existence of this material and gather it together at one access point; it should also enable the reader to obtain as many of these books as possible either from book stores or libraries. A number of these autobiographies were written in the nineteenth century. Some were published at that time and only reprinted for the first time after 1980, whereas some were never published until after 1980. The peruser of this bibliography will find citations for books that were published in the decades preceding 1980, but which have been republished within the defined time frame, sometimes with new material or revisions. For the most part, however, I have not annotated this category of older books. Many of them will have been annotated in one of the several important bibliographies that should be consulted along with this one: Russell Brignano's *Black Americans in Autobiography*, David Brumble's *An Annotated Bibliography of American Indian and Eskimo Autobiographies*, Lynn Woods O'Brien's *Plains Indians Autobiographies*, and Briscoe, et al., *American Autobiography, 1945-1980*.

The entries are arranged alphabetically by author, except in one or two instances. Ethnic identification is provided by the index. Authors who are members of tribal groups are indexed by tribe and by the terms "Native American," or "Native Alaskan." "Chicano-Chicana" is used for American-born authors of Mexican descent. Writers born in Mexico are indexed under "Mexican American." In a few cases, because it seemed as though this is what the writer would wish, "Hispanic" has been used. Although it sounds awkward, and I apologize for this, writers from India have been indexed by the phrase "East Indian American" or "East Indian."

The appropriateness of autobiography as a genre for individuals who view themselves as, or are regarded as being, outside of the western European writing tradition has been explored by a number of theorists. David Brumble discusses this issue as it relates to the oral tradition of most Native American tribal groups in his Book *American Indian Autobiography*. He examines specific examples of types of stories which he would describe as autobiographical in nature even if they do not conform to what is considered to be the western autobiographical tradition, and, therefore, finds that autobiography is a natural means of expression for Native Americans. Frank Chin, in his provocative article, "This is Not an Autobiography," argues that autobiography is an inappropriate form for American writers of Chinese descent. He identifies autobiography with the Christian confessional tradition as exemplified by St. Augustine, and sees no place for Chinese American writers within this tradition.

Susanna Egan makes a powerful case for the power of autobiography as a survival tool for members of marginalized groups, including racial minorities, women, the working class, and gay and lesbian individuals. In her article, "The Changing Faces of Heroism," she describes the typical autobiography of an earlier era typified in the United States by the autobiographies of Ben Franklin, Henry Adams, and Henry David Thoreau. These men wrote toward the end of their lives when their reputations and value to society were already established. They were members of the ruling class. They assumed themselves to be the inheritors, as well as the conduits of a rich cultural heritage, a heritage which, without doubt, would be shared by their readers. In contrast, the new autobiographer, as described by Egan, does not come from the elite. According to Egan, "we now find literary talent and a strong autobiographical impulse emerging from all walks of life. . . . The palm has passed from white, middle class men of distinction to the . . . minorities of our culture who write precisely because of their lack of other kinds of power and their need to be heard" (p. 23). These authors write about rebellion and survival. Rather than looking back on a heroic journey, they are most likely writing in the midst of their lives. The end of the journey is yet to come, the problems they confront are still unresolved, their success or failure remains unevaluated. By writing, they establish their place in history, making their particular experiences, thoughts, and actions part of the permanent written record. Egan maintains that the very act of writing for "this modern crop of autobiographers . . . is not a matter of explanation, apology, or clarification of public record, but entirely a matter of survival" (p. 27).

This fight to affirm the value of self is clearly apparent in the autobiographies of the poet Jimmy Santiago Baca, who describes his prison ordeal; the journalist Jill Nelson, who writes about her experiences at the *Washington Post*; Melba Pattillo Beals, who survived a year-long fight to desegregate Central High School in Little Rock; the poet Louis Rodriguez, who opens his story with his fears for the spiritual and physical survival of his son; Sanyika Shakur, who writes from prison; Elaine Brown, the former Black Panther Leader, who ends her story with her escape from her former comrades; Assata Shakur, who was targeted by the FBI's COINTEL program; and Norma Marcere and Ruthie Bolton, who sought to re-establish a sense of personal value after having been victims of physical and emotional abuse.

By affixing their personal story onto the larger history of

society, these autobiographers have also made it possible for those who share aspects of their recorded experiences to find a place for themselves in this society and in history. Many of the autobiographers included in this compilation relate their feelings upon first discovering their cultural heritage, either through books or from some knowledgeable mentor. Through writing, they gain an entirely new perspective of themselves in the world. These autobiographies, then, provide numerous opportunities for readers with similar experiences to find inspiration.

It is also important to share these stories with those individuals who believe they cannot relate to such narratives, or who would like to believe that they are untouched by the many struggles depicted within the stories. Johnetta Cole writes in her forward to Gloria Wade-Gayles's autobiography that "the recollections of one black woman become the mirror into which each of us can see how alike and how different we are. We can encounter the exquisite diversity and amazing similarity in the human condition" (p. viii). Julius Lester emphasizes the importance of understanding the experiences of others in his essay "Tied in a Single Garment." He writes that

> . . . to understand racism we must use our imaginations
> and enter the lives of others. Understanding racism re-
> quires us to know in the marrow of our beings that the
> way in which we experience the world is not how oth-
> ers always experience it, and more important, the way
> we experience the world is not the only way or even the
> best. (p. 26)

The stories in these autobiographies show us that while our frames of reference and our individual circumstances cause each of us to have a unique outlook and a unique collection of experiences, we share the basic human need for love and acceptance, we share many of the same aspirations, hopes and fears, and we long for a certain spiritual fulfillment.

We are experiencing, in this decade of the nineties, a political backlash against, and an open hostility toward differences of race, socio-economic status, and issues of gender and sexual preference. We need more than ever to understand each other, to have insight into the experiences of all citizens of this country, to acknowledge that we are all, indeed, no matter what our ethnic background or number of years in residence, citizens of the United States. These life stories provide *all* readers with a broad, and perhaps truer sense of U. S. history than it is possible to obtain from a text book or scholarly journal. I consider it a privilege to have encountered each of these books. I have gained new perspective and a deepened understanding of many issues to which I might otherwise have remained oblivious. I hope that these stories will enlighten all of us to the variety of individuals living in this country, and to the myriad cultures which we are fortunate to share. We have all gained from each other, and our "American culture" changes each time a new person arrives. None of us is untouched by the other.

I prepared this bibliography in part for my own children, who are growing up in a small midwestern town. Except for the racially-mixed nature of their own extended family, they lead a fairly homogeneous existence. I hope that the knowledge I have gained in preparing this bibliography can be passed on to them, and that, when at some point they are able to read these life stories, they will develop an understanding of all that it means to be a citizen of this country.

Works Cited

Bloom, Lynn Z. "American Autobiography: the Changing Critical Canon." *Auto/Biography Studies:A/B* 9.2 (Fall 1994): 167-180.

Brignano, Russell. *Black Americans in Autobiography: An Annotated Bibliography of Autobiographies and Autobiographical Books Written Since the Civil War.* Durham, NC: Duke University Press, 1984.

Briscoe, Mary Louise, Lynn Z. Bloom and Barbara Tobias. *American Autobiography, 1945-1980: A Bibliography.* Madison: University of Wisconsin Press, 1982.

Brumble, H. David III. "A Supplement to an *An Annotated Bibliography of American Indian and Eskimo Autobiographies.*" *Western American Literature* 17 (1982): 243-260.

—. *American Indian Autobiography.* Berkeley: University of California Press, 1988.

—. *An Annotated Bibliography of American Indian and Eskimo Autobiographies.* Lincoln: University of Nebraska Press, 1981.

Chin, Frank. "This is Not an Autobiography." *Genre* 17 (June 1985): 109-130.

Egan, Susanna. "The Changing Faces of Heroism: Some Questions Raised by Contemporary Autobiography." *Biography* 10.1 (1987): 20-38.

Lejeune, Philippe. "The Autobiographical Contract" in *French Literary Theory Today*. Ed. Tvetan Todorov. NY: Cambridge University Press, 1982.

Lester, Julius. "Tied in a Single Garment." *Hungry Mind Review*. 31 (September 1994).

O'Brien, Lynne Woods. *Plains Indian Autobiographies*. Western Writers Series. 10. Boise: Boise State College, 1973.

Olney, James. *Metaphors of Self: The Meaning of Autobiography*. Princeton: Princeton University Press, 1972.

Additional Reading

Bataille, Gretchen M. and Kathleen Mullen Sands. *American Indian Women, Telling Their Lives*. Lincoln: University of Nebraska Press, 1984.

Eakin, John Paul, ed. *American Autobiography: Retrospect and Prospect*. Wisconsin Studies in Autobiography. Madison: University of Wisconsin Press, 1991.

Holte, James C. "The Representative Voice: Autobiography and the Ethnic Voice." *MELUS: Society for the Study of the Multi-Ethnic Literature of the United States* 9.2 (June 1982): 25-46.

Kazin, Alfred. "Autobiography as Narrative." *Michigan Quarterly Review* 3 (September 1964): 210-216.

Krupat, Arnold. *For Those Who Come After: A Study of Native American Autobiography*. Berkeley: University of California Press, 1985.

Lidoff, Joan. "Autobiography in a Different Voice: Maxine Hong Kingston's *The Woman Warrior*." *Auto/Biography Studies: A/B* 3.3 (Fall 1987): 29-35.

Nericcio, William Anthony. "Autobiographies at *La Frontera*: The Quest for Mexican-American Narrative." *The Americans Review* 16.3-4 (September 1988): 165-187.

Payne, James Robert, ed. *Multicultural Autobiography: American Lives*. Knoxville: University of Tennessee Press, 1992.

Rayson, Ann. "Beneath the Mask: Autobiographies of Japanese-American Women." *MELUS* 14 (March 1987): 43-57.

Saldivar, Ramon. "Ideologies of the Self: Chicano Autobiography." *Diacritics* (September 1985): 25-34.

Sanders, Mark A. "Theorizing the Collaborative Self: The Dynamics of Contour and Content in the Dictated Autobiography." *New Literary History* 25.2 (March 1994): 445-458.

Sands, Kathleen Mullen. "Telling 'A Good One': Creating a Papago Autobiography." *MELUS* 10 (1983): 55-65.

Stone, Albert, ed. *The American Autobiography: a Collection of Critical Essays.* Englewood Cliffs: Prentice-Hall, 1981.

The Bibliography

1. Aaron, Hank (Henry) (1934-). *I Had a Hammer: The Hank
   Aaron Story.* Written with Lonnie Wheeler. New
   York: Harper Collins Publishers, 1991. ISBN:
   0060163216. 333 pages; photographs.
   Note: Also issued New York: Harper Paperbacks, 1992.
   ISBN: 0061099562.

   In this autobiography, Aaron describes his baseball
   career within the context of the institution's slow integration process. Considering himself to be in the second generation of African American major league ball
   players, Aaron joined the major leagues about nine
   years after Jackie Robinson did in 1954. He broke the
   color line with two other players in the "Sally League,"
   a southern minor league division. Aaron documents
   the influence Jackie Robinson had on the future of
   baseball for all players, black and white, and traces the
   history of desegregation in the major and minor
   leagues. He gives a detailed account of his pursuit of
   Babe Ruth's home run records, and of all the records
   he broke on his way to achieving that goal. As he
   closed in on breaking Ruth's record (714 home runs),
   Aaron encountered virulent racism, receiving death
   threats and mountains of hate mail. Aaron saw his
   breaking Ruth's record as an important event in the
   history of the game and for African American players.
   He finished his career with 755 home runs. Aaron illustrates the difficulties that African American players
   faced in the early decades of desegregated baseball, describes how the improvements came about, and lists
   the changes that still need to be made.

2. Abdul-Jabbar, Kareem (1947-). *Giant Steps*. Written with Peter Knobler. New York: Bantam Books, 1983. ISBN: 0553050443. 324 pages; photographs.
   Note: Also published New York: Bantam, 1985. ISBN: 0553271474.

   In this autobiography, Abdul-Jabbar focuses on his development as a basketball player, starting with his elementary school team participation, and on his conversion to Islam. He discusses his relationship to the Muslim community of Hamaas Abdul-Khaalis in Washington, D.C., and the impact of the spiritual leadership of Hamaas on his life. Abdul-Jabbar describes his professional career in Milwaukee and in Los Angeles, some of his more difficult moments on the court, how he has dealt with fame and public scrutiny, and various issues in his personal life.

3. —. *Kareem*. Written with Mignon McCarthy. New York: Random House, 1990. ISBN: 0394559274. 233 pages; photographs.
   Note: Also published New York: Warner Books, 1990. ISBN: 0446352187.

   This book is based on a diary that Abdul-Jabbar kept during his twentieth and final season as a professional basketball player. He chronicles the daily rigors of the game, provides flashbacks to early moments in his career, and describes the farewell celebrations he received at stadiums around the country.

4. Abernathy, Ralph (1926-). *And the Walls Came Tumbling Down: An Autobiography*. New York: Harper & Row, 1989. ISBN: 0060161922. 638 pages; photographs.
   Note: Also published New York: Harper Perennial, 1990. ISBN: 0060919868.

   Abernathy explains that he was motivated to write this autobiography to leave a record for future generations of life during the Jim Crow Era in the South, and also to describe how it felt to be at the center of the Civil Rights Movement. His detailed account of the Civil Rights Movement begins with the Montgomery Bus Boycott and the development of the Southern Christian Leadership Conference (SCLC). It continues through to Birmingham, to Selma, to the less successful and more difficult protests mounted in the north, and finally to Memphis, where Martin Luther King was assassinated. Abernathy explains the importance of the SCLC doctrine of nonviolence and how it contributed to the successes of the movement as well as to the eventual decline of the SCLC, as younger black leaders with different agendas came forward and attacked the doctrine, dividing the black community. Abernathy concludes his book with an explanation of his support for Ronald Reagan in 1980 and an acknowledgment of it as a strategic mistake, one from which he suffered both personally and professionally.

5. Acosta, Oscar Zeta. *The Autobiography of a Brown Buffalo*. Introduction by Hunter S. Thompson, and afterword by Marco Acosta. New York: Vintage Books, 1989. ISBN: 0679722130. 204 pages.
   Note: Originally published San Francisco: Straight Arrow Books, 1972.

   Acosta's two autobiographical works were reissued posthumously with new introduction and afterword at the instigation of his son, Marco Federico Manuel Acosta. Oscar Zeta Acosta, the model for Hunter S. Thompson's character, Dr. Gonzo, disappeared in 1974 after leaving Mazatlan, Mexico, on a sailboat. The first of the two works, *Autobiography*, describes Acosta's zigzagging interstate sojourn, under the influence of drugs and alcohol. He is on the road to escape from a tedious legal career and to search for his identity. The narrative ends and the next work, *Revolt of the Cockroach People* (see below), picks up with his arrival in Los Angeles in 1968, where he plans to work alongside the Brown Berets, a militant Chicano group, and to write about their movement. He soon rejects his self-designated role as observer and chronicler and instead becomes an active participant, ultimately returning to his legal career and representing individuals active in the Chicano civil rights movement.

6. —. *Revolt of the Cockroach People.* Introduction by Hunter S. Thompson. Afterword by Marco Acosta. New York: Vintage Books, 1989. ISBN: 0679722122. 262 pages.
Note: Originally published San Francisco: Straight Arrow Books, 1973.

See abstract for *Autobiography of a Brown Buffalo* above.

7. Aguero, Kathleen, ed. *Daily Fare: Essays From the Multi-cultural Experience.* Athens: University of Georgia Press, 1993. ISBN: 0820314986:0820314994. 233 pages.

This book is a collection of personal narratives contributed by writers "outside the dominant culture." Although the editor requested no specific subject, she writes in the introduction that the common theme of "relationship to culture and the problem of identity" (p. vii) appears throughout the collection. Editor Aguero concludes her introduction by stating that "we do not have to choose between being purely ethnic or totally assimilated; that instead we may struggle to pay tribute to our differences and cherish what we have in common without compromising either" (p. x). This anthology includes the following writers: Minnie Bruce Pratt, Alberto Alvaro Rios, Judith Ortiz Cofer, Toi Derricote, Yvonne, Kiana Davenport, Garrett Hongo (who has published a memoir *Volcano: A Memoir of Hawaii.* New York, Knopf, 1995), Suzanne Odette Khuri, Robert Peters, Richard Hoffman, Leslie Lawrence, Sam Cornish, Lonny Kaneko, Gary Soto (see separate entries for Soto in this bibliography), Norman Paul Hyett, Joseph Bruchac (who also has essays in *I Tell You Now,* edited by Brian Swann, and *Growing Up Native American,* edited by Patrick Riley, both in this bibliography), and Jack Agüeros.

8. Alexander, Benjamin Harold (1921-). *All the Way Up: Overcoming the Odds.* New York: Vantage Press, 1991. ISBN: 0533095182. 205 pages; photographs.

Alexander examines his family tree and provides a detailed account of his parents' upbringing and early life

together. He had an eventful youth, matriculating at
the University of Cincinnati at the age of 16, attending
college and running his brother's illegal casino while
his brother served in the military during the Second
World War, graduating with a chemistry major, finding employment, and then being drafted himself. A
significant portion of this work is devoted to describing his experiences in a segregated army and how he
worked to keep under control the many tense situations that arose from the racial incidents which occurred between white and black troops in occupied
Japan. Alexander has held many prestigious positions
throughout his career, including eight years as the
president of Chicago State University, which he trans-
formed from a college with an abysmal reputation, beset with fraud and threatened with loss of accredita-
tion, to a well-respected institution.

9. Alexander, Meena (1951-). *Fault Lines: A Memoir*. The
   Cross Cultural Memoir Series. New York: Feminist
   Press at the City University of New York, 1993. ISBN:
   1558610596:1558610588. 226 pages; photographs; poetry.

   Meena Alexander was born in Kerala, India, but spent
   her formative years in the Sudan. She graduated from
   university at age 18 and went to Nottingham, England,
   to attend graduate school, returning to India in her
   mid-twenties. After marrying her American husband,
   she left India for the United States, where she now
   lives in New York. Alexander writes about the psychological effects of being multilingual and of having
   lived for significant lengths of time in four distinctly
   different countries. She was aware of many cultural
   differences, meaning that the expectations placed on
   her as a woman shifted with each country, and these
   differences caused her much personal confusion.
   Alexander includes some of her own poetry, discusses
   her early development as a writer and the poets who
   have influenced her work.

10. Alexander, Theodore Martin. *Beyond the Timberline:*
    The Trials and Triumphs of a Black Entrepreneur.

Edgewood, Maryland: M. E. Duncan and Co., 1992. ISBN: 1878647083. 264 pages; photographs.

Alexander looks back over eighty years to write of his beginnings in Montgomery, Alabama, and examine the people, decisions, and events that led to his success as a pioneering African American and a prominent citizen of Atlanta, Georgia. Alexander places his own experiences within the context of African Americans in Atlanta and the South. Born in 1909, he faced the many obstacles the dominant white society imposed upon African Americans. When during a long-anticipated trip to the North he experienced virulent racism despite that region's lack of institutionalized segregation, he made a conscious decision to stay in the South despite the "diabolical system [which was] conditioning me in my unconscious moments to accept without resentment, a status of inferiority and a circumscribed existence based purely on the circumstance of race" (p. 33). Alexander believed that if he remained in the South he would have the opportunity to effect change. Among many other important accomplishments, Alexander ran for City Alderman in 1957, becoming the first African American to run for office in Atlanta since Reconstruction. Although he didn't win, he ran a close campaign and attracted voters across racial boundaries.

11. Allen, Paula Gunn (1939-). "The Autobiography of a Confluence." *I Tell You Now: Autobiographical Essays by Native American Writers*. Ed. Brian Swann and Arnold Krupat. Lincoln: University of Nebraska Press, 1987. ISBN: 0803227140.

    See entry under *Swann, Brian* for complete list of authors and essays included in this anthology. This essay is also included in Krupat's *Native American Autobiography*. Madison: University of Wisconsin Press, 1994 (see separate entry).

12. Al-Mansour, Khalid Abdullah Tariq (1936-). *Laws Without Justice*. San Francisco: First African Arabian Press, 1990. ISBN: none. 344 pages.

Dr. Al-Monsour, an international legal expert and businessman, presents an account of his own path to success as a lawyer and gives practical advice to those who would emulate him. A significant portion of this book is devoted to the description of a selected number of Dr. Al-Monsour's cases which illustrate specific points in both U.S. and international law. Dr. Al-Monsour is a devout Muslim. His faith was a significant factor in the development of his career, and, thus, an important element of this book.

13. Amos, Wally. *Man With No Name: Turn Lemons Into Lemonade*. Written with Camilla Denton. Lower Lake, California: Aslan Publishing, 1994. ISBN: 0944031579. 154 pages.

Wally Amos, cookie entrepreneur and motivational speaker, writes about how he developed as a businessman and formed a gourmet cookie company, which he eventually lost as a result of financial difficulties. Loss of the company also meant relinquishing the right to use his name or image on any future products. He describes the ten principles that allowed him to keep his self-respect throughout a difficult law suit, and then enter into the chocolate-chip-cookie business once again.

14. Anaya, Rudolpho A. *A Chicano in China*. Albuquerque: University of New Mexico Press, 1986. ISBN: 0826308880. 202 pages; map.

This daily journal kept by Anaya while traveling through China documents his impressions of the country and its people. An experienced world traveler, Anaya writes that this trip held a special significance for him: the Native American portion of his heritage allows him to sense a kinship with the Chinese. He explores this kinship in the journal, noting similarities and differences between the Chinese and Chicano cultures.

15. Anderson, Booker T. *Hanging Tough: Experiencing Life After Birth.* Stockton, California: Koinonia Production, 1983. ISBN: 0866351000. 60 pages; photographs.

This posthumously published book is apparently unfinished, but what exists of Anderson's life story is impressive. He writes that if he had been white, he probably would have been president of the United States, but in his brief life he was a merchant marine, an actor, and a theologian and pastor in the Methodist church. He was also a local politician and civic leader involved in the Civil Rights Movement. In 1957 he arrived in what he describes as crime-ridden Richmond, California, to be pastor of St. Mark's Methodist Church. Soon after his arrival, he organized a political campaign to elect Richmond's first black city councilman. He served on the council himself and was also mayor. In this capacity, Anderson developed the city's first affirmative action policy. In his efforts to get an education or to earn money as a young child to help his family get by, Anderson had to combat the racist society that strove to hold him back. Anderson writes, "What is needed is strong minded, tough willed individuals with a sense of urgency, destiny, courage and the capacity and ability to hang tough in every facet of institutional America, where the bulk of racism takes place" (p. 49).

16. Anderson, Robert Ball (1843-1930). *From Slavery to Affluence: Memoirs of Robert Anderson, Ex-Slave.* Written with Daisy Anderson and Rita Williams Brown. Steamboat Springs, Colorado: Printed by the Steamboat Springs Pilot, 1988. ISBN: none. 90 pages; photographs.
Originally published Hemingford, Nebraska: Hemingford Ledger, 1927. Reprinted in 1967.

17. Anderson, Ruth Bluford (1921-). *From Mother's Aid Child to University Professor.* Iowa City: University of Iowa School of Social Work, 1985. ISBN: none. 136 pages; photographs.

Ruth Bluford Anderson, a professional social worker, writes about her career as a case worker, the director of a county social services program, and finally as a college and university professor of social work. Anderson documents changes in the welfare system from the early thirties, when she herself was a child receiving aid, to the seventies, when she finally resigned her directorship of the Black Hawk County (Iowa) Department of Social Services. As a child on county aid, Anderson remembers a supportive, encouraging atmosphere provided by the social workers and the county (Sioux City, Iowa). By the time Anderson began her career as a professional social worker, society no longer viewed aid as providing support, but instead believed that it created dependence. Her constant fight to counter this negative, and often misinformed, opinion finally took its toll, and Anderson resigned, going into teaching instead. Her teaching career was successful, though not without its personal and professional troubles. In 1982, she was one of four Iowans inducted into the Iowa Women's Hall of Fame.

18. Andrews, Raymond. *The Last Radio Baby: A Memoir*. Illustrated by Benny Andrews. Atlanta: Peachtree Publishers, 1990. ISBN: 1561450049. 221 pages; photographs; illustrations.

Prize-winning novelist Andrews writes about his life from his earliest memories in 1934 up to 1949, when he left home at the age of 15. He affectionately describes in thorough detail his rural Georgia hometown, his church, school, and teachers, his family history and each family member, and many friends and neighbors. Andrews also makes clear the hierarchy of whites and blacks and the code of behavior to be followed by white and black citizens among themselves and toward those of the other race. Though he doesn't leave out the harsh realities of growing up black in the South in the forties, his whole story is told with a lighthearted sense of humor. Andrews writes that he is currently working on another chapter of his life, to be called *Once Upon a Time in Atlanta*, covering the years 1949-1952.

19. Angelou, Maya.
    Angelou began publishing her autobiographies in 1969
    with *I Know Why the Caged Bird Sings*. New York:
    Random House. Also published New York: Bantam
    Books, 1993. ISBN: 0553279378. She published two
    more before 1980: *Gather Together in My Name*. New
    York: Random House, 1974. ISBN: 0394486927. Also
    published New York: Bantam Books, 1985. ISBN:
    0553260669. *Singin' and Swingin' and Gettin' Merry
    Like Christmas*. New York: Random House, 1976.
    ISBN: 0394405455. Also published New York: Bantam
    Books, 1981. ISBN: 0553208748. These three titles are
    also published in a single volume: *Maya Angelou
    Omnibus*. London: Virago, 1991. ISBN: 1853814555.

20. —. *All God's Children Need Traveling Shoes*. New
    York: Random House, 1986. ISBN: 0394521439. 210
    pages.
    Note: The fifth of a five-volume series of autobiogra-
    phies published by Angelou between 1969 and 1986.
    Also published New York: Vintage Books, 1991. ISBN:
    067973404X.

    In 1962, Angelou and her son Guy leave Egypt and her
    South African husband for Ghana, where Guy will at-
    tend university, and Angelou, after seeing him settled,
    will go on to Liberia. However, when her son is in-
    volved in a near fatal car accident, Angelou stays in
    Ghana to help him with his recovery. The rest of the
    book focuses on Angelou's efforts to adapt to Ghana-
    ian life and culture as a member of a circle of African
    American expatriates. Angelou experiences the com-
    fort of being black in a black country and the discom-
    fort of being an immigrant in a foreign country. Cases
    of mistaken identity and unexplainable prescience
    provide Angelou with evidence of her roots in Africa
    and perhaps in Ghana itself. She concludes that
    though black Americans and black Africans have sig-
    nificant societal and cultural differences, there is a
    strong legacy of Africa in black Americans.

21. —. *The Heart of a Woman*. New York: Random House,
    1981. ISBN: 0394512731. 272 pages.

Note: The fourth volume of a five-volume series of autobiographies published by Angelou between 1969 and 1986.
Also published New York: Bantam Books, 1993. ISBN: 0553246895.

In this volume, Angelou describes the end of her career as an entertainer and actress and the commencement of her writing career. She marries Vusumzi Make, a South African Freedom Fighter whom she met in new York while he was a petitioner at the United Nations. Angelou writes about her difficulties as an African American woman married to a man who was not only African but was also involved in an effort which was extremely consuming and dangerous. After Angelou, her husband, and son move to Egypt, Angelou is hired as a writer and editor for the *Arab Observer*, an unusual accomplishment for an American woman. As the marriage deteriorates, Angelou makes plans to leave her husband.

22. Anthony, Earl (1940-). *Spitting in the Wind: The True Story Behind the Violent Legacy of the Black Panther Party*. Santa Monica, California: Roundtable Publishers, 1990. ISBN: 0915677458. 192 pages; photographs.

A graduate of the University of Southern California and a member of the Young Republicans, Earl Anthony was in his final year of law school when he was introduced to radical and black-nationalist politics through his involvement in poverty programs. In 1967, he was the eighth person to join the Black Panther Party. At an early point in his membership, Anthony was approached by FBI agents and coerced into acting as an informer. He later worked for the CIA as well. Although anxious to get on with his life, Anthony found it difficult to sever his ties with the FBI, and this entanglement seriously affected his life in the form of alcohol and drug addiction despite his eventual success as a writer, playwright, and college professor.

23. Archer, Chalmers (1928-). *Growing Up Black in Rural Mississippi: Memories of a Family, Heritage of a Place.* New York: Walker, 1992. ISBN: 0802711758. 156 pages; photographs; bibliography.

Archer's book is both the story of his youth and family and a documentation of black rural life in Mississippi, primarily during the decade of the Depression. Calling his work a history of the ordinary person, he emphasizes the importance of and the need for this kind of scholarship. Archer relies on his memory, oral testimony from family members, and research into conditions and attitudes of the time—including popular sentiment as expressed in local white newspapers immediately after the abolition of slavery through the 1940s. He is able to put the period of his childhood and youth into a broader historical context, thanks to the memories of aunts, uncles, and grandparents born into slavery or within recent memory of its abolition.

24. *As We Lived: Stories by Black Storytellers.* Recorded and written by Jakie L. Pruett with Everett B. Cole. Burnet, Texas: Eakin Press, 1982. ISBN: 0890153094. 146 pages; photographs.

Pruett and Cole present conversations with five African American story tellers who relate episodes from their childhood and retell the stories they were told as they were growing up. The story tellers are Hallie Rooney of Corpus Christi, Texas; Wallace Holland and Mary Jane Bonds of New Palestine, Texas; Rosie Williams of Thomaston, Texas; Lulu V. Jones and John Henry James of Gonzales, Texas.

25. Ashe, Arthur (1943-). *Arthur Ashe: Portrait in Motion.* Ed. Richard Gallen. Written with Frank Deford. New York: Carroll and Graf Publishers, 1993. ISBN: 0786700505. 278 pages; photographs.
Note: Originally published Boston: Houghton Mifflin, 1975. ISBN: 0395204291; New York: Ballantine Books, 1976. ISBN: 0345249046.

This work is a diary covering one year, beginning with the 1973 Wimbledon Tennis Tournament in Wimbledon, England and ending with the same event a year later. It includes an account of Ashe's controversial first trip to South Africa in 1973.

26. —. *Days of Grace: A Memoir.* Written with Arnold Rampersad. New York: Alfred A. Knopf, 1993. ISBN: 0679423966. 317 pages; photographs.
Note: Also published New York: Ballantine Books, 1994. ISBN: 0345386817X.

Ashe began work on this memoir after making public the fact that he had AIDS. He worked on it up until his death in February, 1993. The closing chapter is a letter to his then six-year-old daughter. Although the focus of this book is Ashe's experience with heart disease and AIDS, he also discusses his views on race, education, politics, and sports. He writes about his post-retirement career, including his work as the Davis Cup captain. Ashe addresses some of the criticism he has received over the years because of his quiet approach to racial politics, and also because of his delayed announcement concerning his infection with AIDS.

27. —. *Off the Court.* Written with Neil Amdur. New York: New American Library, 1981. ISBN: 0453004008. 230 pages; photographs.

Ashe wrote this autobiography after undergoing quadruple bypass surgery and subsequently retiring from competition. He states his hope that readers of this book will learn "how Arthur Ashe came to be who he is" (p. 219). To achieve this goal, Ashe writes about his family, crediting them and a close circle of friends for helping him develop a strong sense of self that allowed him to perform comfortably in an otherwise all-white sport. He chronicles his tennis career, from his developing interest during his college years, to balancing a military and amateur tennis career, to his professional years and retirement.

28. Austin, Alberta. *Ne' Ho Niyo' De: No': That's What it Was Like.* Lackawanna, New York: Rebco Enterprises,

1986. ISBN: none. 257 pages; photographs; illustrations; maps.
Note: "Seneca Nation Curriculum Development."

This is a collection of 61 narratives, most, but not all, presented in the first person, contributed by tribal elders of the Seneca, Onondaga, Cayuga, Mohawk, Tuscarora, and Oneida Nations of New York. Each elder provides a brief account of his/her life; some include stories, significant events, and customs. A common concern is the survival of tribal languages and the perceived indifference of the younger generations.

29. Baca, Jimmy Santiago (1952-). *Working in the Dark: Reflections of a Poet of the Barrio*. Santa Fe: Red Crane Books, 1991. ISBN: 1878610082. 168 pages.

This work is a collection of autobiographical essays divided into five sections and a selection of journal entries. The first section describes Baca's discovery of language and poetry, his prison experiences, and his return to San Quentin Prison to act in a movie for which he wrote the script. In writing about his return, Baca discusses his argument against the prison system: the abuses he has seen and his conviction that inmates are more likely to become hardened criminals than to be reformed as a result of their incarceration. In the next section of essays, Baca writes of his love for his family, of individuals who have been a powerful and positive force in his life, and of individuals and institutions which have driven him down to the lowest levels of existence. He describes his weaknesses, his struggles, and his strengths. The reader gains a clear sense of how important the written word in general and poetry in particular are for Baca. Through the writing of these essays, he illustrates what he can do and what he hopes to accomplish with his poetry:

> Still, with the world so set on denying my culture, I am full of insecurities and my life is replete with contradictions, plummeting to mercuric chills and flaring to comet flights. I invite all possibilities of being as long as they don't oppress me. I affirm the right of my people to determine their destiny. I feel rage, hurt, pain, shame—and forgiveness, too. When I walk in the evening, a surge of euphoria from the earth fuses into my heels and hands, into my thoughts—a

light fizz of energy. The delight of being here! Oppressors
step aside to the banks of the road, because I am coming
through. (p. 83)

30. Bacho, Eutiquio de la Victoria (1903-). *The Long Road:
    Memoirs of a Filipino Pioneer.* Seattle: E. V. Bacho,
    1992. ISBN: none. 95 pages; photographs.

31. Baker, Alvis (1916-). *The Bottomless Pit.* New York: Van-
    tage Press, 1981. ISBN: 0533049105. 133 pages.

    Alvis Baker's story begins with the story of his rural
    Georgia childhood, as he grew up on the farm with his
    parents, dependent upon the good will of the white
    landowner. His situation changed when, after the
    death of his father, he needed money to pay for his
    mother's hospitalization. Unable to convince his em-
    ployer to pay him the money that he had earned,
    Baker determined to steal it from him. Thus began
    thirty years of crime and imprisonment. Baker's early
    prison sentences required him to work on a Georgia
    chain gang. He describes the utter brutality of the
    "bosses" who did not hesitate to murder the prisoners
    in cold blood at the least provocation. Baker managed
    to escape a number of times, but finally fulfilled his
    original 12-year sentence in 1966, thirty years after he
    received it. A strong Christian throughout his life,
    Baker ends his story with a statement of his religious
    faith.

32. Baraka, Imamu Amiri (1934-). *The Autobiography of
    LeRoi Jones.* New York: Freundlich Books, 1984.
    ISBN: 0881910007. 329 pages.

    In this examination of his life, Amiri Baraka traces his
    growth and transformation from "white intellectual,"
    to black nationalist, to Marxist-Leninist. After a brief
    time at Howard University and a dishonorable dis-
    charge from the U.S. Air Force, Baraka made his way
    to Greenwich Village, where, now a writer and pub-
    lisher, he gradually became involved with a wide cir-
    cle of white poets and artists. He experienced a radical
    change in his personal philosophy when he took a trip
    to Castro's Cuba with a group of black intellectuals,

consequently rejecting his bohemian life-style and white wife and friends. He then became deeply involved with a number of black organizations, including Black Theater Arts and the Congress of Afrikan Peoples (CAP). His work with the latter led to his commitment to Marxism-Leninism. Baraka sums up his life in the following sentence:

> But I leave you with this, all these words are only to be learned from. The Childhood; music; blues bottomed class distinctions: black, brown, yellow, white; HU [Howard University]; Error Farce [Air Force]; Village time; Harlem sojourn; home-returning black nationalist grown blood red person—all that is like some food for thought, some sounds meant only to say, look at this, dig it, what it means, where I, and some others, been. (p. 313)

33. Barnes, Jim (1933-). "On Native Ground." *I Tell You Now: Autobiographical Essays by Native American Writers*. Ed. Brian Swann and Arnold Krupat. Lincoln: University of Nebraska Press, 1987. ISBN: 0803227140.

See entry under *Swann, Brian* for complete list of authors and essays included in this anthology.

34. Basie, Count (1904-1984). *Good Morning Blues: The Autobiography of Count Basie*. As told to Albert Murray. New York: Random House, 1985. ISBN: 0394548647. 399 pages; photographs.

In this musical autobiography, Count Basie describes the "people and places and happenings" of his nearly sixty-year career in jazz. When he wrote this book, Basie was 80 years old and still touring with his band; he died shortly before the book was published. Count Basie's pure enjoyment of music comes across clearly in his narrative. In his concluding chapter, he writes a little about the rigors of traveling and Jim Crow when his band was the "hottest attraction in the biggest theaters and auditoriums or the top night spot in town" (p. 382). He explains why he did not include much about this aspect of his career in his book:

> [I]t's not because I want anybody to get the impression that all of that was not also a part of [my musical career]. It was. So what? Life is a bitch, and if it's not one damn thing, it's

going to be something else. . . . I'll just say that I was out there trying to do what I was trying to do, which was to play music and have a ball. I'll just say that I was not surprised when things got strange in one way or another. I'll just say that I didn't intend to let anything stop me if I could help it, and that should tell you something. (p. 382-383)

35. Beals, Melba Pattillo. *Warriors Don't Cry: A Searing Memoir of the Battle to Integrate Little Rock's Central High*. New York: Pocket Books, 1994. ISBN: 0671866389. 312 pages; photographs.
Note: Also published New York, Washington Square Press, 1995. ISBN: 0671866397.

Beals was one of nine truly heroic teenagers who integrated Central High School in Little Rock, Arkansas, in 1957. She was 15 years old. This book chronicles her experiences during that traumatic year. Rejected, threatened, verbally and physically abused by the white segregationists, she was also rejected by many in the black community because of the pressure they were receiving from white employers, bankers, and others. In retrospect, Beals writes that she cannot imagine how their parents and NAACP leaders could have let her and her peers follow through with this very dangerous endeavor, and yet, at the time, she felt that it was the right decision. Eight of the nine teenagers finished the year at Central High, one of them graduating, but by the end of the year, publicly posted notices offered rewards for their deaths. Beals was forced to leave Little Rock, moving in with a strange family in Santa Rosa, California, so that she could finish her high school education in safety.

36. Beatus, Henry (1932-). *Henry Beatus, Sr., Hughes*. Interviews conducted and text prepared by Curt Madison and Yvonne Yarber. Alaska Series. North Vancouver, British Columbia: Hancock House, 1980. ISBN: 0888390637. 71 pages; photographs; maps.

Beatus describes his childhood, which he spent with his grandparents in Hughes on the Koyukuk River. Raised in the "old ways" to hunt, fish, and trap, Beatus

compares his early years with those of his own children, noting the changes and the similarities.
For a brief description and list of autobiographies in this Yukon-Koyukuk School District series, see the entry for Moses Henzie.

37. Beetus, Joe (1915-). *Joe Beetus, Hughes.* Interviews conducted and text prepared by Curt Madison and Yvonne Yarber. Alaska Series. North Vancouver, British Columbia: Hancock House, 1980. ISBN: 0888390653. 70 pages; photographs.

Joe Beetus lives along the Koyukuk River and makes his living as a hunter and trapper. In his narrative, he talks about how he learned from his elders and stresses the importance of passing on this wisdom to his own children. Skilled at traditional singing and dancing, Beetus expresses concern at the diminishing number of Natives able to perform these arts. He includes an extensive description of a major Potlatch event, with an account of all the necessary preparations.
For a brief description and list of autobiographies in this Yukon-Koyukuk School District series, see the entry for Moses Henzie.

38. *Beginnings, Japanese Americans in San Jose: 8 Oral Histories/Aru San Noze Nikkeijin No Ayumi.* Ed. Steven Misawa. San Jose: San Jose Japanese American Community Senior Service, 565 North Fifth Street, San Jose, California 95112, 1981. ISBN: none. 121 pages; photographs.

Misawa distinguishes the subjects of these eight oral histories from Issei in general by designating them as Yobiyose, or as having been "called" from Japan by their parents in the United States. In other words, most of these individuals were educated in Japan and raised by grandparents or other older relatives until joining their parents in the United States. A variety of professions, economic and education levels, and view points are represented here, although all subjects have had a connection to San Jose Japantown, and most experienced the internment camps during World II.

They express both approval and disapproval of what they observe to be the directions taken by the Sensei, or third-generation Japanese Americans, and many are pleased to see a renewed interest in learning about Japan, family history, and traditions.

39. Bell, Rose S. (1926-). *Beyond the Strawberry Patch*. Nashville: Winston-Derek Publishers, 1985. ISBN: 0938232762. 126 pages.

Bell provides anecdotes of growing up in rural Arkansas through the 1930s and 1940s. One of seventeen children, Bell writes of a well-organized and loving household with all members contributing to maintaining home and farm. Her sense of duty was often challenged by her love of reading. She writes, "Daddy thought it was a sin to be idle. I thought it was a sin to pick cotton" (p. 51). But all the children were encouraged to get an education, attend college if possible, and to become self-sufficient.

40. Bell, William M. *Black Without Malice: The Bill Bell Story*. Fayetteville, North Carolina: William McNeil Bell, Sr., 1983. ISBN: none. 178 pages.

41. Bell-Scott, Patricia, ed. *Life Notes: Personal Writings by Contemporary Black Women*. New York: W. W. Norton, 1994. ISBN: 039303593X. 427 pages.
Note: Also published New York: W. W. Norton, 1995. ISBN: 0393312062.

Bell-Scott writes that in compiling these autobiographical writings by 50 African American women, she had four objectives:
> (1) [T]o honor the nameless women and girls who have recorded lives in the face of enormous disadvantages; (2) to share the rich experiences lost when our diversity is ignored; (3) to authenticate our ability as self-defining women who can speak for ourselves; and (4) to encourage other generations to write for self-knowledge, empowerment, and posterity. (p. 18)

The ages of the writers range from 8 to 64. They represent both well-known, published writers and unpublished writers. They come from varying vocations, sexual orientations, economic levels, and geographical locations.

42. Belton, David. *Each Night I Die*. Edgewood, Maryland: M. E. Duncan and Co., Inc., 1992. ISBN: 1878647075. 217 pages.

Belton wrote this book while serving a life sentence in a Maryland prison. In and out of reform school and prison from the age of 15, Belton was sentenced for murder at 29. He writes of a happy childhood that began to fall apart after his father suffered a stroke, lost his job, and eventually deserted the family. In writing his life story, Belton examines the prison system, and especially its impact on black men. He also looks at the reasons that black men and women resort to a life on the streets and the reasons behind his addiction to drugs. Belton went through a religious experience shortly after his forty-first birthday, which prompted him to give up drugs and alcohol, become a Christian, and obtain an education. Belton had to come to terms with the tragic circumstances of his life and of the lives of those close to him. He experienced not only the death of many friends, both in and out of prison, but also of close family members, including his wife and his brother, and the imprisonment of his son. Belton hopes that his book will help provide guidance for young people, leading them to make better choices in life.

43. Benson, Joyce. *Last Tag*. Nashville: Winston-Derek Publishers, 1991. ISBN: 1555232779. 194 pages; photographs.

Basing her work on a diary she kept between 1952 and 1960, Joyce Benson writes of her turbulent adolescence in a Pittsburgh housing project and her friendship with Chaya (Charles) Benson, brother of well-known guitarist George Benson. (Joyce married another Benson brother.) She was constantly at odds with her parents, pursuing track and tennis behind their backs and against their will even to the point of burying all the trophies she brought home. Although she was a good student, her parents were concerned that extracurricu-lar activities would interfere with her scholastic achievements, and their concern was the source of their strong, if misguided, opposition. Her parents were also against her friendship with Chaya, despite the fact that they were not romantically involved and were strongly supportive of each other. The story ends with the death of Chaya Benson, who was killed in a street fight at the age of 16.

44. Benton, Horace (1903-). *A Twist of Justice: Gripes*. New York: Carlton Press, 1988. ISBN: 0806230681. 79 pages.

Benton, who grew up in Jasper County, Georgia, "a hell hole for the black man" (p. 9), writes: "I will tell you some of my life's story; at least the things I can remember best and some I wish I could forget" (p. 9). Benton describes the many terrorist acts committed against blacks by individual whites and also of institu-tionalized racism, especially as manifested in the pub-lic school systems. When he became an adult, he determined to leave Georgia and get as many of his family members out as possible. He then settled in Alabama, only to find that life was not significantly improved. As a miner, he moved frequently in both northern and southern states, finally settling in West Virginia, but never finding an escape from racism. In his later years, he created healing ointments which he has had patented, and he describes these in some detail in the final pages of the book.

45. Bernhardt, Clyde E. B. (1905-1986). *I Remember: Eighty Years of Black Entertainment, Big Bands, and the Blues: An Autobiography*. As told to Sheldon Harris. Philadelphia: University of Pennsylvania Press, 1986. ISBN: 0812280180:0812212231. 271 pages; photographs; discography.

Bernhardt was introduced to the blues when Ma Rainey, considered the greatest blues singer at that time, brought her traveling show to his town in 1917. Bernhardt was 12 years old. His first instrument was the kazoo, and he graduated to the trombone at age 16.

He began his professional music career in 1923, when he joined his aunt and uncle's family band—The El-wood Syncopators. He went on to play with many bands and orchestras, performing all over the world. He continued to tour and perform until just before his death in 1986, a few weeks before his book was pub-lished. Bernhardt wrote that "jazz is American her-itage music. It's all we can claim, and when I say we, I'm talking about all Americans. Any color American. We all have something to be proud of" (p. 228).

46. Berry, Chuck. *Chuck Berry: The Autobiography*. New York: Harmony Books, 1987. ISBN: 0517566664. 346 pages; photographs; discography.
Note: Also published New York: Simon & Schuster, 1988. ISBN: 0671671596.

In this autobiography, which he began while serving a year-long prison term for income-tax discrepancies, Berry tells the story of his origins, birth, and life to 1987. His music career got its start while he was serv-ing a sentence at the Algona Intermediate Reformatory as a result of his first and only crime spree. His book provides all the details of his song writing, performing and touring career, his legal problems, and his liaisons. Berry has many accomplishments, both as a musician and a businessman. Faced with a number of serious setbacks through the course of his career, he never al-lowed fate to interfere with his determination and drive.

47. Black, Charlie J. (1934-). *After the Fact: 20/20 Hindsight*. Silver Spring, Maryland: Washington Provider (P. O. Box 5397, Takoma Park Station 20912), 1987. ISBN: none. 267 pages.

While describing his work and teaching experiences, Black also gives the reader a social and political picture of African Americans in Alabama, including their progress through the years and lack of it. Black also writes about his experiences with racism in higher ed-ucation and in the work place, listing some of the institutional means he has used and personal methods he has developed to combat it.

48. Blacksnake, Governor (1753-1859). *Chainbreaker: The Revolutionary War Memoirs of Governor Blacksnake.* Ed. Thomas Abler. As told to Benjamin Williams. American Indian Lives. Lincoln: University of Nebraska Press, 1989. ISBN: 0803214464. 306 pages; portrait; critical notes; bibliography.

This memoir of Governor Blacksnake was dictated in Seneca to Benjamin Williams, who translated it into English. It relates Blacksnake's Revolutionary War experiences and the contributions of the Six Nations of the Iroquois to the establishment of the United States. This edition is accompanied by notes and critical commentary.

49. Blaine, Peter (1902-). *Papagos and Politics.* Tucson, Arizona (949 East Second St., Tucson 85719): Arizona Historical Society, 1981. ISBN: none. 145 pages; photographs; maps.

Born in 1902, Peter Blaine has observed and participated in the many changes affecting the Papago people. He describes the area including and surrounding the San Xavier and Sells Papago Reservations and some of the different characteristics of the communities therein. Blaine discusses the various agricultural methods of the Papago, historically an agricultural people, their livestock practices and their adaptation to life in the desert. He writes that in his memory, San Xavier was completely cultivated, but today he sees very little farming and, because this change saddens him, he stays away from the area. Blaine also covers the land and mineral rights disputes between the federal government and the Papago, and the conflict within the Papago community as well. He gives an account of the clan structure, the variety of dialects found from village to village, and what he sees as the deterioration of a society which has lost sight of the culture and traditions which contributed to its past strength and uniqueness.

50. *Bloods, an Oral History of the Vietnam War.*
    See *Terry, Wallace,* ed.

51. Bolton, Ruthie (1961-) (pseud.). *Gal: A True Life.* Tran-
    scribed by Josephine Humphreys. New York: Harcourt
    Brace & Company, 1994. ISBN: 0151001049. 275 pages.
    Note: Also published New York: Onyx Books, 1995.
    ISBN: 0451406273.

    In the forward to this book, Josephine Humphreys
    writes that "Ruthie Bolton" first attempted to write
    down the story of her life and, having written 58 pages,
    decided to tell her story in the way "southern stories
    are best told: out loud, teller-to-listener." Bolton
    sought Humphrey out to help her with her project,
    and Humphrey takes no credit for the finished prod-
    uct. She asserts that her contributions consisted of
    those of secretary and witness—transcribing and typing
    up the recorded sessions. Bolton would read the typed
    transcripts and expand on what she had dictated. Born
    to a thirteen-year-old mother, Bolton lived with her
    grandparents, who were her de facto parents, and their
    daughters, some of whom were younger than Bolton.
    Her mother, for the most part, did not live at home.
    Her grandfather had a violent nature, and Ruthie and
    her aunt-sisters witnessed the many beatings of their
    mother/grandmother, including the beating that
    finally killed her. After this tragic event, the chil-
    dren were worked and beaten mercilessly by their
    father/grandfather. The tide of Ruthie's nightmarish
    life changed with her second marriage. Her acceptance
    into her husband's family gave her a life she might
    have dreamed of, but never imagined having. Bolton
    reflects on this change:

    > But if I had never met them, I don't know how I would be to-
    > day. Because still today, they are the only people that hug
    > me and tell me they love me. . . . I love them, too; but—I
    > guess I had wanted it from an adult, and I wanted it *al-
    > ready*, to have happened to me when I was little. That is a
    > hard thing to explain—that I want it, but I want it *then*. (p.
    > 191)

52. Bonner, Cleon R. (1911?-). *A Black Principal's Struggle to Survive.* New York: Vantage Press, 1982. ISBN: none. 111 pages; photographs; bibliography.

Bonner was the principal at the Georgia Academy for the Blind from 1950 until 1976. When he began his work there, the school was segregated, and Bonner ran the program, housed in a separate facility, for African American children. The Academy began its painful desegregation process in the mid-1960s. When Bonner was put in charge of the elementary grades, he was faced with overseeing white teachers and employees who were not happy with the idea of being supervised by a black man. He writes that "the sight of a black man in authority was sickening to them" (p. 53). Despite the attempts by his white colleagues to marginalize his role in the school, Bonner was able to achieve many improvements for the school, including the development of a program for the severely handicapped which has been emulated by other schools throughout the world.

53. Boyd, Norma E. (1888-). *A Love that Equals My Labors: The Life Story of Norma E. Boyd.* Washington D.C.: Alpha Kappa Alpha Sorority, 1980. ISBN: none. 143 pages; photographs.

Norma Boyd grew up at the turn of the century, graduating from Howard University in 1909. After retiring from teaching in 1949, she devoted her life to bettering the lives of children by promoting world peace. While at Howard, she helped found the AKA Sorority and its Non-Partisan Lobby, which worked for anti-poverty legislation. Both the sorority and the lobby became national organizations. After World War II, Boyd was involved in working for the establishment of the UN and became an accredited observer in that organization. She also worked with UNESCO's children's book program. In the late 50s, Boyd formed the Women's International Religious Fellowship, whose goal was to promote the UN's Declaration of the Rights of Children, especially Principle 10, which states that "chil-

dren should be brought up in a spirit of universal
brotherhood."

54. Boyer, Ruth McDonald and Narcissus Duffy Gayton.
*Apache Mothers and Daughters: Four Generations of a
Family*. Written with Narcissus Duffy Gayton. Norman: University of Oklahoma Press, 1992.   ISBN:
0806124474. 393 pages; photographs; bibliography.

Falling somewhere between biography and autobiography, this book follows four generations of Apache
women and the history of the Chiricahua Apaches
from about 1848 through 1989. It is co-authored by the
woman representing the fourth generation, Narcissus.
Although Boyer writes the book in the third person,
Narcissus instigated its writing, and it is based largely
on her memories of events as passed on to her in the
oral tradition by her relatives.   The four women,
whose stories are told within the greater context of the
events, tragedies, and changes taking place within the
Apache society, are Dilth-cleyhen, born in 1848; her
first child, Beshad-e, born in 1870; her granddaughter,
Christine, born in 1904; and her great granddaughter,
Narcissus, born in 1924.

55. Brady, Carol Feller (1927-). *Through the Storm Towards
the Sun: A Personal Account of Life in Transition in
Southeast Alaska*. Wrangell, Alaska (P. O. Box 247,
Wrangell 99929): C. F. Brady, 1980. ISBN: none. 64
pages; photographs.

In this reminiscence, Carol Feller Brady describes her
painful childhood.   After the deaths of both her
mother and father, she lived with her older sister.
Carol's sister did not like her and treated her harshly.
Because Carol was needed to care for her sister's children, she missed much of her schooling. After she finally left to continue her studies, school authorities
prevented her from returning to her sister's because
they were aware of how Carol had been treated there.
By the time Carol was a young woman, all of her family had died from illness, fire, or drowning. The final
blow to her sanity was the death of her first husband,

which caused her to resort to drinking. She writes this story as a therapeutic measure and as a message of love to her children.

56. Brady, Paul L. (1927-). *A Certain Blindness: A Black Family's Quest for the Promise of America*. Atlanta: ALP Publisher, 1990. ISBN: 0962372005. 339 pages; photographs; bibliography.

Paul L. Brady writes: "My purpose is to show that the white majority has willfully blinded itself to the humanity and worth of Americans of African descent in order to preserve the best portion for itself" (p. ix). He uses the history of his own family as an example to show 1) how important the African American has been in the building of the United States, and 2) that talent, hard work, and contributions to the good of society do not translate into reward, advancement, or acknowledgment for African Americans. Brady's own adult life included time spent in the navy, which was not segregated but had institutionalized racism; law school at Washburn University which, according to Brady, provided a comfortable environment for African Americans in the midst of segregated Kansas; and, finally, a career in law and politics, pursuing the implementation of civil rights legislation, especially in the areas of housing, education, and employment. Brady writes that he has found that the "special problem of my skin color has far exceeded all other difficulties I have encountered in my efforts to advance myself" (p. 211), and he concludes that this problem is an issue for most African American men and women.

57. Brainard, Cecilia Manguerra. *Philippine Woman in America: Essays*. Quezon City: New Day Publishers, 1991. ISBN: 9711004240. 100 pages; photographs.
Note: 36 previously published essays.

Brainard, who arrived in the United States from the Philippines in 1969, wrote these essays between 1983 and 1988. Some of the themes which she discusses in this collection include what it has meant to her to be an immigrant: she speaks of her experience with

racism, the difficulty of her first trip back to the Philippines and the fundamental changes she underwent because of her immigration; the issues of interracial
marriage; memories of her childhood; and the experience of following the often tragic news from home and
sharing her feelings and reactions with other Filipinos
in the United States. Brainard explains that as a writer,
she has struggled to find "themes and topics that are
true to [her] identity as a Filipino in America," and she
describes the difficulty of writing for an audience that
often does not share her frame of reference.

58. Brave Bird, Mary. *Lakota Woman*. Written with Richard
Erdoes. New York: Grove Weidenfeld, 1990. ISBN:
0802111017. 263 pages; photographs.
Note: Also published New York: Harper Perennial,
1991. ISBN: 0060973897.

"If you plan to be born, make sure you are born white
and male" (p. 4), writes Mary Brave Bird in the opening chapter of her first autobiography. Of Brule
(Lakota) and Caucasian ancestry, Brave Bird has suffered prejudice both from Native American and white
societies. In this book, she writes about the prevalence
of alcoholism and domestic violence on reservations
and about her personal experience with both. She also
speaks of her marriage to Leonard Crow Dog, a Lakota
medicine man, their involvement in the American Indian Movement (AIM), and the FBI siege at
Wounded Knee in 1973.

59. —. *Ohitika Woman*. Written with Richard Erdoes. New
York: Grove Press, 1993. ISBN: 0802114369. 274 pages;
photographs.
Note: Also published New York: Harper Perennial,
1994. ISBN: 0060975830.

Brave Bird's second autobiography recaps some of the
events of *Lakota Woman* and describes the course of
her life since the end of that book. Although these two
books appeared within three or four years of each
other, the second book was actually written fifteen
years after the first. In the early 90s, Brave Bird, con-

fronted with the poverty and despair of reservation life, had descended into a state of continuous alcohol intoxication. After a number of near-fatal accidents and the deaths from accident, domestic abuse, and suicide of many of her friends, she was finally able to begin to recover. Mary Brave Bird continues to struggle against poor employment opportunities and the sense of hopelessness that pervades reservation life for her family, and for all Native Americans. She is also active in the fight against state and federal efforts to make land grabs and to infringe upon Native sovereignty.

60. Brooks, Sara (1911-). *You May Plow Here: The Narrative of Sara Brooks*. Ed. Thordis Simonsen. New York: W. W. Norton, 1986. ISBN: 0393022579. 222 pages; portrait.
Note: Also published New York: Simon & Schuster, 1989. ISBN: 0671638483. Reissued W. W. Norton, 1992. ISBN: 0393308669.

Sara Brooks tells about her childhood growing up on a farm; she describes the crops and planting methods used by her father. Although she was encouraged to attend college, Brooks writes that she had no idea what college was or why she would want to go. Instead, she married at a young age and spent several years in an abusive relationship. Only after many years of hard work was she able to create a situation stable enough to make it possible for her three sons to come live with her. Brooks often refers to her sheltered life and her lack of knowledge of anything beyond the world of her farm experience.

61. Brooks, Velma L. *Velma B.: The Success Story of a Most Dynamic Businesswoman*. N.p.: n.p., 1989. ISBN: none. 242 pages; photographs.

Velma Brooks writes about her drive to achieve success in her chosen field of cosmetology. She has operated a number of successful salons and a school of cosmetology. Brooks began entering hair design competitions in the Dallas area, branched out to other regions of the United States, and finally made her way to international competition, where she won first place. Brooks encourages young people to go into this career because she sees it as a good way to achieve financial independence.

62. Brown, Albert J. *Recollections—by Alaska Native Albert J. Brown: Stories From the Clan House of Raven . . . and Other Random Thoughts.* Ketchikan, Alaska (3310 1st St., Ketchikan 99901): Colleen and Co., 1989. ISBN: none. 134 pages; portrait.

Albert Brown was raised on Prince of Wales Island and later moved to Ketchikan, Alaska. He received an "outside" education and worked for a number of years in Washington, D.C. In this book, he contemplates the changes that have occurred, for good or ill, in Haida culture over his lifetime, and over the past three generations during which most of the modernization has taken place. Brown discusses the impact of Christianity, the Federal Government, and environmental groups on Alaska and Haida society. He presents several legends, describes the making of and uses for totems, and explains the structure and importance of the Haida clan system. Brown both reminisces about the past and looks forward to the future.

63. Brown, Altona (1904-). *Altona Brown: Ruby.* Interviews conducted and text prepared by Curt Madison and Yvonne Yarber. Yukon-Koyukuk School District Biography Series. Fairbanks: Spirit Mountain Press, 1983. ISBN: 091087106X. 128 pages; photographs.
Note: Produced by Yukon-Koyukuk School District of Alaska.

Altona Brown was born during the gold rush in 1904. She was an expert hunter, trapper, and fisher, and continued to be involved in these activities into her eighties. Married at the age of 12 to a 45-year-old man, she gave birth to her first child at 13. Brown presents to the reader a colorful and detailed account of her childhood, describing the lifestyle, customs, and beliefs of her people. Both her mother and father came from families of traditional healers, and Brown describes the significance of this part of her heritage.

For a brief description and list of autobiographies in this Yukon-Koyukuk School District series, see the entry for Moses Henzie.

64. Brown, Cecil (1943-). *Coming Up Down Home: A Memoir of a Southern Childhood.* Hopewell, New Jersey: Ecco Press, 1993. ISBN: 0880012935. 222 pages.
Note: Also published Ecco Press, 1995. ISBN: 0880014148.

Cecil Brown, an acclaimed novelist, writes about his childhood in rural North Carolina. He and his younger brother were raised by their aunt and uncle from a very early age while their father was in prison for the murder of their mother's cousin. Their father was released when Brown was 13, and, against their wishes, the boys were returned to their parents. Brown spent the next several years working on his father's farm and attending school. His discovery of prestidigitation and his father's unexpected purchase of a saxophone were major turning points in Brown's life. The summer before his senior year of high school, he traveled to New York where he worked in a factory, played saxophone in a rhythm-and-blues band, and met a variety of people, both white and black. Brown's visit to New York both inspired and discouraged him because, although he found it free of segregation and overt racism, the whites were still in control, and blacks had to struggle to make a living. Indeed, they suffered the same lack of self-respect as their southern counterparts. Brown returned home for his senior year determined to get away again, but unsure of his choices. His salvation came quickly when he earned a way off the farm in the form of a college scholarship.

65. Brown, Drew T. *You Gotta Believe!: Education + Hard Work - Drugs = American Dream.* New York: W. Morrow, 1991. ISBN: 0688094473. 288 pages; photographs; bibliography.

Note: Also published as *You Gotta Believe!: The In-spiring Life Story of a True American Hero.* New York: Avon Books, 1992. ISBN: 0380710072.

The son of a first generation American Jewish mother and an African American father, Brown grew up in Harlem. His parents were involved in the Harlem night-life scene, and, as a result of their frequent absences, Brown spent a significant amount of time with his Russian grandparents. His past included drug abuse in high school and alcohol abuse as an adult. After recovering from his alcohol addiction, Brown joined the Navy in order to become a pilot and successfully earned his golden wings only after appealing his initial rejection on the basis of discrimination. After a successful tour in the Navy, Brown became a professional motivational speaker with the goal of encouraging youth to forego drugs and get an education.

66. Brown, Elaine (1943-). *A Taste of Power: A Black Woman's Story.* New York: Pantheon Books, 1992. ISBN: 0679419446:0374272565. 452 pages; photographs.
    Note: Also published New York: Anchor Books/ Doubleday, 1994. ISBN: 0385471076.

This book is both the story of Elaine Brown and a history of the Black Panther Party. The first third of *A Taste of Power* is devoted to Brown's childhood, family, and education. Brown's earliest years were spent in the poorest part of North Philadelphia. Her mother, despite their condition of poverty, was determined to give her daughter every advantage. She provided Brown with ballet and piano lessons and arranged for her to attend an exclusive, experimental private school. Brown thrived in the school setting, excelling as both a dancer and a pianist. Brown writes that as a black student in the predominantly-white private schools, she attempted to lead two lives—a black life with her mother and neighborhood friends, and her school life, in which she worked to fit in with her wealthy white classmates. Before graduating from college, Brown moved to Southern California, and it is there that she gradually began to view herself as a black woman, eventually joining the Black Panther Party. Brown describes her increasingly important role within the party. She also describes in detail the war waged on the Black Panther Party by the Los Angeles police force and the FBI. She gives the reader her perspective on how the party operated, its many social and political accomplishments, and the personalities of and her interactions with her fellow leaders in the party.

67. Brown, James R. (1926-). *Jackleg Preacher*. New York: Carlton Press, 1989. ISBN: 0806231874. 113 pages.

Brown focuses on the relationships between black men and black women, white men and black women, and the treatment of black women within black churches. He writes that "the worst sin the black churches committed was throwing out young, pregnant, unmarried black girls" (p. 51). Brown's father turned his own daughter out of the church when she became pregnant. The men suffered no retribution in these cases, and the women were left without any support system. Brown also writes of his experiences in France during the war, and the overwhelming sense of freedom he felt there compared to his life in Georgia.

68. Brown, William Wells (1815-1884). *From Fugitive Slave to Free Man: The Autobiographies of William Wells Brown*. New York: Mentor Books, 1993. ISBN: 0451628608. 296 pages; bibliography.
Note: Includes *Narrative of William Wells Brown, Fugitive Slave* originally published by the Anti-Slavery Office in Boston, 1847. 2nd enlarged edition in 1848; and *My Southern Home, Or the South and Its People*, Boston: A. G. Brown, 1880. Both works were reprinted. The *Narrative* was reprinted in *Puttin' On Ole Massa; The Slave Narratives of Henry Bibb, William Wells Brown, and Solomon Northrup*. New York: Harper & Row, 1969. *My Southern Home* was reprinted by Upper Saddle River, New Jersey: Gregg Press, 1968.

69. Bruchac, Joseph (1942-). "Notes of a Translator's Son." *I Tell You Now: Autobiographical Essays by Native American Writers.* Ed. Brian Swann and Arnold Krupat. Lincoln: University of Nebraska Press, 1987. ISBN: 0803227140.

    See entry under *Swann, Brian* for complete list of authors and essays included in this anthology.

70. Bullock, Clarence C. (1937-). *Bullock: The Autobiography of an Artist.* New York: Vantage Press, 1984. ISBN: none. 58 pages; photographs; reproductions.

    Clarence Bullock, a native of Virginia, briefly describes his childhood and education. He attended graduate school in Pennsylvania with financial aid from Virginia because of the lack of graduate opportunities in his home state for African Americans at that time. Bullock describes his post-graduate art career, including his paintings and exhibitions. He recalls presenting his portrait of John F. Kennedy to the Kennedys at the White House as a high point of his career.

71. Bush, Barney (1945-). "The Personal Statement of Barney Bush." *I Tell You Now: Autobiographical Essays by Native American Writers.* Ed. Brian Swann and Arnold Krupat. Lincoln: University of Nebraska Press, 1987. ISBN: 0803227140.

    See entry under *Swann, Brian* for complete list of authors and essays included in this anthology.

72. Calderon, Erma. *Erma.* Written with Leonard Ray Teel. New York: Random House, 1981. ISBN: 0394517431. 200 pages.

    Erma Calderon grew up with her mother and two sisters in Savannah, Georgia. Her oldest sister, who died at 15 after a sudden illness, had seemingly supernatural powers, which Calderon describes in some detail. Her mother developed a debilitating illness, and, despite the presence of other adults who should have been able to help, Calderon, at the age of nine, had to quit school to nurse her mother until the time of her death. Alone, Calderon was forced into living situations which were intolerable. To escape, she married at the age of 11, and gave birth at 12. Her son was kidnapped by one of her former guardians, and Calderon was only able to find him 14 years later. Calderon recounts her experiences as a child bride trying to find her way in the world, how she cultivated lost familial ties, and finally her years working on Pinkney Island for a wealthy family with whom she was able to share unqualified mutual love and respect for the first time since the death of her mother.

73. Cameron, James (1914-). *A Time of Terror: A Survivor's Story*. Milwaukee: TD Publications, 1982. ISBN: 0937816272. 201 pages.
Note: Also published Baltimore, Maryland: Black Classic Press, 1992 and 1994. ISBN: 093312144X:0933121458.

Cameron was taken from his jail cell by a mob which had just lynched two other African American prisoners. He was beaten almost to a state of unconsciousness and a noose had been placed around his neck when someone intervened. He was returned to his jail cell and transferred to another jail in a different county, where he was fortunate enough to be in the charge of a sheriff who believed in his story and in his character. Cameron had been accused of murder and rape. His own story was that he had agreed to participate in a hold-up with two young men, but ran off when he realized the turn events were taking. A court trial eventually found him guilty of "accessory before the fact to voluntary manslaughter," and he was sentenced to two to twenty-one years in prison. His story details the horror of his arrest and the mob, his stay in jail before the trial, and his prison time after his conviction.

74. Campbell, Bebe Moore (1950-). *Sweet Summer: Growing Up With and Without My Dad*. New York: Putnam, 1989. ISBN: 0399134158. 272 pages.
Note: New York: Ballantine Books, 1989. ISBN: 0345366948.

Campbell writes about her relationship with her

father, who lived in North Carolina while she lived in Philadelphia with her mother and grandmother. Campbell spent each summer with her father in North Carolina, and missed him intensely throughout the rest of the year. Campbell, aware of the absence of men in her female-dominated life, treasured the occasional visits from her father and her uncles—her father's seven brothers. She realizes in retrospect that her father's separation from her daily life was painful and difficult for her, but his evident care and love helped to nurture and sustain her safely into adulthood.

75. Carona, Bert. *Memories of Chicano History: The Life and Narrative of Bert Corona.* Ed. Mario Garcia. Latinos in American Society and Culture 2. Berkeley: University of California Press, 1994. ISBN: 0520082192. 369 pages; photographs.

Carona, the son of a Mexican revolutionary, was organizing on the behalf of the rights of Mexican Americans from a very early age. This book is about a lifetime of working for justice within the labor movement and within a variety of Mexican American political organizations. Indignant at the way Mexican history was being taught in their Texas school, Carona and many of his classmates would argue with the teachers. When this behavior brought on punishment and the threat of expulsion, Carona organized a student strike which resulted in a resolution of the situation in their favor. Carona traces his growth as a political activist and his increasing awareness of having a dual Mexican and American heritage. Though he was born in Texas, his parents were native Mexicans, and Carona spent some of his childhood in Mexico. He spoke English and Spanish fluently, and the customs and traditions of Mexico were practiced in his home, while the family followed American practices in the public sphere. As a student at the University of Southern California, Carona became involved in the Mexican American Movement (MAM), and went on to union organizing and involvement in El Congresso Nacional de Pueblo de Habla Espanol, a militant organization founded in 1939 to further the rights of

Spanish speaking people. These early memberships haunted him during his time in the military. Union members were considered "potential subversives," and Carona was removed from the Air Corps because of his political activities. After the military, Carona returned to union organizing and work with Mexican American groups. In his book he discusses McCarthyism, the FBI, and the red-baiting of the 1950s and 60s; his political associations with Saul Alinsky and César Chavez; and the various aims of the organizations with which he worked. He founded the Mexican American Political Association in the 1960s because the Democratic Party was unwilling to support the needs of Mexican Americans. Carona concludes his narrative with a discussion of the future of Latinos and of Left politics in the United States.

76. Carter, Stephen L. (1954-). *Reflections of an Affirmative Action Baby*. New York: Basic Books, 1991. ISBN: 0465068715:0465068693. 286 pages.

Carter writes about his own education and career from the perspective of having grown up in the era of affirmative action. He explores the various arguments for and against the program. He examines the divisions taking place in the black community over the debate on affirmative action, and expresses his feelings on the difficulty of having that debate take place at all.

77. Cary, Lorene. *Black Ice*. New York: Knopf, 1991. ISBN: 0394574656. 237 pages.
Note: Also published New York: Vintage Books, 1992. ISBN: 0679737456.

Cary writes of her experiences as a student at St. Paul's School in New Hampshire. Cary entered the school as one of its first black women students. She experienced all of the difficulties of adolescence and being away from home with the added difficulties of being black and a woman in a place that was, until only a few years before her arrival, an all-white, all-male institution. Cary, though at many times unhappy with her life at St. Paul's, was academically successful, as well as fully

involved in extracurricular activities, including hold-
ing elected office. As a student, Cary struggled with
two conflicting feelings: should she succeed for herself,
for her family, and for all black people, or was her very
presence in this white institution a betrayal of her
people? In retrospect she writes,

> I began writing about St. Paul's School when I stopped
> thinking of my prep-school experience as an aberration from
> the common run of black life in America. The isolation I'd
> felt was an illusion, and it can take time . . . to get free of il-
> lusions. The narratives that helped me . . . were those that
> talked honestly about growing up black in America. . . . I am
> writing this book to become part of that unruly conversation,
> and to bring my experience back to the community of minds
> that made it possible. (p. 5, 6)

78. Cayaban, Ines V. (1904-). *A Goodly Heritage.* Wanchai,
Hong Kong: Gulliver Books, 1981. ISBN: 9627019801.
151 pages; photographs.

Cayaban provides a family history and a description of
her childhood in the Philippines in a relatively
wealthy household, including some of the traditions
and festivals in which she participated. Education and
moving to the United States were two of Cayaban's
goals. She pursued her education in the Philippines,
attending nursing school, but her move to the United
States seemed elusive. Cayaban presents the details of
her nursing career in the Philippines, and the means
by which she finally achieved her goal of traveling to
the U.S. in 1931. As she left the Philippines, her plans
were to travel to the continental U.S., but Cayaban
never got farther than Hawaii. She gives an account of
her career working first with tuberculosis prevention,
and then as a cancer specialist with the Public Health
Department in Hawaii.

79. Cervantes, John. *My Moline: A Young Illegal Immigrant
Dreams.* Canoga Park, California: Canyon Publishers,
1986. ISBN: 0942568117:0942568125. 167 pages; photographs; illustrations.

Cervantes writes about his youth in the U.S. as an illegal immigrant. His father had traveled in and out of
the United States legally, but conditions changed, and

when his entire extended family had to leave Mexico during the Mexican Revolution, they entered the U.S. illegally. The family followed agricultural work for awhile, finally settling in Moline, Illinois, where Cervantes' father worked with the railroad, and the family lived in a two-room boxcar typical of housing provided for laborers by the railroad companies. Cervantes, who began supplementing the household income at an early age, overcame great odds as well as the objections of a financially-strapped family to attend and graduate from college after the death of his father. In this book, Cervantes gives an account of Moline and its Mexican community during the 1920s. He describes the details of daily life there, including procedures for laundering and bathing. He also discusses the centrality of work in the lives of both adults and children as a means of survival, general preoccupation, and topic of conversation.

80. Chapel, Les (1924-). *The Black Man's Place in America*. New York: Vantage Press, 1991. ISBN: 0533093147. 42 pages.

Les Chapel grew up on a farm in Oklahoma. After his father left, he and his brother experimented with a number of ways to earn money. They eventually moved to California. Chapel describes his road to entrepreneurial success, and offers the six-part formula that helped him achieve that success.

81. Cheffen, Helen Ray. *Some Light, but Viewing the Dark Side*. New York: Vantage Press, 1993. ISBN: 0533091721. 254 pages.

82. Chief Big Eagle.
See *Piper, Aurelius* (1916-).

83. Ching, Frank. *Ancestors, 900 Years in the Life of a Chinese Family*. New York: W. Morrow, 1988. ISBN: 0688044611. 528 pages; photographs; maps.
Note: Also published New York: Ballantine Books, 1989. ISBN: 0449903532.

As the title suggests, this book is an exhaustive history of Ching's family. He was able to piece it together after ˌreceiving the family's ancestral genealogy, accounting for 33 generations, from a half-sister in China. Ching's name was the last to appear on the document. Ching writes about his own life in the final chapters of this work, describing his early years in China, his eventual move to the United States, where he became a journalist for the *New York Times*, and finally his return to China in the 1970s during the United States-China thaw.

84. Chosa, Heart Warrior (1945-). *Heart of Turtle Island: A Trilogy.* Ely, Minnesota: Bearhand Publishers, 1987. ISBN: none. 135 pages (book 1); photographs.
    Note: Book 1: Seven Chalk Hills; Book 2: Thunder Queens; Book 3: Winds of Fire (Books 2 & 3 not yet published).

    In the "Seven Chalk Hills," Chosa relates her life experiences from infancy through her completion of boarding school. She describes this period as the first level of testing on the wheel of life. Chosa (a name which she acquired later in life) and her brother were sent to St. Joseph's Catholic Charity Indian Boarding School, one of a few remaining schools which sought to rid the Indian student of any vestiges of cultural heritage. She recounts four years of life in a school that meted out arbitrary and brutal corporal punishment, and which allowed only short and infrequent visits with her family. Chosa also provides a brief account of the historical background of her tribe, the Turtle Mountain Metís, and their Cree-Scotts-French-Ojibwa heritage.

85. Clark, Septima Poinsette (1898-1987). *Ready From Within: Septima Clark and the Civil Rights Movement.* Ed. Cynthia Stokes Brown. Navarro, California: Wild Trees Press, 1986. ISBN: 0931125049. 134 pages; photographs; bibliography.
    Note: Also published by Africa World Press. Trenton, New Jersey, 1990. ISBN: 0865431736:0865431744.

Clark also published the autobiography *Echo in My Soul*. New York: Dutton, 1962.

Septima Clark, her father born into slavery and her mother a free Haitian, lived most of her life in South Carolina. Always outspoken and ready for change, she was an early activist in the Civil Rights Movement. In this work, Ms. Clark recalls her life-long work for African American rights, beginning with early efforts for voting rights just after the close of World War II and ending officially in 1970, when she retired from the Southern Christian Leadership Conference (SCLC) (after which she continued to work as a volunteer youth advisor). Clark includes details about her family, discusses the status of women involved in the Civil Rights Movement, and tells about some well-known and not-so-well-known leaders from that time. Most notable is Septima Clark's revelation of her willingness to face the anger and disapproval of both whites and blacks in order to fight for justice and change, and to speak out and to take action when few had the courage to stand with her.

86. Clayton, Xernona. *I've Been Marching All the Time: An Autobiography*. Written with Hal Gulliver (1935-). Atlanta: Longstreet Press, 1991. ISBN: 0929264878. 261 pages; photographs.

Clayton writes about growing up in segregated Muskogee, Oklahoma, and moving in her adult years to a segregated Chicago. Her career included work with the Urban League in Chicago, and with the Southern Christian Leadership Conference (SCLC) and Martin Luther King, Jr. in Atlanta. She also worked with the Model Cities Program in Atlanta and pursued a broadcasting career, first as a television talk show host and then as a programming assistant for Ted Turner and Turner Broadcasting. Clayton devotes a significant portion of her book to her personal and working relationship with Martin Luther King and her observations of him during the final months of his life.

87. Clifton, Lucille (1936-). *Good Woman: Poems and a Memoir, 1969-1980.* American Poets Continuum Series 14. Brockport, New York: BOA Editions, 1987. ISBN: 0918526582. 276 pages; photographs.

First edition of the *Memoir* published as a separate work. New York: Random House, 1976. ISBN: 039446155X. This brief memoir includes recollections of Clifton's life and an exploration of her African and slave heritage.

88. Cody, Iron Eyes (1904-). *Iron Eyes: My Life as a Hollywood Indian.* As told to Collin Perry. New York: Everest House, 1982. ISBN: 0896961117. 290 pages; photographs.

Cody's career in Hollywood began when his father's fields were used for the film *Back to God's Country.* After that he went to Hollywood with his father and brother to find work in the popular Westerns that were being churned out. Cody writes that he led a double life "somewhere between white civilization and my Indian heritage" (p. 16). He was not unaware of the stereotype of the Indian he was presenting to the American public and to the world: "The Indians who participated in acting out their role in the myth of the American West, including myself, *became* part of Hollywood" (p. 71). They accepted the portrayal in exchange for good pay and a comfortable life style. Cody never felt at liberty to comment on the characters he played until the years following World War II. With a new consciousness developing in Hollywood, Cody was able to make more demands and to present a more authentic, well-rounded portrait of the Native American. Cody describes his participation in the generally decadent lifestyle that seemed to go with work in the film industry during its early years, and his work and camaraderie with many notable Western film stars.

89. Cole, Johnnetta B. *Conversations: Straight Talk With America's Sister President.* New York: Doubleday, 1993. ISBN: 0385421303. 190 pages.

In the first chapter of *Conversations,* Cole presents a

brief outline of her life up to and including her present position as President of Spelman College. She is the first woman to be president of this all-woman college. In this autobiographical chapter, Cole wishes to present her life within the perspective of the "crucial issues in the lives of African American women, among them: racism, sexism, provincialism, self-help, and education" (p. xiii). In the following chapters, Cole discusses each of these themes separately. Her intention is that this work be a dialogue between herself and her "African American sisters," although others are invited to listen in.

90. Colon, Jesus (1901-1974). *The Way it Was, and Other Writings*. Ed. Edna Acosta-Belen and Virginia Sanchez Korrol. Houston: Arte Publico Press, 1993. ISBN: 1558850570. 127 pages; photographs; bibliography of Colon's writings from 1927-1970.

This work is a collection of short, entertaining vignettes about Colon's early experiences in the United States and portraits of his friends and neighbors. Through his own experiences, Colon writes about a number of issues confronting immigrants in this country, including the complexity of learning the English language, the inability of many Americans to understand and pronounce Spanish names correctly, homesickness, and the difficulties Colon encountered when returning to his native land. Colon also writes about his career as a writer and political activist.

91. Colson, Elizabeth (1917-). *Autobiographies of Three Pomo Women*. Interviews with Sophie Martinez, Ellen Wood, and Jane Adams. Recorded and edited by Elizabeth Colson. Berkeley: Archaeological Research Facility, Dept. of Anthropology, University of California, 1982.
Note: Prepared for publication in 1945 although final editing was never completed. The life-histories appeared in v. 1, *Primary Records in Culture and Personality*, 1956, as a microcard publication by the University of Wisconsin; nothing has been updated for publication in the present format. Republished by the Uni-

versity of California, Berkeley in 1972. Photocopy. [Berkeley, California: University of California, Library Photographic Service, 1982.]

The stories presented are those of Sophie Martinez, Ellen Wood, and Jane Adams. The interviewer, Elizabeth Colson, did little to prompt the women. She essentially got them started and then asked a few questions along the way when clarification was necessary. Ms. Colson provides enough background on the Pomos to give the uninitiated reader a good sense of the demise of a highly-organized society after a century or more of Russian, Mexican, and American intrusion. Appended to the introduction is an annotated bibliography of other life histories of Native Americans of California.

92. Comer, James.
    See *Comer, Maggie*.

93. Comer, Maggie and James P. Comer. *Maggie's American Dream: The Life and Times of a Black Family* a n d *My Turn*. New York: New American Library, 1988. ISBN: 0453005888. 228 Pages.
    Note: Also published New York: Penguin, 1989. ISBN: 0452263182.

    This two-part work includes an oral history of Maggie Comer taken by her son James, and a written autobiography by James Comer himself. Maggie grew up on a farm in the south until she was sixteen years old, with the benefit of only six months of formal schooling. She left to join relatives in East Chicago and married an older man. Together, they raised his daughter from a previous marriage. Maggie battled school officials to ensure that her step-daughter had all of the educational opportunities, including music, that she herself had been denied. Otherwise childless during the first twelve years of her marriage, Maggie eventually gave birth to five children, four of whom survived. She devoted herself to their upbringing, encouraging them to excel in school, work hard, and be proud of their race and heritage. In James Comer's autobiography, entitled "My Turn," he tells the story of his mother's work on behalf of her children, giving her credit for his education and accomplishments. Comer writes that as a black student in a predominantly white student body, both in high school and as an undergraduate, he always felt an immense pressure to be the best at everything, both because he felt the responsibility of representing his race and because of a sense that the white majority demanded it. He decided to attend Howard University for medical school so that he could enjoy the luxury of being a black student in a black student body.

94. Concepcion, Jaime E. (1921-). *From My Rearview Mirror.* Metro Manila, Philippines: Tambay Kay Lim Sports Foundation, 1989. ISBN: none. 133 pages.

Concepcion was born and raised in the Philippines, fought against the Japanese invasion during World War II, and was part of the Bataan Death March and a prisoner of war. A U.S. citizen since 1961, Concepcion attended graduate school at New York University, worked for the Agency for International Development (AID) during the Vietnam War, following which he was stationed in Mauritania. Concepcion has tried to have legislation passed that would grant Filipino World War II veterans full veterans' rights which they have been denied despite the fact that the Philippines was a commonwealth of the United States (receiving independence in 1946 after the end of the war). He has many criticisms of the United States with regard to their presence in the Philippines historically and in the present. Concepcion speculates that the United States holds a grudge against countries that legitimately champion their own interests: "In most situations you cannot be pro-your own country without being viewed at the same time, as being anti-American" (p. 106). He predicts difficulties in the future with U.S.-Filipino relations.

95. Conner, Douglas L. *A Black Physician's Story: Bringing Hope in Mississippi.* Written with John F. Marszalek.

Jackson: University of Mississippi, 1985. ISBN: 0878052798. 183 pages; photographs.

Conner reached adulthood anxious to create change in a system that allowed segregation and discrimination. He grew up in segregated Mississippi, attended all black schools and colleges, and was drafted into a segregated armed forces during World War II. His first experience with an integrated educational system occurred when he was chosen to participate in the Walter Reed Army Hospital medical training program. Conner eventually completed his medical training at Howard University in Washington, D.C. He set up practice in Starkville, Mississippi, where he was one of the few African Americans to complete the voter registration process. It took a full year for him to complete the process, because it involved paying the poll tax twice over a twelve-month period. Conner became involved in state and national politics, partly at the urging of Medgar Evers.

96. Cook-Lynn, Elizabeth (1930-). *"'You May Consider Speaking About Your Art . . .'." I Tell You Now: Autobiographical Essays by Native American Writers.* Ed. Brian Swann and Arnold Krupat. Lincoln: University of Nebraska Press, 1987. ISBN: 0803227140.

See entry under *Swann, Brian* for complete list of authors and essays included in this anthology.

97. Cooper, Michael J. *No Slack.* Written with Theodore J. Lynn. Albuquerque, New Mexico: CompuPress, 1987. ISBN: 0944009026. 116 pages; photographs; glossary.

In this book, Cooper urges young men who pursue basketball to take their education seriously. He himself did not and at one point was removed from eligibility. Although he went on to be a successful professional basketball player, Cooper stresses that many players don't make it, some may have a professional career that lasts no more than four years, and for long term success, an education with plans for the future is essential. Cooper provides a detailed discussion of his philosophy, strategies, and techniques.

98. Corral, Jesus C. (1912-). *Caro Amigo: The Autobiography of Jesus C. Corral.* Tucson, Arizona: Westernlore Press, 1984. ISBN: 0870260596. 238 pages; photographs.

Corral's family was from Sonora, Mexico, and he spent his first years in the mining town of Camanea—a town he describes as dirty and crime-ridden. The family left Camanea for the agricultural town of Scottsdale, Arizona, in 1919. Corral was inspired artistically when he traveled back to Sonora with his mother and observed the artwork of a boy not much older than himself. He spent his life working on developing as an artist while trying to support himself and, later, his growing family. Throughout these years, Corral had many experiences and worked for a variety of people. Not until much later in life, during his second marriage, was he able to realize his dreams of commercial success as an artist while running his own restaurant and building a house in Mexico.

99. Crow Dog, Mary.
See *Brave Bird, Mary.*

100. Cruikshank, Moses (1906-). *The Life I've Been Living.* Recorded and compiled by William Schneider. Oral Biography Series 1. Fairbanks: University of Alaska Press, 1986. ISBN: 0912006234.

Cruikshank describes his life growing up along the Yukon River. He tells of learning about animals, hunting, and survival from the "old timers"; working with missionaries; working in the mines and on the railroad; and finally, in retirement, working with children, telling stories about the early days, in the Parent-Child Center of the Fairbanks Native Association.

101. Cuero, Delfina (1900-1972). *Delfina Cuero: Her Autobiography, an Account of Her Last Years, and Her Ethnobotanic Contributions.* Ballena Press Anthropological Papers 37. Menlo Park: Ballena Press, 1991. ISBN: 0879191236:0879191228. 98 pages; map; photographs.
Note: Originally printed Pasadena, California: Castle Press, 1968. Baja California Travel Series 12; and

Riverside, California: Rubidoux Printing Company, 1970. "An Account of Her Last Years" and "Her Ethnobotanic Contributions" were written by Florence Connolly Shipek.

Cuero was a member of the Kumeyaay Tribe, whose traditional homeland extended approximately 50 miles on either side of the U.S.-Mexican border. Used to living by hunting, gathering, and fishing, the Kumeyaay had also had gardens, but during Cuero's childhood they were unable to settle down long enough to plant because the land had been taken over by newcomers to the California/Mexico area. They were eventually forced to lead a subsistence existence with fewer and fewer areas on which to rely. She gives a detailed explanation of the kinds of food they ate, where and how they came by the food, and how it was prepared. She also describes some recreational activities, ceremonies, and rites. Many rites which served as a means for educating children, not only in the specific religious beliefs and customs of the Kumeyaay, but also as valuable survival methods, had been forbidden by Catholic missionaries, and this restriction contributed to the degradation of the tribe. Cuero relates some of the difficulties in her own coming of age and adult life, and also in the lives of her children.

102. David, Jay, ed. *Growing Up Black: From Slave Days to the Present: Twenty-Five African-Americans Reveal the Trials and Triumphs of Their Childhoods.* New York: Avon Books, 1992. ISBN: 0380766329. 276 pages.
Note: Originally published New York: W. Morrow, 1968. This edition contains new material.

This is a collection of excerpts from material published in the nineteenth and twentieth centuries. This edition has been updated to include materials published since 1970, all of which are represented separately in this bibliography. The excerpts from the following works are not represented in this bibliography because of their original publication dates: *A Man Called White* by Walter White, 1948; *Dark Symphony* by Elizabeth Adams, 1942; "The Afternoon of a Young Poet," in *Anger and Beyond: The Negro Writer in the U.S.* by M. Carl Holman, 1966; *Memoirs of a Monticello Slave: The Life of Isaac Jefferson*, (n.d.); *Narrative of the Life of Frederick Douglass, An American Slave*, (1846); *Up From Slavery* by Booker T. Washington, (1901); *The Black Man's Burden* by William H. Holtzclaw (1915); *Manchild in the Promised Land* by Claude Brown (1965); *The Long Shadow of Little Rock* by Daisy Bates, 1962; and *Coming of Age in Mississippi* (1968).

103. Davis, Angela Yvonne. *Angela Davis - An Autobiography*. New York: International Publishers, 1988. ISBN: 0704342324:070434209X. 400 pages.
Originally published New York: Random House, 1974. ISBN: 0394489780. Also published New York: Bantam Books with title *Angela Davis; With My Mind on Freedom. An Autobiography*, 1974. ISBN: 0553117955.

104. Davis, Miles (1926-1991). *Miles, the Autobiography*. Written with Quincy Troupe. New York: Simon & Schuster, 1989. ISBN: 0671635042. 431 pages; photographs.
Note: Also published New York: Simon & Schuster, 1990. ISBN: 0671725823.

Miles Davis became seriously interested in music when he was 12 years old and never turned back. He was involved professionally with top-level jazz musicians—Billy Eckstine, Dizzie Gillespie, Charlie "Bird" Parker—by the time he was 18. Davis chronicles his professional career and describes his work with many great musicians, both known and unknown. He also describes in some detail his relationships with women, his serious problems with drug addiction, and his struggle with poor health in the latter part of his life. It is clear from this work that Davis was a consummate musician, one who was never satisfied with the status quo. He looked for new ideas both from the younger jazz musicians and from contemporary composers trained in the classical tradition, and thus had a style that was constantly evolving.

105. Dayton, Roger (1921-). *Roger Dayton, Koyukuk*. Interviews conducted and text prepared by Curt Madison

and Yvonne Yarber. North Vancouver, British Columbia: Hancock House, 1981. ISBN: 088839067X. 85 pages; photographs; maps.
Note: Produced by the Yukon-Koyukuk School District of Alaska.

Roger Dayton describes his family, relating some of his earliest memories and the stories passed on to him by his elders. He tells of his experiences hunting and fishing and of how he learned the necessary skills from his father and other older male relatives. Dayton compares formal schooling to learning outdoor skills from the elders, noting that "of course you'd tell your kids to learn as much as you can in school. Then when you take them out you just teach them what your father taught you when you were a kid. . . . There's not much difference between going to school and learning the outdoor life. . . . They learn to make a living" (p. 77).
For a brief description and list of autobiographies in this Yukon-Koyukuk School District series, see the entry for Moses Henzie.

106. De Vergee, Winston W. *Assignment in Hell*. New York: Vantage Press, 1991. ISBN: 0533085179. 119 pages; photographs.

107. Delany, Samuel. *The Motion of Light in Water: Sex and Science Fiction Writing in the East Village, 1957-1965.* New York: Arbor House/W. Morrow, 1988. ISBN: 0877959471. 302 pages; portrait.
Note: Also published New York: New American Library, 1989. ISBN: 0452262321; New York: Masquerade Books, 1993. ISBN: 1563331330.

Delany examines his life from the time his father died when Delany was 18 until he began a six-month sojourn in Europe at the age of 24. He spent the intervening years in the East Village with poet Marilyn Hacker. Their relationship as writers, friends and lovers, lovers of others, mutual supporters, and, to some extent, rivals is the main focus of this fragment of Delany's life. Both Hacker and Delany were recog-

nized as exceptional writers while still in their teens.
Delany had two novels published by the time he was
21, and Hacker was the recipient of many prizes and
awards. Delany's homosexuality figures prominently
in his book. He writes, "So, I thought, you are neither
black nor white. You are neither male nor female.
And you are that most ambiguous of citizens, the
writer. There was something at once very satisfying
and very sad, placing myself at this pivotal suspen-
sion" (p. 52). Delany includes samples of Hacker's poetry throughout this work.

108. Delany, Sarah Louise and A. Elizabeth. *Having Our Say:
The Delany Sisters' First 100 Years.* Written with Amy
Hill Hearth. New York: Kodansha International, 1993.
ISBN: 156836010X.
Note: The Delany sisters have also published *The De-
lany Sisters' Book of Everyday Wisdom.* Written with
Amy Hill Hearth. New York: Kodansha International,
1994. ISBN: 1568360428.

The Delany sisters were 101 and 103 at the time this
book was published. Their father, born a slave, began
life as a freeman by becoming a mason and then attending St. Augustine's College in North Carolina. He
eventually became an Episcopal Bishop and the principal of St. Augustine's. Their mother, another St.
Augustine's graduate, was born free and later became
matron of the college. The sisters were members of a
large family. The college campus and their well-educated, highly respected parents, shielded the girls from
much of the misery experienced by African Americans
during the early decades of freedom. Yet the sisters
remember experiencing the change from reconstruction to the institution of the Jim Crow laws and the
widespread practice of lynching, during their childhood. Elizabeth (called Bessie) nearly became the victim of a white mob. The sisters are very close and
have lived together most of their lives, but they have
developed different approaches to handling and sur-
mounting racism. Both women pioneered in their
fields as blacks and as women. Bessie earned a doctoral
degree in surgical dentistry and was the second woman

licensed to practice in New York. Sadie was the first black high school teacher of domestic science in the New York City system. The chapters are narrated alternately by the two sisters, with Hearth contributing a chapter of background information at the beginning of each section. Both sisters comment on the need for blacks to be better than whites to succeed in the United States. Bessie states that

> when you are colored, everyone is always looking for your faults. If you are going to make it, you have to be entirely honest, clean, brilliant, and so on. . . . So you don't have to be as good as white people, you have to be *better or the best*. When Negroes are average *they fail*, unless they are very, very lucky. Now if you're average and *white*, honey, you can go far. Just look at Dan Quayle. If that boy was colored he'd be washing dishes somewhere. (p. 154)

109. Delorme, Eugene P. *Chief: The Life History of Eugene Delorme, Imprisoned Santee Sioux.* Written with Inez Cardozo-Freeman. American Indian Lives. Lincoln: University of Nebraska Press, 1994. ISBN: 0803214693. 218 pages; photographs; bibliography.

The first three chapters of this book were recorded by Delorme while he was in prison; the final chapter was written ten years later, after he had been released. Born on the reservation but raised in the city, Delorme did not grow up with a strong Native American identity or with much knowledge of his Dakota heritage. He became more involved with this culture through his contact with other Native American prisoners. He began stealing with his brother at an early age, mostly bringing home food to supplement the family's meager supplies. It was a pattern he was never able to break, although he had periods of time, mostly while in prison, where he was able to conform to society's expectations for suitable behavior, even to complete his education through college graduation. But outside of prison, Delorme was unable to resist drug and alcohol addiction for long. His last chapter concludes with the sentiment that he felt that he was better off in prison than on his own.

110. Dickerson, Leon. *Life Within Two Decades 1960-1980: Poetry, Essays and Photographs.* Lawrenceville, Virginia: Brunswick Publishing Corporation, 1988. ISBN: 1556180268. 115 pages; photographs.
Note: Autobiographical essays, poetry, and photographs.

In this collection of essays, Dickerson writes about his childhood in the segregated South and in Harlem; his experiences as a young revolutionary and poet; his descent into drug addiction; and finally his reawakening and return to school to earn a Masters Degree in Social Work from Adelphi University.

111. Dorris, Michael. *The Broken Cord.* New York: Harper & Row, 1989. ISBN: 0060160713. 300 pages; photographs; bibliography.
Note: Also published New York: Harper Perennial, 1990. ISBN: 0060916826.

Dorris, an anthropologist, writer, and sometime aerobics instructor, tells the story of his son, Adam, whom he adopted at the age of three. Dorris was aware that Adam had been abused, neglected and malnourished, and that he was at least mildly retarded. He writes of his first meeting with Adam and his instant and intense commitment to and love for him. Adam's limitations remained a puzzle, however, until Dorris learned about Fetal Alcohol Syndrome (FAS) and saw other children who were suffering from this affliction. At this point, Dorris realized that Adam, too, was affected by the syndrome. Dorris began to research this disease with a passion, studying Native Americans on reservations in particular. He provides detailed information as to the cause of FAS/FAE (Fetal Alcohol Effect), and the nature of children born in this condition. Apparently, very little can be done beyond providing a safe and nurturing environment for these victims of parental alcohol abuse. Dorris, honestly and with humor, describes his life with Adam, and the difficulty of caring for a child, healthy or otherwise, as a single, working parent. He concludes this work at the point where Adam leaves home to live in a half-way house, revealing the emotional struggle to relinquish some parental responsibility and daily involvement. Dorris also includes Adam's life story as Adam himself wrote it.

112. Dudley, Joseph Iron Eye (1940-). *Choteau Creek: A Sioux Reminiscence*. Lincoln: University of Nebraska Press, 1992. ISBN: 0803216904. 179 pages.
Note: Also published New York: Warner Books, 1994. ISBN: 0446395196.

Dudley grew up with his elderly grandparents, William and Bernice Bourisseau, near Choteau Creek, on the Yankton Sioux Reservation in South Eastern South Dakota. This book is in honor and in memory of them. He writes that his grandparents cared for him, feeding and clothing him, though they were always in a state of economic poverty. They also provided Dudley with a rich spiritual life, one which was both Christian and connected to traditional Sioux beliefs. He stayed with his grandparents, spending brief periods with his father or mother, until he was able to set out on his own. Dudley became a Methodist minister, and served two small parishes not far from where he grew up.

113. Durham, Jimmie (1940-). "Those Dead Guys for a Hundred Years." *I Tell You Now: Autobiographical Essays by Native American Writers*. Ed. Brian Swann and Arnold Krupat. Lincoln: University of Nebraska Press, 1987. ISBN: 0803227140.

See entry under *Swann, Brian* for a complete list of authors included in this anthology.

114. Early, Gerald Lyn. *Daughters: On Family and Fatherhood*. Reading, Massachusetts: Addison-Wesley Publishing Co., 1994. ISBN: 0201627248. 234 pages; photographs.

Early writes about himself in the context of his family and in the role of father and husband. He notes that he was happy to be the father of daughters because he grew up without a father or brothers, and never learned to socialize well with men. He includes brief excerpts from his daughters' diaries (which were given to him for the book on their own initiative) and includes many of their impressions and responses to family events. Early maintains in his initial chapter that he writes only about his own family and experiences and does not seek to represent any group of people.

115. Eaton, Hubert Arthur (1916-). *Every Man Should Try*. Wilmington, North Carolina: Bonaparte Press, 1984. ISBN: none. 360 pages; photographs.

A successful doctor in New Hanover County, North Carolina, Eaton was shocked out of complacency when, as a witness in a court trial, he was asked to swear on a Bible marked "colored." The fact that even the Bible could be segregated jolted him into action to effect change. Eaton worked to improve and integrate local schools and medical facilities, first within the strictures of the segregated South, and then within the court system. He gives a detailed account of a case involving his youngest daughter, *Carolyn Eaton, et al., v. New Hanover County Board of Education*, which was aimed at speeding up the pace of desegregation in the public schools. This case was in the courts from 1964 through July 1971. Eaton also worked to end discrimination and inequities in the welfare and Medicaid system, and to increase voter registration in the African American community. (In 1952 only 1,800 out of 23,000 eligible African Americans were voting in New Hanover County.) He discusses his family's relationship with Althea Gibson, the African American tennis player who went on to win two Wimbledon singles championships. Eaton and his family provided Gibson with a home and moral and financial support while she returned to high school at the age of 19 to earn her diploma. An avid tennis amateur himself, Eaton had his own tennis courts built because of the poor condition of courts available for use by African Americans.

116. Edenso, Christine. *The Transcribed Tapes of Christine Edenso*. Transcribed by Vesta Johnson, Robert Cogo,

and Nora Cogo. Anchorage: Materials Development Center, Rural Education, University of Alaska, 1983. ISBN: none. 45 pages; photographs.

Christine Edenso recorded her story in Haida, a rapidly vanishing language, in 1980 at the age of 91. In her narrative, Edenso describes fishing and the uses for the different parts of the fish. She also explains the gathering of a variety of vegetation used for food, medicines, and basket making. Edenso includes in her narrative a discussion of the effects of alcohol use on native life, and she tells the legend of the "Red Coho."

117. Edwards, Harry (1942-). *The Struggle That Must Be: An Autobiography*. New York: Macmillan, 1980. ISBN: 0025350404. 350 pages.

Harry Edwards grew up in a family of eight children. When their mother left, the oldest daughter, not yet a teenager, took responsibility for the family, including two infants. Their father stopped in periodically to make sure that they had food. Edwards describes a childhood of abject poverty without adequate shelter, services, or parental care. He writes that "we had fallen into the chaotic and nightmarish world of people who the combined forces of history, society, and biography have condemned to the status of so much excess baggage and human debris" (p. 3-4). Edwards became involved in organized sports in junior high school, and he was eventually encouraged to go out to California to seek an athletic scholarship at one of the state universities. He eventually achieved this goal and attended San Jose State University (SJU). What seemed a golden opportunity soon deteriorated into a mire of racism and stereotyping. Edwards describes the situation of the few black athletes attending SJU during those early years of integration, and his own personal experiences with racism from both coaches and fellow athletes. Edwards was one of the few black athletes of his day to graduate from SJU, and he went on to pursue a doctoral degree in sociology from Cornell University and to teach at the University of California at Berkeley. Before attaining his position at Berkeley,

Edwards gained a national reputation as the organizer of the Negro Boycott of the 1968 Olympics and became the subject of long-term FBI surveillance. His political activities led to an initial denial of tenure at UC Berkeley, which was overturned after it became an international incident.

118. Ekada, Henry. *Henry Ekada: Nulato.* Interviews conducted and text prepared by Yvonne Yarber and Curt Madison. Yukon-Koyukuk Biography Series. Fairbanks: Spirit Mountain Press, 1986. ISBN: 0910871094. 64 pages; photographs; maps.
Note: Produced by Yukon-Koyukuk School District of Alaska.

Ekada tells stories of growing up, family, and work in the Alaskan interior along the Yukon River. Ekada's father was Japanese and his mother was Athapascan. He describes some of the difficulties experienced by his family because of their Japanese heritage and customs.
For a brief description and list of autobiographies in this Yukon-Koyukuk School District series, see the entry for Moses Henzie.

119. Elaw, Zilpha (b. 1790?).
See *Lee, Jarena.*

120. Elizondo, Virgilio P. *The Future is Mestizo: Life Where Cultures Meet.* Oak Park, Illinois: Meyer-Stone Books, 1988. ISBN: 094098928X. 109 pages.
Note: Translation of *L'avenir est au Metissage.* Paris: Nouvelles Editions Mame, 1987. Also published New York: Crossroad, 1992.

Elizondo describes himself as a middle-aged priest, native, and life-time resident of San Antonio. This work, though autobiographical, is more a vision of the future than the study of a life. Elizondo had a happy childhood, always aware and proud of his Mexican heritage. This combination made it possible for him to survive the discrimination he inevitably faced as he moved out of the secure confines of his family and neighborhood. In setting out his vision, Elizondo examines the different cultures that make up his Mestizo background—U.S.-Anglo, Spanish, Indian—and concludes that no one heritage presents the sole model for existence, but all together make up a "new human." He writes, "I was rich in mixture, but I was not mixed-up! . . . I was *not just* U.S.-American and *not just* Mexican but fully both and exclusively neither" (p. 23). Having traveled widely and spent extended periods of time in a number of different countries, Elizondo came to realize that the populations of most nations are the product of mixed heritage: "The idea of pure seems to appear only when people forget their origins. All modern-day nations and cultures are products of a 'mesticizing' process that often has long been forgotten" (p. 101). Elizondo also addresses the fears that some have expressed concerning multiculturalism: "Americanism is not disappearing, but it is radiating a new image and experiencing a new soul—no longer the face and voice of a soloist, but the countenance and heart of an entire symphony" (p. 94).

121. Ellis, Jerry. *Walking the Trail: One Man's Journey Along the Cherokee Trail of Tears.* New York: Delacorte Press, 1991. ISBN: 038530448X. 256 pages; maps; bibliography.
Note: Also published Thorndike, Maine: Thorndike Press, 1993. ISBN: 1560548851:1560546425; New York: Delta, 1993. ISBN: 0385308264.

Jerry Ellis, of mixed Cherokee and European ancestry, was raised in Fort Payne, Alabama. His ancestors had been forced to relocate to Fort Payne or one of twelve other camps and then were led on a 900-mile march to Oklahoma during the winter of 1838. Ellis wished to become closer to this piece of Cherokee history by making the walk himself, only in reverse—from Oklahoma to Fort Payne. This book describes his two-month-long sojourn, the places he passed through, the people he met, his thoughts and emotions. Ellis met both Indians and non-Indians, most of whom were supportive of his walk. His hopes were that his effort would help to affix the tragic event of 1838, during which 4,000 Cherokees died, in the minds of all Americans.

122. Estes, Bernice Q. *They Called Me Sweetgrass*. Bellevue, Washington: Sweetgrass Publishing, 1990. ISBN: 0964443856. 79 pages; photographs.

Bernice Estes describes life with her grandparents on the Mandan Reservation in North Dakota. She left this community at 18, and married soon after. Her married life included a loving relationship with her husband, but economic hardships, health problems, and difficulties with her children. A psychic, Estes describes her many visions and dreams.

123. Fairbanks, Evelyn (1928-). *The Days of Rondo*. St. Paul: Minnesota Historical Society Press, 1990. ISBN: 0873512553:0873512561. 182 pages; photographs.
Note: An abridged version is also available on cassette tape.

Fairbanks writes about growing up with her adoptive family in the Rondo District of St. Paul, Minnesota, a black community that was erased by the highway department to make way for Interstate 94 in the 1960s. Fairbanks describes her school years and what it was like to be black in Minnesota: the positive aspects of her family and community, and the negative aspects of discrimination. She tells about visits to relatives in Macon, Georgia, and finally her career and adult years. She explains that the Rondo District was changing even before the highway was built through it, but that former residents remember their life there with fondness. An annual celebration called Rondo Days is held, according to Fairbanks, "to remember and recreate at least the atmosphere of our community" (p. 182).

124. Farmer, James (1920-). *Lay Bare the Heart: An Autobiography of the Civil Rights Movement*. New York: Arbor House, 1985. ISBN: 0877956243. 370 pages; photographs.
Note: Also published New York: New American Library, 1985. ISBN: 0452258030.

Farmer begins his story by describing his role as a Congress of Racial Equality (CORE) leader and participant in the Freedom Ride into Mississippi in 1961. He emphasizes the fear and uncertainty that he and other participants felt as they prepared to make the trip after the violent mobbing of a previous Freedom Ride to Alabama, but he also speaks of the urgent need of all the participants to carry out their commitment. Farmer then goes on to document his long association with non-violent activities, beginning in the early 1940s with his work for the Quaker organization Fellowship of Reconciliation (FOR), and including his position as national director of CORE.

125. Faulkner, Audrey Olsen, et al. *When I was Comin' Up: An Oral History of Aged Blacks*. Hamden, Connecticut: Archon Books, 1982. ISBN: 0208019529. 221 pages; bibliography.
Note: "Life histories of elderly black people in Newark, New Jersey from tape-recorded reminiscences collected as a project of the Rutgers Graduate School of Social Work."

The thirteen subjects of this collection of oral histories were selected from one public housing project in Newark, New Jersey. The purpose of the collection is to document the lives of those who participated in the great northern migration of African Americans from the South.

126. Fields, David. *Growing-up in a Rural Setting*. Ontario: Vesta Publications, 1983. ISBN: 0919301800. 76 pages; illustrations.

Fields grew up in rural Alabama and, after finishing high school, eventually made his way to Detroit, Michigan. Arriving there while the city was still recovering from the riots of 1967, he was shocked by how dangerous life was and realized that it was not the "promised land" he had expected to find. Although he was not encouraged by anyone at his high school to attend college or pursue a professional career—the only employer to attend the high school job fair was the

U.S. Military—Fields was determined to do both. He describes his positive experiences at an all-black college and then, returning to Detroit, his career as a parole officer working with individuals addicted to drugs and alcohol. Ironically, Fields found that he himself was a substance abuser with a serious alcohol problem. He writes about the extent of his addiction and the effect that it had on his family life. Afraid to seek help because of his work but unable to help himself, Fields explored transcendental meditation (TM). His experiences with TM enabled him to become sober within two months.

127. Fields, Mamie Garvin (1888-). *Lemon Swamp and Other Places: A Carolina Memoir*. Written with Karen Fields. New York: Free Press, 1983. ISBN: 0029101603. 250 pages; photographs.

Mamie Fields narrates the story of her family, describes her neighbors and neighborhood, and relates the events and customs of her life in Charleston, South Carolina, from her birth in 1888 to her retirement from teaching in 1948. Fields testifies to the richness of Charleston's African American culture, but also recounts the many restrictions placed on African Americans by the white society—restrictions that held fast according to both written and unwritten law. After training to be a teacher, Fields taught in several rural schools. She describes what was and wasn't provided by the state and the difficulty many children had attending school during the brief period it was officially offered them. Fields also provides insight into the high infant and maternal mortality rate, giving a personal account of her own loss and the losses suffered by her extended family and friends.

128. Fisher, Charles B. (1840?-1903). *Diary of Charles B. Fisher*. Transcribed and edited by Paul E. Sluby and Stanton L. Wormley. Washington, D.C.: Columbian Harmony Society, 1983. ISBN: none. 106 leaves; photographs.

Fisher kept this diary during his two years in the navy, beginning in 1862. In this diary, Fisher recorded the daily activities of shipboard life, described the members of the crew, and provided accounts of their battles.

129. Fisher, Te Ata.
     See *Te Ata*.

130. Fong-Torres, Ben. *The Rice Room: Growing Up Chinese-American: From Number Two Son to Rock 'n' Roll.* New York: Hyperion, 1994. ISBN: 0786860022. 260 pages.
     Note: Also published New York: Plume, 1995. ISBN: 0452274125.

     Fong-Torres, formerly a *Rolling Stone* editor and rock 'n' roll DJ, now a freelance writer, was born in 1945 to Chinese immigrant parents. In his life story, Fong-Torres gives the reader a taste of the times, chronicling his musical preferences along with his childhood, adolescence, and college years, his ups and downs with women, and his work in journalism and rock 'n' roll. In describing his relationship with his parents, who spoke Cantonese with only a smattering of English, Fong-Torres focuses on the difficulty of communication during a time when the "generation gap" of the late 60s and early 70s was unbridgeable, even in households where everyone spoke the same language. Fong-Torres writes: "This is one of the great sadnesses of my life. How ironic, I would think. We're all well educated, thanks in part to our parents' hard work and determination; I'm a journalist and a broadcaster—my *job* is to communicate—and I can't with the two people with whom I want to most" (p. 5).

131. Foote, Julia A. J. (1823-1900).
     See *Lee, Jarena*.

132. Forbes, Jack D. (1934-). "Shouting Back to the Geese." *I Tell You Now: Autobiographical Essays by Native American Writers.* Ed. Brian Swann and Arnold Krupat. Lincoln: University of Nebraska Press, 1987. ISBN: 0803227140.

See entry under *Swann, Brian* for a complete list of authors included in this anthology.

133. Ford, Nick Aaron. *Seeking a Newer World: Memoirs of a Black American Teacher.* Great Neck, New York: Todd and Honeywell, 1983. ISBN: 0899622771. 285 pages; photographs.

Ford became a teacher both at the high school and college level after experiencing great difficulty himself in obtaining an education. Both former slaves, Ford's parents were well educated for their time, and they were determined that Nick receive an even better education than their own. When his father died, his mother went to extremes to get Nick through high school. Although it seemed both economically and strategically impossible, Ford completed high school and went on to get a college degree as well. Later in life he earned an M.A. and a Ph.D. Ford taught literature and specialized in African American literature. He published *The Contemporary Negro Novel* in 1936. He completed his teaching career as the Alain Locke Professor of Black Studies at Morgan State University and as a consultant for Black Studies programs nationwide.

134. Forman, James (1928-). *The Making of Black Revolutionaries.* 2nd ed. Washington, D.C.: Open Hand Press, 1990. ISBN: 0940880113:0940880105. 568 pages.
Note: First edition published New York: Macmillan Co., 1972.

James Foreman writes that this book is an "attempt to illustrate the development of [himself] and of others within the context of a racist, brutal, sexist, and anti-Semitic society" (p. xix). In this second edition, Foreman strengthens his original position in support of women's rights. After reading through 3,000 pages of his personal files from the FBI and CIA, he is able to document the government's role in the destruction of the Student Nonviolent Coordinating Committee (SNCC).

135. Forten, Charlotte L. *The Journal of Charlotte L. Forten: A Free Negro in the Slave Era.* Ed. Ray Allen Billington. New York: W. W. Norton, 1981. ISBN: 039300046X. 286 pages; bibliography.
Note: Originally published New York, Dryden Press, 1953.

A school teacher living in the North, Forten kept this journal from May 24, 1854, through May 15, 1864. The editor has chosen to delete certain sections of the diary.

136. Fortunate Eagle, Adam. *Alcatraz, Alcatraz!: The Indian Occupation of 1969-1971.* Photographs by Ilka Hartmann. Berkeley, California: Heydey Books, 1992. ISBN: 0930588517. 155 pages; photographs; map.

Adam Fortunate Eagle tells the story of the takeover of Alcatraz by "The Indians of All Tribes" in 1969. He explains the roots of the movement, which began in the 1950s with the U.S. Government's efforts to move Native Americans out of the reservations and into urban areas. Thus, by 1969, there were thousands of Indians in the San Francisco Bay Area who had been relocated from all over the country. Many of them experienced a strong sense of displacement and a need to regain traditional culture. The goals of the takeover included making the island a center of Native arts, history, and education. Fortunate Eagle describes his role in the occupation as an organizer who provided support from the mainland. He tells of the successes and failures of the occupation, and of its long term benefits: it provided a catalyst to awaken and instill pride in Native Americans throughout the U.S. despite the fact that its immediate goals were not met.

137. Francis, Lelia (1904-). *Your Mind is Your Life, Your Word is Your Bond: An Autobiography.* The Black Contemporary Lives Series. Dayton Ohio (402 Salem Ave., Dayton 45406): Fells Johnson Techni-write, Inc., 1989. ISBN: none. 128 pages; photographs.

Francis' father, who was born into slavery and bought both his and his mother's freedom, told his children that they should neither work for or rent from anybody. He owned a five-acre farm in Saltlick, Kentucky, where Francis grew up, which allowed the family to be self-sufficient. Francis took his advice to heart, and, after a period of time spent as a teacher and as a cosmetologist, she entered into the real estate business with her husband and her brother in Dayton, Ohio. Through this enterprise, they were able to assist Dayton's African American community by opening up white neighborhoods to black families.

138. Frias, Gus. *Barrio Warriors: Homeboys of Peace.* Los Angeles: Diaz, 1982. 181 pages; photographs.
Note: Also published as *Barrio Patriots: Killing and Dying for America.* 2nd ed., revised and enlarged. Los Angeles: n.p., 1989.

This personal testimony was written by Frias after eight years as a volunteer for the End Barrio Warfare Movement. His story begins in 1970 with the National Chicano Moratorium, a major demonstration organized to protest the large number of Chicano deaths in Vietnam. Frias was 15 at the time and ready to enter high school. He then describes the pressures and dangers of attending high school with members of rival barrios and the difficulty of concentrating on classroom activities and schoolwork. His involvement in barrio rivalries (Frias purposely avoids the use of the term "gang") ends in 1972 with the murder of his best friend. The normal sequence of events would be for a murder to lead to revenge, but this death awakened Frias to the senselessness of murder following murder. He resolved to dedicate his life to ending what he refers to as the Chicano Civil War:

> In search of a diabolic revenge, I found, instead, a path to an altruistic frontier—one centered in respect, trust, and sincere Chicano understanding. I can still remember facing the two dynamic paths of justice: one implying further fratricide through the barrio's law of 'reclamar'; the other expressing brotherhood, peace, awareness, and clean pride through Chicanismo. (p. 34)

The rest of this work chronicles Frias's experiences: organizing, recruiting, and providing inspiration for the End Barrio Warfare Movement; struggling to dispel the suspicions his transformation raised in his barrio associates; his success as a student and his attendance at the University of Southern California and Hastings Law School (San Francisco). Frias sets forth his analysis of and solutions for the problems faced by young boys and men in the barrios of California, clearly depicting the magnitude of the loss to families and the Chicano people caused by barrio rivalries. This book, which includes many moving photographs and poems inspired by the End Barrio Warfare Movement, is a symbol of Frias's dedication to the movement.

139. Fukuda, Yoshiaki (1898-1958). *My Six Years of Internment: An Issei's Struggle for Justice.* Translated by the Konko Church of San Francisco. San Francisco: Konko Church of San Francisco, 1990. ISBN: none. 150 pages; photographs.
Note: First English edition of *Yokuryu Seikatsu Rokunen*, 1957.

A Japanese national and a civic and spiritual leader, Fukuda was arrested immediately after the bombing of Pearl Harbor and subsequently interned with other Issei and German and Italian prisoners of war on the grounds that he was a spy for the Japanese. He describes conditions of the POWs as being superior to his own both in terms of housing, services, and space provided. He became a spiritual adviser to his fellow internees, and details the psychological effect of internment on the Japanese, ranging from servility to militancy. Among the last to be released, Fukuda began writing about the forced relocation in the Japanese American press, and also in a petition for redress to the United States Government (February 10, 1957). This book includes a copy of the petition in which he documents specific extreme treatment of individuals and challenges the general legality of the whole operation within the context of domestic and international law. Besides the general issue of the relocation and internment of Japanese nationals and Japanese Americans living in the United States, Fukuda addresses the threat of forced deportation for many Issei after the war, the plight of ethnic Japanese who were deported to the United States from Peru, Colombia, and other

South American Countries during the war and then
threatened with deportation to Japan after the war, and
finally of the need to restore U.S. citizenship to those
Nisei who renounced it during their internment.

140. Funderburg, Lisa. *Black, White, Other: Biracial Americans Talk About Race and Identity.* New York: W.
Morrow, 1994. ISBN: 0688118240. 391 pages; photographs.

Funderburg interviewed individuals who met the cri-
terion of having "one biological parent who identified
as black and one who identified as white" (p. 15). The
book is the result of interviews with 65 people conducted during 1992. Interviewees were essentially responding to the request that they tell about their lives,
their ideas about race, and their racial identity. The
book is divided into chapters such as "Parents and
family," "Neighborhood," "School," "Work," "Love
and Romance," "Religion and Politics," and "The Next
Generation."

141. Gaines, Patrice. *Laughing in the Dark: From Colored Girl
to Woman of Color—A Journey From Prison to
Power.* New York: Crown Publishers, Inc., 1994. ISBN:
0517594757. 295 pages.

Gaines decided to turn her life around when she
found herself in prison charged with possession of
drugs, waving to her young daughter through a small
frosted pane of glass in the prison wall. The change,
however, was difficult to make. Drugs were alluring,
employment was not easy to come by, and Gaines
seemed to be attracted to the "wrong" kind of men, a
practice she attributed to her low self-esteem and lone-
liness. After one more near miss with prison while
still on parole, Gaines finally did change the direction
of her life. She attended classes that led to her being
hired by the *Charlotte Observer* as a secretary. She
then became a reporter at the *Miami News,* and went
on to the *Washington Post,* where she covered city
news. This book is based on an article she wrote for
the *Post* about her early years and experiences with

drugs, jail, rape, unwanted pregnancy, and despair. She was moved to write this story after observing girls and women in Washington, D.C., who seemed to be going through experiences similar to her own. This award-winning article served as an emotional release for Gaines. It also provided her with opportunities to give inspirational speeches to women in prison, teenage girls in crises, and young men in court assigned to rites-of-passage programs.

142. Galvan, Jesse (1937-). *The Way Back: The Autobiography of Jesse Galvan, Jr.: Businessman, Comedian, Federal Employee.* San Antonio: Watercress Press, 1992. ISBN: 0934955255. 123 pages; photographs.

Texas businessman Jesse Galvan provides an account of his life, and the legal problems he ran into as a member of the loan division of the SBA.

143. Garcia, Lionel G. *I Hear the Cow Bells Ring: Growing Up in South Texas.* Houston: Arte Publico Press, 1994. ISBN: 1558851143. 205 pages.

These autobiographical vignettes are a "testament to the love and joy of being raised as a Mexican American in deep South Texas" (p. 14). Garcia writes of growing up in the comfortable town of San Diego in Duval County, Texas, a town populated predominantly by Mexican Americans. Religion played a prominent role in this Catholic town, permeating daily life. Large extended families watched out for the children in a communal manner, creating a sense of security and well-being despite economic hardship. Garcia provides portraits of various family members and community members, including the town priest; accounts of various boyhood activities and antics; and descriptions of farming and ranching.

144. Garcia, Mario T.
    See *Carona, Bert.*

145. Gardner, LeRoy (1924-). *Prophet Without Honor*. St. Paul: Neo Life Publications, 1991. ISBN: none. 173 pages.

146. Gates, Henry Louis, ed. *Bearing Witness: Selections From African-American Autobiography in the Twentieth Century*. New York: Pantheon Books, 1991. ISBN: 0679735208:0394585224. 385 pages; photographs; bibliography.

This book is a collection of 28 autobiographical essays and excerpts originally published between 1904 and 1990. Many of the excerpted works are included in this bibliography. The following works in Gates's book are not otherwise a part of this bibliography and were originally published in journals or essay collections: Fannie Barrier Williams, "A Northern Negro's Autobiography," 1904; Marita Bonner, "On Being Young— A Woman—and Colored," 1925; Zora Neale Hurston, "How it Feels to be Colored Me," 1928; Alice Walker, "Beauty: When the Other Dancer is the Self," 1983; Houston A. Baker, Jr., "What Charles Knew," 1987; and Bell Hooks, "Black is a Woman's Color," 1989.

147. Gates, Henry Louis , Jr. *Colored People: A Memoir*. New York: Knopf, 1994. ISBN: 0679421793. 216 pages.
Note: Also published New York: Vintage Books, 1995. ISBN: 0679421793.

Gates was four when *Brown vs. Topeka Board of Education* made illegal the institutionalized "separate-but-equal" policies of the South. Consequently, he began his education attending a newly-integrated school and experiencing life quite differently from his parents, older relatives, and even from his older brother six years his senior. Gates takes the reader through the important phases of his life, including his mother's depression and his subsequent religious conversion; the strict code of behavior which he adopted but which was eventually moderated under the influence of an Episcopal priest; and his transformation from "Negro" to "black." He describes his town, extended family and friends, and the changes that occurred as integration took hold in their small community of Piedmont, West Virginia. Gates writes: "Only later did I come to realize that for many of the colored people in Piedmont . . . integration was experienced as a loss. The warmth and nurturance of the womblike colored world was slowly and inevitably disappearing . . ." (p. 184).

148. Gayton, Narcissus Duffy.
See *Boyer, Ruth McDonald*.

149. Gibson, Bob (1935-). *Stranger to the Game*. Written with Lonnie Wheeler. New York: Viking, 1994. ISBN: 0670847941. 286 pages; photographs.

Bob Gibson tells the story of his athletic career, the preparation for which began on neighborhood baseball teams coached by his dedicated and hard-working brother. He continued to develop his skills on high school and college teams where he focused on basketball, as a player with the Cardinals' minor league, and in the off-season, with the Harlem Globe Trotters. These activities finally culminated with his major league career as a pitcher for the Cardinals. Playing minor league baseball in Georgia and attending major league spring training in Florida, Gibson was not immune to racial attacks. He experienced some discrimination breaking into the major leagues, some hostile comments from "fans," and problems with one manager. His team experience, however, was very positive. Gibson writes about the exceptional camaraderie of the Cardinals, which he believes helped them become a championship team in the 1960s. Gibson closes his book with a discussion of how baseball has changed, his own professional reputation, and a review of the possible reasons why, at the time of the writing of this book, he had been unable to find work in major league baseball after his retirement.

150. Gilbert, Roland (1947-). *The Ghetto Solution*. Written with Cheo Tyehimba-Taylor. Waco, Texas: WRS Publishing, 1993. ISBN: 1567960219. 187 pages; photographs.

Gilbert grew up in the Acorn Housing project in Oakland, California, and managed to survive a rough childhood. He describes himself as sexually active at 8, a father at 13, and married with two more sons at the age of 19. He became part of a group which successfully robbed banks for one year before they were caught by the FBI. After serving three years of a fifteen year prison term, Gilbert was released. He attended college and graduate school and ran a successful business until he became the victim of cocaine addiction. A religious conversion helped him to turn his life around. He formed Simba, Inc., which operates on the belief that "[p]eople are more important than objects and each of us has the power to choose our own behavior in spite of other people and circumstances. Simba exists to save our ghetto children" (p. 34). Simba, Inc., provides an extended family type of environment for young boys, as well as spiritual and motivational support. Its activities, goals, and some of its successes are described by Gilbert in this work.

151. Giovanni, Nikki. *Racism 101*. New York: W. Morrow, 1994. ISBN: 0688043321. 203 pages.
Note: Also published New York: Quill, 1994. ISBN: 0688142346.

A collection of loosely related essays which look at issues of literature, art, and history, as well as Giovanni's own life and memories.

152. Glancy, Diane (1941-). "Two Dresses." *I Tell You Now: Autobiographical Essays by Native American Writers*. Ed. Brian Swann and Arnold Krupat. Lincoln: University of Nebraska Press, 1987. ISBN: 0803227140.

See entry under *Swann, Brian* for a complete list of authors included in this anthology.

153. Glen, Isabella C. *Life on St. Helena Island*. New York: Carlton Press, 1980. ISBN: none. 79 pages.

Glen writes about everyday life on the Island of St. Helena in South Carolina. A teacher herself, in her narrative she emphasizes the schools of St. Helena and the teachers that taught in them from the mid-nineteenth century on. She mentions the African American teacher Charlotte Forten, who came to teach the newly-freed slaves just after emancipation. As a child, Glen studied under her older brother who was just 17, the same age as many of his students, when he began teaching. In the early days after emancipation, the African American children received a classical education. As time passed, however, the academically-oriented curriculum was dropped for a more "practical" program in which the children were taught farming techniques, basketry, and other related skills instead. Glen discusses methods of crop production and food preparation, holidays and other festive occasions, and the customs, beliefs, and religious practices of the community. Glen also writes about her work and life away from the Island in New York and Philadelphia.

154. Golden, Marita. *Migrations of the Heart: A Personal Odyssey*. Garden City, New York: Anchor Press, 1983. ISBN: 0385175191. 234 pages.
Note: Also published New York: Ballantine Books, 1987. ISBN: 0345346696.

Marita Golden marries a Nigerian man whom she met while attending Columbia University. She moves to Nigeria with him, and the cultural differences begin to manifest themselves more and more prominently. Polygamy, male marital sovereignty, and personal freedom are some of the issues she confronts. Golden pursues a teaching and writing career while in Nigeria to help with family finances and to shore up her own deteriorating ego. As her marriage falls apart, she seeks advice from her African American friends also married to Nigerians. She is told that if she wants to keep her son, who by Nigerian law belongs to the father, she will have to escape back to the United States. Although this decision is difficult because of her love for Nigeria, Golden leaves the country rather than risk the loss of her son.

155. Gonzales, George L. *The Other Side of the Coin*. Ogden, Utah: n.p., 1987. ISBN: none. 126 pages; photographs;

documentation.
Note: Caption title: Autobiography of George L. Gonzales: 65 Years of Life Combined With 35 Years of Joys and Sorrows at Hill Air Force Base, Utah.

George Gonzales writes about his Navy and civil service career as well as his contributions to the Latino/a community in Utah through his television and radio talk show programs. His program, "The Other Side of the Coin," had as its theme "what it is to be a minority in the State of Utah." Gonzales also provides a history of his family in Mexico and includes his childhood memories of growing up on his grandfather's ranch in New Mexico. His primary motivation for writing this book was to vindicate himself of accusations concerning his competence made by supervisors at the Hill Air Force Base, where Gonzales was employed for 37 years.

156. Gonzalez, Ray. *Memory Fever: A Journey Beyond El Paso del Norte*. Seattle: Broken Moon Press, 1993. ISBN: 0913089494. 223 pages.

Poet Gonzalez has written a collection of brief essays which represent a series of memories and impressions of his experiences growing up in El Paso, Texas. Important elements which have contributed to his development as an individual and a writer are explored. Some of the elements are the people, natural landscape, and wildlife of El Paso and the Texas and New Mexico deserts. Gonzalez writes about his ties to the desert in the essay "The Active Poet": "In order to write poetry from the heart, I had to confront the land where I grew up. I found an immense solitude among the cactus and rocks, and I discovered that the force of my poems rose from a mysterious connection to the desert" (p. 97).

157. Goodbird, Edward. *Goodbird the Indian: His Story*. As told to Gilbert L. Wilson. Illustrated by Frederick N. Wilson. St. Paul: Minnesota Historical Society Press, 1985. ISBN: 0873511883. 78 pages; engravings; map.
Note: Originally published: New York: F. H. Revell, Co., 1914.

This work has been reprinted with new introductory material by Mary Jane Schneider, providing information about both Wilson and Goodbird, explaining the circumstances that brought them together and Wilson's relationship to Goodbird's tribe. Schneider also points out which portions of the work are Wilson's additions, what parts have been censored, and which parts are truly the words of Goodbird. This work was originally part of a series of educational books for children sponsored by the Council of Women for Home Missions. In his life story, Goodbird describes the traditional ways in which he was brought up and how those traditions were set aside or weakened through the influence of schools and churches or because they were directly forbidden by federal law.

158. Gooding, James Henry (1837-1864). *On the Altar of Freedom: A Black Soldier's Civil War Letters From the Front*. Amherst: University of Massachusetts Press, 1991. ISBN: 0870237454. 139 pages; engravings; maps; bibliography.
Note: Also published New York: Warner Books, 1992. ISBN: 0446394149.

These civil war letters were originally written for weekly publication in a Massachusetts newspaper. In them, Gooding documented the formation of the country's first black regiment, the 54th Regiment of Massachusetts. Gooding wrote about the beginning of the regiment and its members, their camp life, and the battles they fought. He also discussed issues of justice, focusing on the inequitable pay received by the black troops. Through his writings, Gooding helped persuade Congress to end the pay discrimination. Before the end of the war, however, Gooding was imprisoned in the notorious Andersonville Prison, where he died.

159. Gordon, Jacob U. *Narratives of African Americans in Kansas, 1870-1992: Beyond the Exodust Movement*. Lewiston, New York: E. Mellen Press, 1993. ISBN: 0773493506. 302 pages; photographs; bibliography.

This is a collection of 35 brief narratives, both oral and written, by African Americans living in Kansas. The narrators represent a variety of socio-economic and education levels. Although the narratives vary in content, most authors give some family background, and many describe life in a segregated Kansas, and analyze how and why changes in this system occurred.

160. Gordy, Berry. *To Be Loved: The Music, the Magic, the Memories of Motown: An Autobiography.* New York: Warner Books, 1994. ISBN: 044651523X. 432 pages; photographs.

Gordy began promoting music and musicians at a very early age by taking a friend of his door to door and having him sing for the neighborhood at 50 cents a song. This entrepreneurship led to the development and success of Motown Records headquartered in Detroit, Michigan. Gordy describes his early professional days writing songs and promoting groups. As head of Motown Records, Gordy worked with Smokey Robinson and the Miracles, Diana Ross and the Supremes, Stevie Wonder, the Jackson 5, and many other artistically and commercially successful groups. Gordy sold his music empire to MCA in 1988 because it had become more difficult for him to reap a profit, and because of his developing interests in film production.

161. Grayson, George Washington (1843-1920). *A Creek Warrior for the Confederacy: The Autobiography of Chief G. W. Grayson.* Ed. W. David Baird. The Civilization of the American Indian 189. Norman: University of Oklahoma Press, 1988. ISBN: 0806121033. 181 pages; photographs; bibliography; maps.

Grayson's manuscript waited some sixty years for publication and was, perhaps, only intended for the eyes of his family. Educated in the western classical tradition, Grayson was among the few Native American leaders of his time able to write his own story. Of mixed-blood, or Métis heritage, Grayson provides rare insight into the views and influence of a Métis elite within the Creek Nation. This autobiography tells the story of the Creek Nation, its tribal framework, and its troubles and inner controversies. It also describes the U.S. Government's dealings with the Creeks specifically and the tribes removed to Oklahoma in general. Grayson ends his autobiography with the establishment of the Dawes Commission in March 1893, which led to the dissolution of the tribal governments of the Oklahoma tribes and the allotment of their land.

162. Green, Ely (1893-). *Ely: An Autobiography.* Athens: University of Georgia Press, 1990. ISBN: 0820312347. 246 pages.
Reprint, with new introduction. Originally published New York: Seabury Press, 1966.

163. Greene, Lorenzo Johnston (1899-). *Working with Carter G. Woodson, the Father of Black History: A Diary, 1928-1930.* Baton Rouge: Louisiana State University Press, 1989. ISBN: 0807114731. 487 pages; photographs; bibliography.

Greene documents the two years of his life spent working with prominent African American historians Carter G. Woodson and Charles H. Wesley, giving his impressions of their scholarship, contributions, and personalities. Woodson has been named by many as the "father of Negro history," having founded the Association for the Study of Negro Life and History (ASNLH) and *The Journal of Negro History*, and originated Negro History Week. Greene, who worked as a research assistant and field worker for Woodson and the ASNLH, calls this record of that period in his life a "potpourri of the economic, social, and political conditions under which Negroes lived in their communities at that time" (p. 1).

164. Greenfield, Eloise (1929-), Lessie Jones Little (1906-) and Pattie Ridley Jones (1884-?). *Childtimes: A Three-Generation Memoir.* New York: Harper Trophy, 1993. ISBN: 0064461343. 175 pages; photographs; drawings.
Note: Originally published New York: Thomas Y. Crowell, 1979. ISBN: 0690038755; New York: Scholas-

tic, 1979. ISBN: 0590467298; New York: Harper Collins, 1979. ISBN: 0690038747.

This work presents the childhood memories of three black women—grandmother, mother, and daughter—who grew up between the 1880s and 1950s in Parmele, North Carolina, and Washington, D.C.

165. Gregory, Dick (1932-). *Nigger: An Autobiography*. Written with Robert Lipsyte. New York: Washington Square Press, 1986. ISBN: 0671626116. 209 pages; photographs.
Originally published New York: Dutton, 1964.

166. Guerrero, Salvador. *Memorias, a West Texas Life*. Ed. Arnoldo DeLeon. Lubbock: Texas Technical University Press, 1991. ISBN: 0896722511:0896722554. 126 pages; illustrations; map.

This series of short narratives is about ordinary people making something of themselves through their own efforts and resolve. Guerrero's family moved to northern Mexico close to the Texas border to escape the Mexican Revolution. For some time they crossed back and forth over the Texas-Mexico border following the availability of field work, until they finally settled permanently in San Angelo, Texas. Guerrero writes of segregated movie theaters, separate and unequal schools, and the first challenges to that system. Because of his family's work in the fields, Guerrero was never able to attend more than three months of school at a time. When he did attend, the classes were only held half days because of overcrowded conditions. Guerrero had to walk over 35 blocks to attend school for three hours a day. He describes the kind of work available to Mexican Americans, the recreational activities, and his World War II experiences, which included participation in the invasion of Normandy on D-Day. After his discharge from the armed services, Guerrero was involved in a number of political and civic activities. He was the first Mexican American to become elected County Commissioner in Ector County, Texas.

167. Haizlip, Shirlee Taylor. *The Sweeter the Juice: A Family Memoir in Black and White.* New York: Simon & Schuster, 1994. ISBN: 0671792350. 271 pages; illustrations; photographs; bibliography.

Of African, white, and Native American heritage, Haizlip sets out to discover that part of her mother's family which had "passed" for white, and traces her family history back to 1680 on her mother's side and to 1820 on her father's. This book relates both her family's history and her search for her lost relatives. While still young children, Haizlip's mother and her mother's youngest brother were abandoned by their father shortly after the death of their mother, presumably because of their more African features and darker skin color, and they were raised by their black relatives. The rest of the family, a brother and a sister, were taken with the father to live as whites in white society. The "white" children, in fact, grew up knowing little or nothing of their black heritage until Haizlip succeeded in reuniting the family. Haizlip's search for her family causes her to reconsider the meaning and significance of race and skin color. She points out in her introduction that some "geneticists have said that 95 percent of 'white' Americans have widely varying degrees of black heritage. . . . 75 percent of all African-Americans have at least one white ancestor and 15 percent have predominantly white blood lines" (p. 15).

168. Hale, Janet Campbell. *Bloodlines: Odyssey of a Native Daughter.* New York: Random House, 1993. ISBN: 0679415270. 187 pages.
Note: Also published New York: Harper Perennial, 1994. ISBN: 0060976128.

In this collection of essays, Hale contemplates the art of autobiography as she writes about her past. In remembering her childhood and youth, she studies her dysfunctional family, the psychological abuse she received from her mother and sisters, and her family's mixed-blood heritage. Hale relies on a combination of memory, conjecture, and historical research to write her story.

169. Hampton, Lionel. *Hamp: An Autobiography.* Written with James Haskins. New York: Warner Books, 1989. ISBN: 0446710059. 286 pages; photographs; discography.

Jazz great Lionel Hampton tells the story of his life from childhood through the present. The extended family in which he was raised, included a grandmother who was a faith healer and an uncle who consorted with Al Capone. His first serious percussion teacher was "hard-hitting" virtuoso drummer Sister Petra at Holy Rosary School in Collins, Wisconsin. Hampton went on to be a top drummer with the Chicago Defender Youth Band. While still in his early teens, he headed for Southern California to start his professional career. Hampton pioneered the use of vibraphones as a jazz instrument, and continues to experiment with new jazz forms.

170. Hanna, Mark (1882-1964). *Man of the Canyon: An Old Indian Remembers His Life.* As told to Richard G. Emerick. Orono, Maine: Northern Lights, 1992. ISBN: 1880811065:1880811073. 170 pages; photographs; maps. Note: Originally recorded in 1953.

Hanna relates memories of the significant events in his life from babyhood to old age, describing childhood activities and his mother's strict and often violent method of raising him. He tells of witnessing the Ghost Dance, which was started by the Paiute shaman Wavoka in the 1890s and, many years later, his observation of and participation in the Hopi Snake and Butterfly dances. Other significant experiences include three brief marriages, encounters with white racist society, including the deaths of two friends at the hands of brutal policemen, and work in and around a Japanese internment camp. Hanna explains the importance of horses to the Havasupai, the generally peaceful nature of the Havasupai, and their relations with neighboring tribes who were often belligerent to them. In his later years, he was given the gift of healing with song. Hanna describes a healing and the ailments which he is and is not capable of treating.

171. Harewood, John W. (John Wilfred) (1909-). *The Hare-wood Heritage: An Autobiography*. The Black Contemporary Lives Series. Dayton, Ohio (402 Salem Ave., Dayton 45406): Fells Johnson Techni-write, Inc., 1989. 144 pages.

172. Harjo, Joy (1951-). "Ordinary Spirit." *I Tell You Now: Autobiographical Essays by Native American Writers*. Ed. Brian Swann and Arnold Krupat. Lincoln: University of Nebraska Press, 1987. ISBN: 0803227140.

   See entry under *Swann, Brian* for a complete list of authors included in this anthology.

173. Hawkins, Dwight (1938-). *Survival in the Square*. Written with Morrie Greenberg. Northridge, California: Brooke-Richards Press, 1989. ISBN: 0962265209. 152 pages; photographs.

   When he was 11, Dwight Hawkins was in a car accident which shattered his left leg below the knee. Although told that he would not be able to participate in sports, Hawkins began a professional boxing career when he was just 15. At 18, he was the California Bantam weight Champion. Hawkins writes about pacing oneself as an athlete and the need to plan for the future. He retired from boxing at the age of 29, and has devoted himself to youth work since that time.

174. Hawkins, O. *Chili: Memoirs of a Black Casanova*. Los Angeles: Holloway House, 1985. ISBN: 0870672584. 216 pages.

175. Hayslip, Le Ly (1949-). *Child of War, Woman of Peace*. Written with James Hayslip. New York: Doubleday, 1993. ISBN: 0385421117. 374 pages.
   Note: Also published New York: Anchor Books, 1994. ISBN: 0385471475.

   Hayslip left Vietnam with her two sons in 1970, while the Vietnam War was still in progress. Together they flew to San Diego to join her American husband, whom she had met in Vietnam, and thus began her odyssey in the United States. Her story is one of cultural conflict. Hayslip recalls that San Diego might as well have been the moon, because it was so completely foreign to her: from the behavior of her in-laws, to the food she had to cook, to the language. She spent the next thirteen years trying to adapt through two failed marriages and two abortive engagements. But Hayslip did become a successful businesswoman, and raised three sons and five Vietnamese foster children. After a return visit to Vietnam, Hayslip decided to do something for her people and began the process that would allow her to build a medical clinic in her home village.

176. —. *When Heaven and Earth Changed Places: A Vietnamese Woman's Journey From War to Peace.* Written with Charles Jay Wurts. New York: Doubleday, 1989. ISBN: 0385247583. 368 pages.
Note: Also published New York: Plume, 1990. ISBN: 0452271681.

After nearly two decades in the United States, Hayslip recalls her childhood in the village of Ky La, which lay midway between North and South Vietnam. Born in 1949, her youth was spent in a war-torn country: first the war of independence against France, which led to the division of Vietnam in 1954, and then the civil war. She describes her reasons for supporting the Viet Cong, the reality of the war for the Vietnamese versus the view of the war by the West. Hayslip recalls the terrifying years of the war, her departure for the United States in 1970, and her brief return to Vietnam and her reunion with her family in 1986. She writes that in this book she will try to explain to the American soldier "who your enemy was and why almost everyone in the country you tried to help resented, feared, and misunderstood you" (p. xiv).

177. Heard, Regie. *Regie's Love: A Daughter of Former Slaves Recalls and Reflects.* Written with Bonnie Langenhahn. Menomonee Falls, Wisconsin: McCormick and Schilling, 1987. ISBN: 0961821213. 166 pages; photographs.
Note: An expanded and illustrated edition was issued by McCormick and Shilling in 1989.

Heard grew up in Washington, Arkansas. Her mother and father were both born into slavery. Her father, who was literate and had obtained a knowledge of legal matters, was a deputy sheriff and assisted poor people with legal problems. Heard's parents insisted on her attending school and on her training to be a teacher. She did follow this career but after her marriage and move to Milwaukee found that there were few opportunities for African American teachers there. She and her husband began working together as live-in domestic help. They worked for several generous employers and were able to save enough money to open a quality restaurant, none being available to African Americans in Milwaukee at that time.

178. Henry, Thomas W. (1794-1877). *From Slavery to Salvation: The Autobiography of Rev. Thomas W. Henry of the A.M.E. Church*. Introduction and an historical essay by Jean Libby. Jackson: University Press of Mississippi, 1994. ISBN: 0878056904. 139 pages; photographs. Note: Originally published as *Autobiography of Rev. Thomas W. Henry of the A.M.E. Church*. [Baltimore: n.p., 1872].

Henry's autobiography tells the story of a free African American living in the slave state of Maryland. It reflects the increasingly restrictive laws aimed at limiting the activities of individuals like him, and it also tells the story of the African Methodist Episcopal (A.M.E.) Church in its earliest days. Henry elucidates its role in the abolitionist movement: the church functioned as a venue for free religious expression and as an important social organization for African Americans of the South and North. Henry describes his many hardships as an African American individual and as a leader of a developing African American church.

179. Henzie, Moses (1901-). *Moses Henzie: A Biography of Allakaket*. Interviews conducted and text prepared by Curt Madison and Yvonne Yarber. Alaska Series. North Vancouver, British Columbia: Hancock House, 1980. ISBN: 0919654819. 63 pages; photographs; map.

Moses Henzie, born about 1930, leads a traditional life based on hunting, trapping, and fishing. He is a master at many native crafts, including sled- and boat-building and making snowshoes, caribou rope, and fish baskets. Henzie and his wife continue to follow the beliefs and practice the rituals taught them by their elders. His was the first autobiography prepared by the Yukon-Koyukuk School District, which has sponsored the publication of autobiographies of residents in the 11 villages which it serves. The intent was to make available readings in dialect for school age children, providing them reading materials in familiar speech, perhaps offering a better reading experience, and also giving them the opportunity to learn about their traditional culture. The following names are those of other subjects in the series which are included in this bibliography: Roger Dayton, Henry Ekada, Madeline Solomon, Edwin Simon, Goodwin Semaken, Altona Brown, Joe Beetus, Henry Beatus, Sr., John Honea, Martha Joe, Edgar Kallands, Billy McCarty, Simeon Mountain, Oscar Nictune, Josephine Roberts, Peter John, Frank Tobuk, and Andrew Isaac.

180. Herbert, Belle. *Shandaa In My Lifetime.* Recorded and edited by Bill Pfisterer with the assistance of Alice Moses, and edited by Mary Jane McGary. Transcribed and translated by Katherine Peter. Fairbanks: Alaska Native Language Center, University of Alaska, 1988. ISBN: 0912006307. 207 pages; photographs.
Note: Written in Gwich'in Athapascan and English.

This oral history is distinctive in that it attempts to replicate in writing the manner in which the stories were delivered. The recorder/transcribers did very little to the text and presented them in the order in which Herbert told the stories. They provided line breaks and spaces in the text to indicate short and long pauses. When this oral history was prepared in 1980, Belle Herbert was somewhere between 105 and 127 years old. Because of the events she was able to remember, the editors believed her to have been close to 120 years old, meaning that she was born shortly after the first white men arrived. In this work, Herbert describes events from her childhood and married life. Hunting methods, games, food preparation, shelter and clothing, the transition to Christianity, and the division of labor are among the many aspects of life described by Herbert in this unique work.

181. Herrera, Jess Robert (1924-). *Memories of My Life*. San Francisco: J. R. Herrera, 1992. ISBN: 1881156001. 224 pages.

182. Higa, Thomas Taro. *Memoirs of a Certain Nisei/Aru Nisei No Wadachi: 1916-1985*. Ed. Elsie Higa. Translated by Mitsugu Sakahara. Kaneohe, Hawaii: Higa Publications, 1988. ISBN: 0944985009. 164 pages; photographs.

Higa was born in Hawaii in 1916. His parents sent him and his siblings to be raised and educated by his grandparents in Okinawa, which was a common practice, Higa writes, because life in Hawaii was too hard for the Japanese immigrants "to entertain the notion of spending time to rear their children" (p. 3). Higa describes his youth in Okinawa and Osaka, and then his return to Hawaii, where he was drafted into the United States Army before the bombing of Pearl Harbor. After the bombing, the Japanese American battalions in Hawaii were disarmed and sent to training camps on the mainland. Higa was eventually sent to the front in Italy, wounded, and returned to the United States. After his recovery, he was sent by the War Relocation Authority and the Japanese American Citizens League on what became a seven-month speaking tour to at least 75 cities in 40 states, and to all the relocation camps except for Tule Lake. During his lectures, he reassured Japanese American families about the conditions of the Nisei soldiers and dispelled rumors that had been spreading about abuses at the front. After his speaking tour, Higa was sent to Okinawa, where he started the Okinawa War Victim Relief Campaign. When World War II ended, Higa took part in the movement to gain naturalization rights for Japanese Americans. He also produced a film and wrote a book about Japanese American immigrants in Hawaii.

183. Higashide, Seiichi. *Adios to Tears: The Memoirs of a Japanese-Peruvian Internee in U.S. Concentration Camps*. Honolulu: E & E Kudo, 1993. ISBN: none. 256 pages; photographs; maps; bibliography.

Higashide immigrated to Peru from Japan after a childhood of poverty. Living in a Japanese community, Higashide married a Nisei, eventually set up a successful business, and became active in Japanese-Peruvian civic affairs. Thus, he was on the first blacklist issued by the Peruvian government after the bombing of Pearl Harbor. He spent a period of time in hiding but was eventually arrested and deported to the United States as were over 2,000 other Central and South American ethnic Japanese. Higashide gives an account of life in the Crystal City Internment Camp in Texas. After the war, Higashide and the other Japanese deported to the United States were classified as illegal aliens and thus became subject to a second deportation to Japan. After a legal battle, Higashide and his family were able to stay in the United States (they were not allowed back into Peru), where they had to struggle with a new language as well as housing and employment discrimination. Higashide first published this book in Japanese, and has had it translated into both English and Spanish.

184. Highwalking, Belle (1892-1971). *Belle Highwalking: The Narrative of a Northern Cheyenne Woman*. Ed. Katherine M. Weist. Billings, Montana: Montana Council for Indian Education, 1991. ISBN: none. 66 pages; photographs; bibliography; maps.
Note: Recorded 1970-1971. First published in 1979 by Montana Council for Indian Education.

Highwalking recorded her life story in the Cheyenne language. It was then translated with the help of her daughter-in-law. Because Highwalking died shortly after completing her recording, Weist, the editor and instigator of the project, chose to leave the text much as she received it, without significant editing or rearranging. Highwalking describes the events of her life, her relatives and acquaintances, the old ways and the changes that have taken place over the course of her life, and some of the problems of modern society. She also retells several stories.

185. Hill, Mary Nell. *From Darkness to Glorious Light.* N.p.: S.C.A. International, 1984. ISBN: none. 163 pages. Note: This is a collection of poems with a short autobiography of the author.

186. Hilliard, David. *This Side of Glory: The Autobiography of David Hilliard and the Story of the Black Panther Party.* Written with Lewis Cole. Boston: Little, Brown, 1993. ISBN: 0316364215. 450 pages; photographs.

Hilliard relates his story and that of the Black Panther Party. He was born in Alabama, the youngest of a large family, and moved to Oakland, California, at the age of 11. He became close friends with Huey Newton and his family during his first months in Oakland. It was after the Watts Riots (1965) that Hilliard learned of Newton's formation of the Black Panther Party and the Ten Point Program. Hilliard writes of his involvement with the party, observing its rise and fall. In the final portion of his book, Hilliard describes his imprisonment, his eventual release during the eclipse of the party, and his subsequent lapse into alcoholism and drug addiction. A year and a half after Hilliard's recovery, Huey Newton was killed. Hilliard concludes his book with an assessment of Newton's accomplishments and a coming to terms with Newton's long-term dependence on alcohol and drugs. He is finally able to place in perspective for himself and for posterity the significance of his own role as Chief of Staff of the Black Panther Party, and the many sacrifices which he and many other Black men and women made in pursuing and realizing the party's goals.

187. Hinton, Eddie (1947-). *Locker Room to Boardroom: Superbowl Player Eddie Hinton's Strategies for Tackling Life's Choices, Challenges, and Changes.* As

told to Lynne Washburn. Sugar Land, Texas: Candle Publishing Co., 1988. ISBN: 0942523342:0942523334. 183 pages; photographs.

An avid athlete who participated in organized basketball, track and field, baseball, and football from the time he was in fifth grade, Hinton became a star collegiate football player at the University of Oklahoma and was a first-choice draft of the Baltimore Colts. Hinton describes the difficulty of succeeding in professional sports, and of his own struggle to survive five years without significant injury so that he could receive a pension. His career and marriage ended at the same time, leaving Hinton in a deep depression and involved in self-destructive activities. Hinton eventually recovered and set out to start his own business, becoming quite successful. Realizing how many other professional athletes had had experiences similar to his own, Hinton set up a nonprofit organization called Exec-U-Team, which assists athletes in making the transition from sports to a business career.

188. Hodges, Willis Augustus (1815-1890). *Free Man of Color: The Autobiography of Willis Augustus Hodges*. Ed. Willard B. Gatewood. Knoxville: University of Tennessee Press, 1982. ISBN: 0870493531. 97 pages; engravings; maps; bibliography.

Hodges was born free to free, property-owning parents in Virginia. His grandmothers were also free, whereas both of his grandfathers were born into slavery. Hodges was a dedicated abolitionist, risking his life to teach and preach to the slaves who lived near his parental home. He also promoted the abolitionist cause during his frequent residencies in New York. Hodges' autobiography was written as an abolitionist tract although it was not published until after his death. He describes the many hardships endured by and cruelties visited upon slaves as well as the free people of color living in the South. Hodges ran into resistance and outright hostility from both southern whites and southern free African Americans who had suffered retribution after the Nat Turner rebellion.

189. Hogan, Linda (1948-). "The Two Lives." *I Tell You Now: Autobiographical Essays by Native American Writers.* Ed. Brian Swann and Arnold Krupat. Lincoln: University of Nebraska Press, 1987. ISBN: 0803227140.

See entry under *Swann, Brian* for a complete list of authors included in this anthology.

190. Honea, John. *John Honea, Ruby.* Interviews conducted and text prepared by Curt Madison and Yvonne Yarber. North Vancouver, British Columbia: Hancock House, 1981. ISBN: 0888390734. 85 pages; photographs; maps.
Note: Produced by Yukon-Koyukuk School District of Alaska.

Honea describes life in Ruby, Alaska, a relatively large and bustling town in the interior of the state. He did not have relatives to teach him the techniques of hunting, trapping, fishing, and fish preparation, so Honea was largely self-taught. Once he married, his wife's parents helped him improve his fishing and trapping skills. Honea was raised by his oldest sister, who was a full-blooded Indian. Honea's parentage, however, was mixed, and this caused him some anguish while growing up: "It was hard for me to learn English. I think my mind was set more on the Native way than the White man way. I didn't know which was right" (p. 41). Lorraine Honea, Honea's wife, also contributes material to this autobiographical work.
For a brief description and list of autobiographies in this Yukon-Koyukuk School District Series, see the entry for Moses Henzie.

191. Horn, Gabriel (1947-). *Native Heart: An American Indian Odyssey.* San Rafael, California: New World Library, 1993. ISBN: 1880032074. 293 pages; bibliography.

Gabriel Horn describes his spiritual visions and his work with the American Indian Movement (AIM). Because of their devotion to traditional Native practices, Horn and his Ojibwa wife have worked with children as teachers and parents to instill in them the history of Native peoples on this continent and to give them a sense of pride in their heritage. Horn is not registered with any tribal group and has had his ethnic identity challenged. His militant politics have put him at the center of many tribal controversies and at odds with the FBI.

192. Horton, John Benjamin (1904-). *Flights From Doom: The Autobiography of the Life, Observations, Experiences and Involvements in America of an African-American Journalist, Author and Publicist in the United States.* Louisville, Kentucky: J. Benjamin Horton and Associates, 1990. ISBN: none. 126 pages.

193. Hosaka, Fred T. *Shortchanged in America: A Story of Hardship.* Coquille, Oregon (HC 83, Box 5770, Coquille 97423): F. T. Hosaka, 1993. ISBN: none. 175 pages; photographs.

This book is, to some degree, a family history. Hosaka gives an account of his father's immigration to the United States and marriage to Hosaka's mother. He also describes his childhood and agricultural life in Southern California as part of a Japanese American community during the first two decades of the twentieth Century. Families were already experiencing cultural confusion and widening gaps between immigrant parents and quickly-assimilating children when the bombing of Pearl Harbor added many changes which increased the confusion: arrests, curfews, the draft, business losses, and of course, evacuation and relocation. Hosaka's father was arrested the February following the attack and was interned separately from the rest of the family. Hosaka was among those who answered "No-No" to the infamous loyalty questions, Numbers 27 and 28 on the questionnaire distributed to all Issei and Nisei in the camps by the War Relocation Authority (WRA). (If the Issei were to answer "no" to either of these questions, he or she would become a person with no country since at that time Asian immigrants were not allowed to become naturalized U.S. citizens; a no answer on the part of the Nisei meant a renunciation of U.S. citizenship and deportation at the end of the war. Many of the Nisei who did renounce their citizenship were exonerated later on after it was proved that they had done so under duress and in exceptional circumstances.) He explains the significance of taking this stand, why he chose to do so, and the impact it had on his family. Hosaka eventually reversed his stand so that his family could remain together (his father died shortly before he was to be reunited with the rest of the family) and because answering "No" to the two loyalty questions meant deportation to Japan.

194. Howell, Roy Carlton. *Little Chocolate Soldier*. Huntington, West Virginia: University Editions, 1992. ISBN: 1560021985. 289 pages.

Howell spent his first years with his heroin-addicted parents. After his mother's conviction on felony charges, he went to live with grandparents in Detroit, Michigan. He found the transition to a more structured, conservative household somewhat difficult, but learned to love his grandmother, heeding her advice and direction. Howell's aunts and uncles, still children, followed various paths, some taking to the streets as did his own mother, and some completing their education and pursuing careers. He writes of the atrocious conditions of his high school and the difficulty of staying away from drugs and crime. Although the family lost two sons to heroine overdoses, Howell managed to resist drugs and attend college and law school. His life did not run smoothly despite these successes, and he describes the many setbacks which he and his family faced, including illnesses, unemployment and homelessness.

195. Hudson, Hosea. *Black Worker in the Deep South: A Personal Record*. 2nd ed. New York: International Publishers, 1991. ISBN: 0717806839. 130 pages.
First edition published in 1972 by International Publishers. ISBN: 0717803732:0717803627.

196. —. *The Narrative of Hosea Hudson: The Life and Times of a Black Radical*. Ed. Nell Irvin Painter. New York: W. W. Norton, 1994. ISBN: 0393310159. 400 pages; photographs; bibliography.

Originally published as *The Narrative of Hosea Hudson: His Life as a Negro Communist*. New York: Harvard University Press, 1993

197. Hum-ishu-ma/Mourning Dove (1888-1936). *Mourning Dove: A Salishan Autobiography*. Ed. Jay Miller. American Indian Lives. Lincoln: University of Nebraska Press, 1990. ISBN: 0803231199:0803282079. 265 pages; photographs; bibliography.
Note: Mourning Dove is the pen name of Christine Quintasket.

Mourning Dove wrote out of a desire to provide sympathetic representations of Native Americans to counter those currently in fashion. She received criticism for her literary efforts from both white and native people, and her motivation to write her autobiography was, in part, to answer this criticism. This work is as much a story of her people as of herself. She describes Salishan traditions, the role of the woman in a marriage, the care of children, and hunting and fishing practices. Mourning Dove also touches on the difficulty her people were faced with giving up their migratory practices and attempting to shift to an agricultural way of life.

198. Hungry Wolf, Adolf and Beverly. *Shadows of the Buffalo: A Family Odyssey Among the Indians*. New York: W. Morrow, 1983. ISBN: 0688016804. 288 pages; photographs.

The authors explain, "We want to share the following experiences with you, hoping to show that ours is but one of a multitude of ancestral paths that can still be traveled and learned from, even though we belong to a contemporary society" (p. 7). Beverly is a member of the Blood Indian tribe of Canada, and Adolf, a white man, immigrated to the United States from Germany. Influenced by childhood dreams and the back-to-nature movements of the 60s, Adolf dedicated his life to living off the land and learning traditional Indian ways. It was through the connections he had made with Blackfoot elders that he met Beverly. Together they have devoted themselves to learning and relearning the traditional Blackfoot way of life. Many Native Americans have been suspicious of Adolph's motives, and in writing this book he hopes to put some of these doubts to rest.

199. Hungry Wolf, Beverly. *The Ways of My Grandmothers*. New York: W. Morrow, 1980. ISBN: 0688036651. 256 pages; photographs.

This book consists primarily of the stories of the lives of the old women of the Blood tribe, a division of the Blackfoot Nation. The women are either related to Hungry Wolf or are close friends. Hungry Wolf provides some details of her own efforts to learn about, to live, and to raise her children in the traditional Blood manner. Many of the stories that she has collected from the women are related in the first person.

200. Hunt, Annie Mae (1909-). *I am Annie Mae: An Extraordinary Woman in Her Own Words: The Personal Story of a Black Texas Woman*. Written with Frieda Werden. Ed. Ruthe Winegarten. Austin, Texas: Rosegarden Press, 1983. ISBN: 0961034009. 151 pages; photographs; bibliography.
Note: 2nd edition published in 1984. ISBN: 0961034017; 3rd edition published in 1989.

Annie Mae Hunt grew up in Washington County, Texas. Well into her adult years, both she and her family persevered against intense racism and racially motivated violence, which included intimidation, murder, and rape. Hunt became a political activist, and the events of her life, her political work, and the stories of her grandmother who was born into slavery, are described in this book. It was produced as a musical in 1987.

201. Hunt, Marsha (1946-). *Real Life*. London: Chatto and Windus, 1986. ISBN: 0701130261. 258 pages; photographs.

Hunt grew up in North Philadelphia in what she describes as "the reservation," her term for predominantly black neighborhoods. She gives an account of her streetwise but secure childhood there, a security that was interrupted by her mother's decision to move to California. She attended the University of California, Berkeley during the mid-sixties, but dropped out to travel to England, where she became part of the music scene. She describes her own developing music, acting, and modeling career and her relationships with many well-known rock musicians, especially Mick Jagger.

202. Hunter, Latoya. *The Diary of Latoya Hunter: My First Year in Junior High*. New York: Crown, 1992. ISBN: 0517585111. 131 pages.
Note: Also published New York: Vintage Books, 1993. ISBN: 0679746064.

Born in Jamaica, Hunter moved to New York City in 1986 when she was eight years old and wrote the journal that comprises this work between the ages of 12 and 13. Having read an article about Hunter's grade school graduating class in which Latoya was singled out for her exceptional writing abilities, the editor of this book sought her out and eventually contracted with her to keep a diary for ten months—which would then be published. Hunter writes about adjusting to a new school, conflicts with her mother, love, and friendship.

203. Hunter-Gault, Charlayne. *In My Place*. New York: Farrar, Straus, Giroux, 1993. ISBN: 0374175632. 257 pages; photographs.
Note: Also published New York: Vintage Books, 1993. ISBN: 0679748180.

Charlayne Hunter-Gault came of age with the Civil Rights Movement. Approached by members of the Atlanta Committee for Cooperative Action (ACCA) during her senior year of high school in 1959, Hunter-Gault was convinced, along with her classmate Hamilton Holmes, to test the state's segregation laws by seeking to enter the University of Georgia. Two years later, both Holmes and Hunter-Gault matriculated at the

University.   Hunter-Gault describes in detail the events which accompanied this revolutionary event. She acknowledges the value of the support she received from friends and family, who provided her "with the suit of armor and determination that I needed as I began my journey to the horizons" (p. 3). Hunter-Gault describes herself as fairly ordinary, smart, and ambitious, but interested in enjoying life. Her assessment of the Atlanta Student Movement explains how an ordinary person might achieve something so extraordinary:

> [W]e could see in a new light both our past and our future. We could see that past—the slavery, the segregation, the deprivation and denial—for what it was: a system designed to keep us in our place and convince us, somehow, that it was our fault, as well as our destiny. Now, without either ambivalence or shame, we saw ourselves as the heirs to a legacy of struggle, but struggle that was, as Martin Luther King taught, ennobling; struggle that was enabling us to take control of our destiny. . . . [W]e did not see ourselves or the other young people demonstrating . . . as heroes to be praised, celebrated, or fretted over. We were simply doing what we were born to do. (p. 144)

204. Huntington, Sidney (1915-). *Shadows on the Koyukuk: An Alaskan Native's Life Along the River.* As told to Jim Reardon. Anchorage: Alaska Northwest Books, 1993. ISBN: 088240427X. 235 pages; map; bibliography.

Huntington, born to an Athapascan mother and an English-Scots father and raised under the influence of both cultures, provides some history of white influence on the Athapascan culture and way of life: what has changed and what has remained the same. His mother died suddenly when he was five, but his maternal relatives continued to be involved with his upbringing. Huntington learned to trap, hunt, and fish from his father, who combined Athapascan and European practices. Along with accounts of his own adventures in Alaska's interior, Huntington also includes events from the lives of his Athapascan relatives and traditional stories passed on to him by Athapascan elders.

205. Huntley, Jobe. *I Remember Langston Hughes: An Auto-biography*. New York: J. Huntley, 1983. ISBN: none. 105 pages; facsimiles; music.

206. Hurmence, Belinda, ed. *Before Freedom, When I Can Just Remember: Twenty-Seven Oral Histories of Former South Carolina Slaves*. Winston-Salem: J. F. Blair, 1989. ISBN: 089587069X. 135 pages; photographs.

Hurmence selected these twenty-seven oral histories from the 284 taken in South Carolina by the Library of Congress through the Federal Writers' Project of the 1930s.

207. —, ed. *My Folks Don't Want Me to Talk About Slavery: Twenty-One Oral Histories of Former North Carolina Slaves*. Winston-Salem, North Carolina: J. F. Blair, 1984. ISBN: 089587038x:0895870398. 103 pages; bibliography.

Hurmence selected these twenty-one oral histories from the 176 taken in North Carolina by the Library of Congress through the Federal Writers' Project of the 1930s. She writes in her introduction about the difficulty of limiting the number of selections: "Nearly every individual expressed some special viewpoint that I felt reluctant to omit" (p. xiii). Hurmence decided to make her selection based on age, choosing the narratives of those who were at least ten years old at the time of the emancipation.

208. Huynh, Jade Ngoc Quang (1957-). *South Wind Changing*. St. Paul, Minnesota: Graywolf Press, 1994. ISBN: 1555971989. 305 pages.

Huynh was born in 1957 and grew up in the village of An Tan on the Mekong River in South Vietnam. He was 12 years old when the Tet Offensive brought the war to his village. In this book, Huynh writes about his family's effort to survive the war and its bloody aftermath. He describes his experiences with the Viet Cong's postwar purges and their indoctrination programs; his year-long imprisonment in a labor camp and subsequent escape; his many attempts to flee the country; his arrival in a Thai refugee camp; and his eventual settlement in Vermont.   Huynh and his brother, who escaped with him, were able to bring over his ten surviving siblings to the United States. Huynh concludes his story with an expression of profound sadness at his continued separation from his parents and two older brothers who remained in Vietnam, and at the memory of his family as it was before the war.

209. Hyun, Peter. *Man Sei!: The Making of a Korean American*.   Honolulu: University of Hawaii Press, 1986. ISBN: 0824810414. 186 pages; photographs.

Man Sei!, which essentially means "Long live Korea!," became a forbidden expression during the Japanese occupation.   This narrative is about the Hyun family's involvement in the Korean Independence Movement. Hyun's father was involved in the planning and carrying out of the March 1st, 1919, demonstration against Japan (see the book by Margaret Pai for another account of this event), and then became a member of the Korean Provisional Government in Exile in Shanghai.   Hyun, raised in Japan-occupied Seoul, escaped to Shanghai in 1920 with his mother and seven brothers and sisters. He writes of his childhood in Seoul, his years as a "Young Revolutionary" for Korean independence in Shanghai, and then finally of leaving China for Hawaii with members of his family. Hyun continues his story in his 1995 publication *In the New World: The Making of a Korean American*.   Honolulu: University of Hawaii Press.   ISBN: 0824810414.

210. Imahara, James M. *James Imahara, Son of Immigrants*. As told to Anne Butler Poindexter.   Baton Rouge: Imahara Nursery, 1982. ISBN: none. 81 pages; photographs.

Imahara writes about the racial discrimination suffered by Japanese Americans from the time they began arriving in the United States in the 1890s until after

World War II. Born in 1903, Imahara was among the oldest of the Nisei and, fluent in both Japanese and English, was able to help immigrants as they arrived, assisting many Issei at the time of the evacuation and relocation during World War II. For his services, Imahara later received the designation of National Treasure from the Japanese Government. Imahara describes building up his farm during the pre-war years and then losing everything at the time of the evacuation. He refused to return to California at the war's end and moved his family to Louisiana. Imahara documents the difficulty his family faced trying to start over again with the $25.00 given them by the U.S. Government upon their dismissal from the internment camps.

211. Isaac, Andrew (1898-). *Andrew Isacc*. Interviews conducted and texts prepared by Yvonne Yarber and Curt Madison. Fairbanks: Central Alaska Curriculum Consortium, 1988. ISBN: 0961952008. 64 pages; photographs.
Note: Based on interviews with Chief Andrew Isaac in November, 1983, and June, 1985.

Andrew Isaac is a "traditional" chief of the Athapascan people. He is descended from the "four great chiefs" from whom he learned the old ways. He describes caribou hunting, the use and care of dogs, learning to make snow shoes at the age of ten, and the communal way of life in which his people lived in earlier days. Isaac hopes to leave a message for the young people through this book: to encourage them to learn about the old ways and to treasure their land—to hold on to it.

212. Iwata, Buddy T. (1918-). *Portrait of One Nisei: His Family and Friends*. Modesto, California: Ink Spot, 1986. ISBN: none. 248 pages; photographs.

Iwata opens this work with a list of events in his life which include attending Stanford University, internment at the Amache Relocation Camp in Colorado, teaching the Japanese language for the war office dur-

ing World War II, and getting settled into business after the war. He had three goals: contributing to the
educational system; becoming assimilated into the
mainstream of life in the United States; and enhancing
world peace in general and peace between the United
States and Japan in particular. He provides some par-
ticulars as to how he achieved these goals. The rest of
his book is a collection of his speeches and documents
relating to the war years and his career.

213. Jackson, Bo (1962-). *Bo Knows Bo: The Autobiography of
a Ballplayer*. Written with Dick Schaap. New York:
Doubleday, 1990. ISBN: 0385416202. 218 pages; photographs.

One of ten children raised by his mother in a three-
room house in rural Alabama, Bo Jackson was a
fighter and self-described "hoodlum" who managed to
reform himself before entering high school, where he
dedicated himself to sports and to getting into college.
While attending Auburn University, Jackson participated in three sports: football, track and field, and baseball. He describes the ups and downs of being a high-
profile collegiate athlete; the pressures of responding
to or ignoring public opinion and the press; his decision to begin his professional career in baseball; and
then his determination to add football to his professional agenda. Jackson also tells about his devotion to
his wife and three children, and his activities with
children who are sick, abused, or neglected.

214. Jackson, Clyde Owen. *In This Evening Light*. Hicksville,
New York: Exposition Press, 1980. ISBN: 0682494798.
113 pages.

Jackson describes the conditions in which he grew up:
poverty, segregation, discrimination, and limited employment opportunities. These were the conditions of
the South in particular, and the United States generally, during his childhood in the Depression years. He
asks the reader how one makes something of him- or
herself when confronted with such desperate and often humiliating formative years, and mentions the

names of several well-known African Americans who broke color barriers to become famous in a variety of fields. The bulk of this book is devoted to the presentation of articles and speeches written by Jackson which, he writes, help to answer this question.

215. Jackson, George. *Soledad Brother: The Prison Letters of George Jackson*. Chicago: Lawrence Hill Books, 1994. ISBN: 1556522304. 339 pages.
Note: Originally published New York: Coward-McCann, 1970. This new edition includes a forward by George Jackson's nephew, Jonathan Jackson, Jr., the original introduction by Jean Genet, and a brief autobiographical essay.

This collection of letters and a brief autobiography were published less than a year before Jackson was killed, allegedly trying to escape from prison. He was in the tenth year of a "one year to life" prison sentence—seven years of which were spent in solitary confinement. In the autobiography and letters, Jackson reveals his efforts to survive in a hostile and desolate prison environment and leaves a clear testament to his revolutionary vision, as well as making a case for his status as a political prisoner. The letters are written to his parents, his defense team, and to a few friends, including Angela Davis.

216. James, Kay Coles. *Never Forget: The Riveting Story of One Woman's Journey From Public Housing to the Corridors of Power*. Written with Jacquelline Cobb Fuller. Grand Rapids, Michigan: Zondervan, 1992. ISBN: 0310482003. 182 pages.

James tells the story of how she progressed from the daughter of a struggling mother on public assistance to a successful business woman. She writes that she was able to leave the housing projects when so many of her friends did not because of the moral and spiritual support provided by her parents. James is a prominent spokeswoman for the anti-abortion movement, and she explains many of her political and philosophical views on family, AIDS prevention, and teen sexuality.

217. Jamison, Judith. *Dancing Spirit: An Autobiography.*
     Written with Howard Kaplan. New York: Doubleday,
     1993. ISBN: 0385425570. 272 pages; photographs.
     Note: Also published New York: Anchor Books, 1994.
     ISBN: 0385425589.

     Jamison gives an account of her dancing career, begin-
     ning with her early studies at the age of 6 with Marion
     Cuyjet in Philadelphia. Following graduation from
     Fisk University, she danced professionally with the
     Philadelphia Dance Academy and the Alvin Ailey
     Dance Theater, and directed her own company known
     as the Jamison Project. She was one of Ailey's featured
     dancers, and he choreographed many works for her in-
     cluding "Cry," which helped to solidify Jamison's rep-
     utation. Jamison describes her friendship and her
     working relationship with Ailey and other members
     of the company and the dance world. Jamison had an
     international reputation, and was extraordinary in her
     profession because of her height of 5'10". After Ailey's
     death, Jamison inherited directorship of the Alvin
     Ailey Dance Theater.

218. Jerry, Daisy. *My Life Story - A Sharecropper's Daughter.*
     Ed. Connie Gross and Joyce Johnson Balkum.
     Rochester, New York: Eastern Printing and Publishing
     Co., 1984. ISBN: none. 74 pages; photographs.
     Note: Poetry by Joyce Johnson Balkum.

     Jerry grew up with an abusive, alcoholic father. After
     he murdered her mother, she and her nine brothers
     and sisters moved in with their grandparents, but be-
     cause of their meager income, all of the children had
     to work very hard at home and at various occupations
     to help support the family. Jerry describes her difficult
     life, including three unsuccessful and abusive mar-
     riages. She concludes her life story with an account of
     how she overcame this history of adversity by seeking
     out training and establishing her own daycare center.

219. Joe, Martha (1896-). *Martha Joe, Nulato*. Interviews conducted and text prepared by Yvonne Yarber and Curt
Madison. Yukon-Koyukuk Biography Series. Fairbanks: Spirit Mountain Press, 1987. ISBN: 0910871140.
56 pages; photographs.
Note: Produced by Yukon-Koyukuk School District of
Alaska.

Martha Joe recalls stories told to her by her elders, including that of the Nulato Massacre of 1851. One of
the few people to escape this late night, surprise attack
by the men of another village was Joe's grandmother.
Growing up in a time of transition, Martha Joe was
brought up with some of the older traditions: taking
part in the coming of age ritual and a forced marriage
shortly after reaching puberty. She also attended a
mission school where she was exposed to the Christian
religion. Joe laments her old age and her inability to
find and prepare the food which she grew up eating,
and also the failure of the generations following her to
learn their native language.
For a brief description and list of autobiographies in
this Yukon-Koyukuk School District series, see the entry for Moses Henzie.

220. John, Peter. *Peter John: Minto*. Interviews conducted and
text prepared by Yvonne Yarber and Curt Madison.
Yukon-Koyukuk School District Biography Series.
Fairbanks: Spirit Mountain Press, 1986. ISBN:
0910871124. 64 pages; photographs; maps.
Note: Funded and produced by the Yukon-Koyukuk
School District.

Peter John was raised in the traditional manner, learning a subsistence existence of hunting, fishing, and
trapping. He writes that he believes in the old ways
and is disillusioned with the changes that have occurred in the Athapascan way of life. He speaks with
frustration about the white encroachment on Athapascan land, especially with regard to the damage caused
by mining, and the trend of hunters flying in to the
area and over-trapping for sport. John also discusses
the importance of preserving the language and the

Minto (Tanana Athapascan) dialect, and describes efforts that are being made to ensure its survival. For a brief description and list of autobiographies in this Yukon-Koyukuk School District series, see the entry for Moses Henzie.

221. Johnson, Gertrude. *Look Where He Brought Me From.* Orrville, Ohio: Gertrude Johnson, 1989. ISBN: none. 51 pages; photographs.

222. Johnson, James Weldon (1871-1938). *Along This Way: The Autobiography of James Weldon Johnson.* New York: Penguin, 1990. ISBN: 0140184015. 418 pages. Originally published New York: Viking Press, 1933. 418 pages; illustrated; includes index.

223. Johnson, Lyman T. (1906-). *The Rest of the Dream: The Black Odyssey of Lyman Johnson.* As told to Wade Hall. Lexington: University Press of Kentucky, 1988. ISBN: 0813116740. 230 pages; photographs.
Note: Oral autobiography based on interviews from 1979-1987.

Lyman Johnson grew up in Columbia, Tennessee, and eventually settled, working as a high school history teacher, in Louisville, Kentucky. All four of his grandparents were born into slavery and both of his parents were well-educated, his mother graduating from high school and his father from college. Johnson specialized in Southern History throughout his own education, which included nearly three years of graduate school at the University of Michigan. His aim was to find out the truth, and then to debunk the noted Southern historians who had painted a romantic picture of the Old South, including a glorification of slavery. In his own classroom he was always in the middle of a controversy because he refused to teach from the book. A strong believer in civil disobedience, Johnson taught the concept to his students and led them in many sit-ins and pickets, slowly opening up the lunch counters, stores, and hotels of Louisville. Johnson writes, "conditions are better now, but I'm not going to glorify and embellish a society that once used fear and violence to keep Negroes in their place" (34).

224. Johnson, MayLee. *Coming Up on the Rough Side: A Black Catholic Story.* Written with Anne Barsanti. South Orange, New Jersey: Pillar, 1988. ISBN: 0944734014. 88 pages.

MayLee Johnson was an honor student until, as a fifth grader, she was placed in the class of an overtly racist teacher. This, coupled with her belief that she was ignored at home, sent her into a downward spiral. She failed fifth grade, spent more and more time in the streets, and finally was arrested and sent to a girls reform school. Johnson relates how a priest with whom she had had some previous contact arranged for her to be released from the school and then helped her to become involved with some of the church-sponsored community programs. His interest and her involvement in these programs helped Johnson follow through with school and develop a more constructive lifestyle. Her lack of self esteem, however, was too strong, and Johnson struggled with one setback after another over the years. After one particularly low period, she began to make decisions that brought more order to her life. She describes the work, effort, and determination it took for her gradually to move forward, and the support of her church community that enabled her to live independently with her two children.

225. Jones, Bessie (1902-). *For the Ancestors: Autobiographical Memories.* Collected and edited by John Stewart. Urbana: University of Illinois Press, 1983. ISBN: 0252009592. 203 pages; photographs; bibliography.
Note: Also published Athens: University of Georgia Press, 1989. ISBN: 0820311731.

Jones, founder of and performer with the Georgia Sea Island Singers, was born in Georgia in 1902. Her grandfather was born in Africa and sold into slavery in Virginia. She learned many songs and games from him, and in this book, she discusses their origins, how they were used by the slaves, and the meanings behind the words. She also describes the formation of the Singers, its history, the various members, and the importance of its role in keeping alive the traditional songs which they perform.

226. Jordan, Michael (1963-). *Rare Air: Michael on Michael.* Ed. Mark Vancil. Photographs by Walter Iooss. San Francisco: Collins Publishers, San Francisco, 1993. ISBN: 0002553899:0006382568. 112 pages; photographs.

In this photographic essay, Jordan describes his life at home with his wife Juanita and three children. He explains his competitive philosophy, his pre- and postgame procedures, and his thoughts and actions while on the court. Jordan also discusses the pressures of being a celebrity and role model.

227. Kalifornsky, Peter (1911-1992). *A Dena'ina Legacy/ K'TL'EGH'I SUKDU: The Collected Writings of Peter Kalifornsky.* Written with James M. Kari and Alan Boraas. Fairbanks: Alaska Native Language Center, University of Alaska, Fairbanks, 1991. ISBN: 1555000436. 485 pages; photographs; bibliography.
Note: Written in English and Tanaina.

Chapter seven of this collection of writings by Kalifornsky covers various moments and events in his life. One of the last speakers and only writer of the Kenai dialect of the Athapascan language, Kalifornsky writes about being raised by his aunts after his mother's death and how he learned to hunt and trap from his uncle. He describes various hunting and trapping experiences, his travels through California teaching and lecturing in the 1970s, and his efforts to reestablish the tradition of potlatches. In the rest of this collection, Kalifornsky gives the history of the Dena'ina (Tanaina), describes their beliefs and customs, discusses the language, and retells many stories and legends.

228. Kallands, Edgar. *Edgar Kallands, Kaltag.* Interviews conducted and text prepared by Yvonne Yarber and Curt

Madison. Yukon-Koyukuk School District Biography Series. Fairbanks: Spirit Mountain Press, 1982. ISBN: 0910871000. 64 pages; photographs; maps.
Note: Produced by Yukon-Koyukuk School District of Alaska.

Edgar Kallands's father was from Nova Scotia and his mother was Athapascan. His mother died when he was nine years old, and after this he spent most of his time with the white inhabitants of the area. His father taught him farming, growing mostly hay and vegetables. After his father's death, Kallands spent more time with Native people and relearned the Athapascan language. He worked on the steam boats, ran a small store, and trapped. As a mail carrier, Kallands participated in the "serum run"—dog sled teams relayed the serum to Nome to combat the diphtheria epidemic. This historic run was the inspiration for the Iditirod Dog Sled Race.
For a brief description and list of autobiographies in this Yukon-Koyukuk School District series, see the entry for Moses Henzie.

229. Kegg, Maude (1904-). *Portage Lake: Memories of an Ojibwe Childhood.* Transcribed and edited by John D. Nichols. Minneapolis: University of Minnesota Press, 1993. ISBN: 0816624151. 272 pages; bibliography.
Note: Also published Edmonton, Alberta: University of Alberta Press, 1991. Kegg also wrote *Gabekanaansing/At the End of the Trail: Memories of Chippewa Childhood in Minnesota with Texts in Ojibwe and English.* Published Greeley, Colorado: Museum of Anthropology, University of North Colorado, 1978. Occasional Publications in Anthropology: Linguistics Series 4; and *Gii-ikwezensiwiyaan/When I was a Little Girl: Memories of Indian Childhood in Minnesota.* Published Onamia, Minnesota: Kegg, 1973.

Nichols has recorded a set of Kegg's stories about her childhood and organized them by season. Spring stories relate the activities surrounding the collection and preparation of maple syrup; summer stories describe the gathering of bulrushes and berries, and the variety of wildlife to be found in the Portage and Mille Lacs Lakes area; fall stories center around the ricing; and winter stories describe snow, ice, hunting, and trapping. Kegg includes some traditional stories and descriptions of special celebrations, rituals, and games.

230. Kelley, Jane Holden (1928-). *Yaqui Women: Contemporary Life Histories.* Lincoln: University of Nebraska Press, 1991. ISBN: 0803277741. 265 pages; maps; bibliography.
Originally published Lincoln: University of Nebraska Press, 1978. ISBN: 0803209126.

231. Kenny, Maurice (1929-). "Waiting at the Edge: Words Toward a Life." *I Tell You Now: Autobiographical Essays by Native American Writers.* Ed. Brian Swann and Arnold Krupat. Lincoln: University of Nebraska Press, 1987. ISBN: 0803227140.

See entry under *Swann, Brian* for a complete list of authors included in this anthology.

232. Khanga, Yelena. *Soul to Soul: A Black Russian American Family, 1865-1992.* Written with Susan Jacoby. New York: W. W. Norton, 1992. ISBN: 0393034046: 0393311554. 318 pages; photographs.

Herself a third generation Russian citizen, Khanga's maternal grandparents met in an American jail cell after a Communist Party demonstration. Her grandfather was black, a descendent of slaves; her grandmother was a naturalized American of Jewish and Polish descent. They married and left the United States to live in Russia. Khanga's father was an African independence leader from Zanzibar. He met Khanga's mother while studying in Moscow, and was assassinated in his own country a year after Khanga's birth. In this book, Khanga explores her family history and seeks out her roots on three continents.

233. Kikuchi, Charles. *The Kikuchi Diary: Chronicle From an American Concentration Camp: The Tanforan Journals of Charles Kikuchi.* Ed. John Modell. Urbana:

University of Illinois Press, 1992. ISBN: 0252062833.
253 pages; photographs.
Originally published University of Illinois Press, 1973.
ISBN: 0252003152.

234. Kikumura, Akemi (1944-). *Promises Kept: Life of an Issei
     Man*. Rev. ed. Novato, California: Chandler and
     Sharp Publishers, Inc., 1991. ISBN: 0883165635:
     0883165627. 132 pages; photographs.

     Although the subject of this book is her father,
     Kikumura writes in the first person, and many of her
     own experiences, thoughts, and interpretations are
     worked into the story. The chapter "Going Home" is
     about her visit to her father's family in Japan. Her ex-
     periences there lead her to imagine what her parents'
     life would have been like had they stayed in Japan.
     She concludes that it would have been easier. On the
     other hand, Kikumura feels she would not have en-
     joyed the life she would have had in Japan. The
     telling of her father's story is an exploration of her
     own life. Joan Lidoff writes in her article "Autobiog-
     raphy in a Different Voice: Maxine Hong Kingston's
     The Woman Warrior" (*Auto/Biography Studies*. 3.3
     [Fall 1987]) that "Today we often find women's autobi-
     ographies written as biography . . . a number of daugh-
     ters writing their own story as a subplot of their par-
     ents'. The story of the other is foreground; one's own
     story emerges from the interstices, and the back-
     ground" (p. 30).

235. King, Charles H. *Fire in My Bones*. Grand Rapids, Michi-
     gan: W. B. Eerdmans Publishing Co., 1983. ISBN:
     0802835708:0802800378. 326 pages.

     King writes about his entry into the ministry and the
     political events and personal experiences leading to
     the development of his theology which embraced a so-
     cial gospel, "the gospel of earthly redemption" (p. 43),
     and also signaled his growing political commitment.
     He became deeply involved in the sit-ins, marches,
     and demonstrations which characterized the Civil
     Rights Movement, and eventually gave up his parish

to devote his energies to political issues: "[M]y ten-year tenure had changed me from being a Negro to becoming a black man. . . . I began to disdain the weak theological shorings of the traditionalists, and I sought for a new philosophy of religion which was both religiously sustaining and secularly fulfilling" (p. 112). Immediately after his retirement, King took charge of the Human Relations Commission in Gary, Indiana. In this book he describes the changes that took place within the black church in response to the political climate and growing influence of militant groups. King documents his initial contacts and interactions with various black militant groups and his personal response to their philosophy. After completing his work with the Human Relations Commission, King went on to work with other politically active groups, including the Urban Crisis Center in Atlanta. He also worked with the Lutheran Church, offering racial awareness seminars. He speaks of a turning point for himself in his work with white Americans which led him to develop a new series of seminars using the "encounter" method. King describes this seminar and its purpose in some detail: "My purpose is to convince white people to change. If they don't change, it actually spells the end of a future for many, many blacks" (p. 313). "The problem is white racism. The problem is discrimination. The problem is racial prejudice. . . . The answer is the will and power of white society and white institutions to change. They must change" (p. 317).

236. King, Coretta Scott. *My Life with Martin Luther King, Jr.* Rev. ed. New York: Henry Holt, 1993. ISBN: 030810221. 372 pages.
    Originally published New York: New York, Holt, Rinehart, and Winston, 1969.

237. Kingman, Dong (1911-). *Paint the Yellow Tiger.* New York: Sterling Publishing Co., 1991. ISBN: 0806983167. 128 pages; illustrations by the author.

    Born in Oakland, California, in 1911, Dong Kingman had just begun kindergarten when his father decided to move the family to Hong Kong. Kingman writes about his earliest artistic inclinations which, as a child, he manifested through sidewalk drawings outside his home. After being sent back to the United States with his brothers, Kingman attended art school while operating his own restaurant. Although initially discouraged by his art teacher, Kingman did not believe that his passion for art could be so strong and his talents so weak. He began working with water colors, and the story of his successful career as an artist is documented in this book. Every page includes a sketch or a water color by Kingman, many created specifically for this book.

238. Kingston, Maxine Hong. *China Men*. New York: Knopf, 1980. ISBN: 0394424638. 308 pages.
Note: Also published New York: Vintage Books, 1989. ISBN: 0679723285.

In *Woman Warrior* (1976) and *China Men*, Kingston presents autobiographical material together with her interpretations of Chinese myths and legends, and the history of her family and of China based on her knowledge of the facts as well as the workings of her imagination. In *China Men*, Kingston writes that she was anxious to visit China, to explore her ancestral village, and to "compare China, a country I made up with what country is really out there" (p. 87). As suggested by the title, Kingston's earlier work focuses on women and their status in China and among Chinese Americans: how the conflicts between traditional Chinese culture, its American permutations, and Western American culture have shaped her mother and herself. *China Men* illustrates the problems and opportunities presented by the culture clashes from the context of the men in Kingston's family: her father, brother, grandfathers, and other male relatives from her past and present.

239. —. *The Woman Warrior: Memoirs of a Girlhood Among Ghosts*. New York: Knopf, 1976. ISBN: 0394400674. 209 pages.
Note: Also published New York: Vintage Books, 1989. ISBN: 0679721886.

See Kingston's *China Men* for a description of this work.

240. Kochiyama, Yuri (1921-). *Fishmerchant's Daughter: An Oral History*. Written with Arthur Tabier. New York: Community Documentation Workshops, St.-Mark's-in-the-Bowery, 1981. 2 volumes; photographs.

Kochiyama relates the story of her life before, during, and after World War II, and the relocation of 110,000 West Coast Japanese Americans to internment camps. Already aware of hostility toward and prejudice against Japanese Americans from her experiences looking for work and being excluded from unions, Kochiyama was nonetheless shocked by the internment. Her father was arrested as an enemy alien, and died shortly afterwards. FBI agents were present at his funeral to make note of those who attended. At the end of the war and the dissolution of the camps, many Japanese Americans had no home to which they could return, and they continued to be viewed as the enemy by many white Americans. After her marriage, Kochiyama moved to New York, where she and her husband hosted many traveling Japanese American soldiers and students. Kochiyama also writes about her involvement with the "Hiroshima Maidens," young girls who were victims of the atomic bomb and had come to the United States for medical treatment.

241. Krupat, Arnold, ed. *Native American Autobiography: An Anthology*. Wisconsin Studies in American Autobiography. Madison: University of Wisconsin Press, 1994. ISBN: 0299140202. 546 pages; photographs.
Note: Also published in paperback. ISBN: 0299140245.

This anthology presents complete autobiographical essays and excerpts from larger works spanning a period of almost 300 years. The works in this anthology, as distinguished by Krupat, represent two types of autobiography. The first type Krupat calls "Indian Autobiography." In this type, the subject speaks through an interpreter to the recorder/editor, who is often, though not always, an anthropologist. Krupat calls the second type "Autobiographies by Indians," with the text written by the subject of the narrative. Krupat divides the work into seven sections and has written an introduction for each section and for each excerpt. Sections six and seven fall within the restrictions of this bibliography; that is, they include at least some works published after 1980. Section six contains excerpts or essays by "mixed-blood" writers including Momaday, Rose, Vizenor, and Hogan. The essays by Vizenor and Hogan also appear in *I Tell You Now: Autobiographical Essays by Native Americans*, 1987 (see entry in this bibliography under individual essayists or under editor, Swann). Section seven, "Traditional Lives Today," contains the stories of Native Americans "intimately acquainted with the ways of the dominant, non-Indian culture but whose lives are nonetheless guided by traditional values." Individuals whose life histories are presented here are Fools Crow, Albert Yava or Big Falling Snow, Peter Kalifornsky, Angela Sidney, Annie Ned, and Kitty Smith. Entries for the entire works from which these excerpts are taken are listed separately in this bibliography.

242. Ladd, Jerrold (1970-). *Out of the Madness: From the Projects to a Life of Hope.* New York: Warner Books, 1994. ISBN: 0446517445. 195 pages.

Ladd tells the story of his childhood in a West Dallas housing development. He describes his home as a "Hitler camp," where filth, insect infestation, oppressive heat, and hunger were his daily companions. His father left, abandoning his drug addicted wife and their three children to a situation where there was little or no income, and little or no attention to their essential needs. Ladd's story is about his determination not to repeat the failures of his mother and father, and of many of the adults in his neighborhood—to avoid drugs, alcohol, and violence—and to take care of his children no matter what. In this work, Ladd addresses the importance of a knowledge of one's heritage and his own regeneration at learning about his African and African American heritage: "My discovery of dead literary role models permanently cured my doubt and made me bind back to the fundamental truth. Knowing the great accomplishments of my people, when they existed in their own civilizations, started a chain reaction that would change the foundation of my mind" (p. 175). He currently writes, and, at the time of the writing of this book, had started up a small company to produce films and books for African Americans.

243. Lamar, Jake. *Bourgeois Blues: An American Memoir.* New York: Summit Books, 1991. ISBN: 0671691910. 174 pages.
Note: Also published New York: Plume, 1991. ISBN: 0452269113.

Lamar, a graduate of Harvard and writer for *Time Magazine*, writes about his relationship with his father, who was ambitious and hardworking, but also controlling and often violent. As Lamar sorts through his feelings for his father and struggles with decisions about his role as an African American writer, he reviews his experiences at his alma mater and *Time*, two bastions of white male tradition, considering the subtle and not-so-subtle impact that his race has had on him and those around him.

244. Lame Deer, Archie Fire (1935-). *Gift of Power: The Life and Teachings of a Lakota Medicine Man.* Written with Richard Erdoes. Santa Fe: Bear and Co., 1992. ISBN: 0939680874. 280 pages; photographs.

Archie Fire Lame Deer recounts his childhood with his maternal grandfather, a traditional Lakota Indian and medicine man. Although his grandfather died when Lame Deer was 11, his teachings have remained with Lame Deer throughout his life. After his grandfather's death, Lame Deer was sent to a Catholic boarding school, where an attempt was made to stifle his Indian identity and spirituality. Two years later, Lame Deer ran away from the boarding school, and it was about this time that he met his father, John Lame Deer, also a medicine man, for the first time. Many years later, John Lame Deer, on his deathbed, transferred his spiritual power to his son, Archie, who then followed the path that led him to fulfill his father's and his grand-father's vision for him. Lame Deer explains what it means to be a medicine man. The term in English, according to Lame Deer, does not express the true nature of the spiritual leader, nor does it account for the variety that exists among medicine men. At the time of the writing of this book, Lame Deer was lecturing on Indian spirituality and traditions throughout Europe and the United States.

245. Lane, Lois W. *The Last of the Thirteen Growing Up in Georgia*. New York: Vantage Press, 1988. ISBN: 0533075645. 77 pages.

Lois Lane describes her status as the baby of a family of thirteen children. She lost her mother when she was just seven years old and was subsequently cared for by her aunt, but Lane felt that any opportunity to better herself would be up to her. She arranged for her own education and was able to complete a college degree and earn teaching credentials while also providing some financial assistance to family members at home. Lane writes of many adverse situations, including mistreatment and neglect from older siblings and injustices in the work place.

246. Lee, George P. (1943-). *Silent Courage: An Indian Story: The Autobiography of George P. Lee, a Navajo*. Salt Lake City: Deseret Book Co., 1987. ISBN: 0875790569. 359 pages; photographs.

George P. Lee spent his early childhood living a traditional Navajo life on the Navajo reservation in the Four Corners area, herding sheep and migrating between summer and winter hogans with his family. His family also worked as migrant fieldworkers for two months out of each year. Lee stresses the poverty in which his family lived, and the alcoholism from which his father and many in his extended family suffered. But he also writes of a happy childhood and a strong sense of being loved. As migrant workers, members of his family were attacked both verbally and physically. Their attackers were motivated by virulent racism. Lee writes that "[d]espite having to venture into a white man's world and be treated worse than dogs, we were Navajo through and through. Deep inside, we had unconditional respect for ourselves. We were true to our Navajo heritage and this gave us . . . a higher understanding of nature and of life" (p. 84). Lee became a member of the Church of Jesus Christ of Latter-Day Saints (LDS) when his mother checked that particular box on a boarding school application. Required by the school to choose an "Anglo" religion, she chose that of a respected white friend. This friend of the family later talked Lee's parents into letting him participate in a special foster family program sponsored by the Mormon church. Lee describes adjusting to this new family; the difficulties of making the transition from home life on the reservation, to home life in Utah and back again; and his continued dedication to the church and his work with the Navajo people through the church.

247. Lee, Jarena (b. 1783-), Zilpha Elaw (b. 1790?-) and Julia A. J. Foote (1823-1900). *Sisters of the Spirit: Three Black Women's Autobiographies of the 19th Century*. Ed. William L. Andrews. Religion in North America. Bloomington: Indiana University Press, 1986. ISBN: 0253352606:0253287049. 245 pages; bibliography.

This work reprints autobiographies of three female African American evangelists originally published in the nineteenth century. Jarena Lee was born to free parents in 1789. She arranged for the publication of her autobiography, *The Life and Religious Experiences of Jarena Lee* in 1836 and again in 1839. A revised version was published in 1849. She used this work as a conversion tool which she passed out at religious meetings. Lee was preaching with the African Methodist Episcopal (A.M.E.) Church in Philadelphia at a time when women were not licensed to do so. Zelpha Elaw, born about 1790 also to free parents, became a self-supported itinerant preacher sometime after 1823 and included a sojourn to the slave states and a visit to England as part of her spiritual travels. She published her *Memoirs of the Life, Religious Experience, Ministerial Travels, and Labors of Mrs. Zilpha Elaw* about 1846. Julia A. J. Foote, born in 1823, was the daughter of former slaves who had purchased their freedom. She began her preaching career shortly after becoming a member of the A.M.E. Zion Church. Her preaching was not acceptable to the church leaders, and she was forced out of the membership. Foote continued as an itinerant evangelist. She published *A Brand Plucked From the Fires* in 1879 and again in 1886. Nearly a decade after this second publication, she became the first woman ordained as deacon in the A.M.E. Zion Church.

248. Lee, Joann Faung Jean (1950-). *Asian American Experiences in the United States: Oral Histories of First to Fourth Generation Americans From China, the Philippines, Japan, India, the Pacific Islands, Vietnam, and Cambodia.* Jefferson, North Carolina: McFarland & Co., 1991. ISBN: 0899505856. 228 pages; photographs.
Note: Also published New York: The New Press, 1992. ISBN: 1565840232 with the title *Asian Americans: Oral Histories. . . .*

Lee presents here 52 interviews with 40 subjects described by the subtitle of the book. Oddly enough, "Korea" was left out of the title, although Korean Americans are represented in this collection. Lee writes that she "aimed to come as close as possible to Asian American attitudes and lifestyles as defined by their cultural past and American present" (p. xi). As one might expect from such a broad selection of subjects, a range of experiences and outlooks, can be found within these interviews. The book is divided into three sections: "Living in America," "Aspects of Americanization," and "Interracial Marriage."

249. Lee, Mary Kuang Sun Paik (1900-). *Quiet Odyssey: A Pioneer Korean Woman in America.* Ed. Sucheng Chan. Seattle: University of Washington Press, 1990. ISBN: 0295969466. 201 pages; photographs; bibliography.

Mary Kuang Sun Paik Lee tells the story of her family's immigration to the United States, their struggles to make a living in the face of racially-discriminatory labor laws, employers who exploited their workers, and the Great Depression. Although her parents were never able to get beyond a subsistence existence, the children, as they grew up, had better opportunities and prospered. Lee writes: "The fourth generation of young Koreans growing up in comfortable homes with every advantage open to them will find it difficult to realize the sacrifices made by the first generation. It is very gratifying to me to see the progress our family has made from poverty to where we are today" (p. 134). Lee provides some family history. Both her mother and father were from relatively prosperous families and were well educated. Lee's grandmother, educated by Christian missionaries at a time when few Korean women had the opportunity to learn, established the first girls' school in Pyongyang. Although she does not dwell on discrimination, Lee devotes a chapter to describing the kind of overt and covert discrimination that she and other racial minorities faced in the California of her youth and early adult years. The editor provides a brief history of Korea, chapters on Korean-American family farms, rice growing, and a bibliographic essay of books on Korea and Korean Americans.

250. Left Handed (1868-?). *Left Handed, a Navajo Autobiography*. Recorded and edited by Walter and Ruth Dyk. New York: Columbia University Press, 1980. ISBN: 0231049463. 578 pages; photographs.
Note: Translated from the Navajo.

This is the sequel to *Son of Old Man Hat; a Navajo Autobiography*. New York: Harcourt Brace, c1938. (Also published Lincoln, Nebraska: University of Nebraska Press, 1967. ISBN: 0803250541 and reissued in 1996. ISBN: 0803279582.) In *Son of Old Man Hat*, Left Handed covered the years of his life from childhood through maturity. This volume discusses three years at the end of the 1880s when Left Handed was in his twenties. His narrative reveals the difficulties he encounters in his relationship with his wife, and elements of daily life including such subjects as witchcraft, religion, the Navajo clan system, seasonal migrations connected to the herding of sheep, and the care of cattle and horses. This narrative is a detailed account including daily minutiae and conversations.

251. Leighton, Alexander H. (1908-).
See *Lucky*.

252. Lester, Julius. *Lovesong: Becoming a Jew.* New York: Henry Holt, 1988. ISBN: 0805005889. 248 pages; photographs.
Note: Also published New York: Arcade Publishers, 1991. ISBN: 1559701757. Lester's earlier autobiography is *All is Well*. New York: W. Morrow, 1976. ISBN: 0688030459.

Lester's great-grandfather was a German-Jewish immigrant, and his great-grandmother was a former slave. As a child asking questions, Lester did not receive much information about his great-grandparents, but because many of his experiences had some connection with Judaism, he looks back on his life as a spiritual journey leading finally to his conversion to Judaism. He writes of growing up as the son of a Methodist minister and community leader and recalls his responses to religious events, the Bible, and his father's strict moral vision. Lester writes about his feelings for and involvement in the Civil Rights Movement, and particularly about the role he played in the controversy that developed over the movement toward community control of schools in New York. Lester presents his story year by year, documenting the changes he underwent spiritually, emotionally, and socially—not without a sense of humor.

253. Lewis, Lloyd (1904-). *Life is for Living: An Autobiography.* The Black Contemporary Lives Series. Dayton, Ohio (402 Salem Ave., Dayton 45406): Fells Johnson Techniwrite, Inc., 1989. ISBN: none. 112 pages; photographs.

Born with the entrepreneurial spirit and growing up with the dream of "carloads" of money, Lewis set out in his adult years to succeed in business. A graduate of Wilberforce College in Ohio, Lewis' first job was as a physical education director at a branch of the Dayton YMCA. He describes the segregated nature of that institution. Despite the YMCA's own institutional racism, it was the only place for African American boys to play basketball, since they weren't allowed on high school teams. Lewis was able to break some color barriers while working at the YMCA. He became chairman of Dayton's Fifth Street Branch, and the first black chairman with a vote. He writes that at first he had a voice but no vote: "After the Board got through listening to me, they concluded it was easier to give me a vote than to listen to me talk so much" (p. 67). In 1939, Lewis, with other members of the black civic organization known as the Dayton Frontier Club, attempted unsuccessfully to persuade the local high school to integrate its programs, but later, in the '50s, he helped to organize a successful attempt to integrate the local Hospital.

254. Lightfoot, Claude M. (1910-). *Chicago Slums to World Politics: Autobiography of Claude M. Lightfoot.* Written with Timothy V. Johnson (1952-). New York: New Outlook, 1987. ISBN: 0878981659. 226 pages; photographs.

Claude Lightfoot documents his 60-year membership in the United States Communist Party. Joining in 1931 after becoming discouraged by the Democratic Party, Lightfoot quickly took on leadership roles. He explains why he joined the Communist Party and why he has remained with them. He notes that the work of the Communist Party in black neighborhoods was quite evident during the 30s. There was no such evidence of Democratic or Republican Party work. He also writes that "when I joined the Communist Party I was 'free at last.' From that moment on, I did not have to bow and scrape before the man. I was my own man" (p. 203). Lightfoot was arrested under the Smith Act during the McCarthy era and was under virtual house arrest for ten years while his case was in the courts. He was eventually acquitted of charges brought against him by the U.S. Government. Immediately upon his acquittal, he returned to Party work and only limited his activities because of health problems. Lightfoot records his experiences as a soldier during World War II, the treatment he received as an African American soldier and as a prominent member of the Communist Party, and also of his work in the Civil Rights Movement through the auspices of the Communist Party.

255. Lin, Alice Murong Pu (1942-). *Grandmother Had No Name*. San Francisco: China Books and Periodicals, 1988. ISBN: 0835120457:0835120341. 220 pages.

Lin describes her aunts and uncles to reveal the expectations of and possibilities for women in China, and the past and current state of marriage and child-rearing there. She combines her childhood memories of living in China with her experiences as an adult during a return trip in 1979, nearly 30 years later. Lin arrived in Michigan to attend the University during the era of the Civil Rights Movement. As part of her graduate studies, she worked with recent immigrant families. This contact allowed Lin to verify her own sense of what she could accomplish as a woman in America and compare it with her possibilities in China. She finds both stark contrasts and surprising similarities. Lin addresses American stereotypes of Asian women and the low value placed on female children in the climate of China's one-child policy. Lin is anxious to work for changes to improve the status of women in both countries.

256. Linda B. (Nguyen Thi Loan). *Edge of Survival: Vietnam, the Other Side*. Charleston, South Carolina: Ashley Publishing, 1993. ISBN: 0963716700. 240 pages; maps. Note: From title page: "The true story of a young girl's growth and experiences in war-torn North and South Vietnam; not as seen by foreigners or the soldiers who fought that terrible war, but by those who were most deeply affected: the Vietnamese people."

Linda B. writes about growing up in Vietnam between the years of 1951 and 1969. She has memories of a beautiful land, a loving family, and close friends. Her "peaceful existence" ended when her village was invaded and her father murdered. From that point on, her life was a continuous struggle for survival. She eventually left Vietnam after marrying an American soldier. Linda B. is currently working on a new book, *Bui Doi.*

257. Ling, Jing Chuan (1930-). *Odyssey in the Forest.* Tacoma, Washington: All My Somedays, 1982. ISBN: none. 69 pages; photographs.
Note: Written as part of the All My Somedays/Living History project sponsored by the Pierce County Library and the Tacoma Public Library.

Ling writes about her childhood in the predominantly white community of Tacoma, Washington. Her father, an herb doctor, arrived in Tacoma in 1906 and brought her mother over from China in 1924. Her parents raised ten children during the years of the depression. Ling describes her early friendships and schooling. She recalls the disappearance of the Japanese after the bombing of Pearl Harbor, and that she and her siblings wore a special badge which identified them as Chinese.

258. Lipscomb, Mance (1895-1976). *I Say Me for a Parable: The Oral Autobiography of Mance Lipscomb, Texas Blues Man.* As told to A. Glenn Alyn. New York: W. W. Norton, 1993. ISBN: 039303500X. 508 pages; photographs; map; discography; filmography; song index.
Note: Also published New York: Da Capo Press, 1994. ISBN: 030680610X.

Lipscomb tells about his family, childhood, farming experiences and musical life in this oral account of his life. Provided with very little formal education, Lipscomb learned the basics of reading and writing from an itinerant tutor. His father was a professional fiddler, and he got Lipscomb started on the fiddle. Lipscomb became a guitarist and singer as well. In 1961 he was invited to take part in the Berkeley Blues Festival, and went on to tour throughout the rest of the continental United States. He also made a number of recordings with Arhoolie and Reprise Records. Lipscomb, also a tenant farmer, describes the hardships and inequality of that life:

> I call myself a slave until I got somewhere along about foedy-five years of age. I had to go by the landowner's word. Do what he said ta git a home ta stay in. And then when I make my crop, why he sold the cotton, an figgered it out his own way. An brought me out in debt. I didn clear no money til nineteen foedy-five in my whole life. (p. 299)

259. Loan, Nguyen Thi.
     See entry for *Linda B.*

260. Loftus, Mitzi Asai. *Made in Japan and Settled in Oregon.* Coos Bay, Oregon: Pigeon Point Press, 1990. ISBN: none. 177 pages; photographs.

Loftus grew up in Hood River, Oregon. Her parents immigrated from Japan, her father arriving in 1904 and her mother coming as a "picture bride" in 1911. Loftus describes her childhood and her parents' child-rearing practices and expectations. Loftus relates the events of the evacuation and internment that followed the bombing of Pearl Harbor, and her family's subsequent return after the war to neighbors, both hostile and friendly. The difficulties of returning were compounded by the news of the death of her older sister who had been raised in Japan and been the victim of a firebombing during the war. Loftus traveled to Japan on a Fulbright grant in 1957. While teaching there, she was able to meet many relatives, including her sister's surviving son.

261. Lone Dog, Louise. *Strange Journey: The Vision Life of a Psychic Indian Woman.* Ed. Patricia Powell. Happy Camp, California: Naturegraph Publishers, 1990. ISBN: 0879612061:087961207X. 105 pages; illustrations.

Louise Lone Dog describes her experiences with the spirit world as a child and as an adult. She tells of her

visions and their significance for the future of human-
kind.

262. Lopez, Arcadia H. (1909-). *Barrio Teacher*. Houston: Arte
Publico Press, 1992. ISBN: 1558850511. 81 pages.

Arcadia Lopez' earliest memory is of the revolution in
1913 and her family's flight from Mexico. They crossed
the border, settling first in Laredo and then San Antonio. Lopez describes her neighborhood in a San Antonio barrio and the poverty of her family and her
neighbors. She writes of her college years during
which she balanced work and study, finally achieving
her goal of becoming a teacher. In her 46 years as an
elementary-school teacher, Lopez pioneered bilingual
education and continued to direct a bilingual training
program after her retirement. About her first experiences with bilingual education, Lopez writes:

> Previous to the bilingual education experiments, only about
> one third of my [first grade] students performed well enough
> to merit promotion . . . so, I worked with the project whole
> heartedly. I saw the change in the students immediately.
> They became more alert and they felt good about them-
> selves. (p. 67)

263. Lorde, Audre. *Zami, a New Spelling of My Name:
Biomythography*. The Crossing Press Feminist Series.
Trumansburg, New York: The Crossing Press, 1982.
ISBN: 0895941236:0895941228. 256 pages.

Lorde writes that the "[i]mages of women flaming like
torches adorn and define the borders of my journey,
stand like dykes [sic] between me and the chaos. It is
the images of women, kind and cruel, that lead me
home" (p. 3). In Lorde's story of her childhood growing up in New York City during World War II, she describes her relationships and experiences with her
mother, aunts, female teachers, and female friends and
lovers. It was in high school that Lorde first began to
meet other girls with whom she could identify and
who shared her interest in words and poetry. The girl
to whom Lorde felt closest committed suicide before
her senior year, and images of her reappear throughout the work. This book is at once a coming-of-age

story and an homage to the women Lorde has loved most.

264. Loving, Neal V. (1916-). *Loving's Love: A Black American's Experience in Aviation.* Smithsonian History of Aviation Series. Washington: Smithsonian Institution Press, 1994. ISBN: 1560983426. 288 pages; photographs.

Loving tells the story of his life-long devotion to flying and aircraft design and construction. He was first struck with this love of flight at the age of 10, took his first ride at 14, and joined the Ace Flying Club, an all-black organization, when he was 16. He attended a technical high school which allowed him to work on aeronautic design and construction. Loving describes his experiences building gliders, learning to fly, starting his own glider construction company, and flying after he became an accomplished pilot. Although he faced many obstacles due to racial discrimination, including segregated airports and limited opportunities for lessons and employment that would take advantage of his expertise in engineering and design, Loving was determined to do what he loved, and he succeeded. He emphasizes the importance of absolute attention to detail both in building an aircraft and in flying one. Loving describes two accidents, both of which were the result of taking short cuts and disregarding warning signs. One of these accidents, which nearly cost him his life, was due to his own impatience. As a result of the accident, Loving was in the hospital for over six months and lost both legs. This loss did not keep him from his aviation dreams, and, in fact, most of his accomplishments as a pilot and airplane designer occurred after the accident.

265. Lucas, Maria Elena (1941-). *Forged Under the Sun: The Life of Maria Elena Lucas.* Ed. Fran Leeper Bus. Women and Culture Series. Ann Arbor: University of Michigan Press, 1993. ISBN: 0472094327:0472064320. 314 pages; photographs; bibliography.

Lucas grew up with migrant farm workers, on the edge of poverty. Discouraged by her teachers, her father, and the harvesting schedule from getting an education, Lucas kept diaries and wrote as an emotional release. Married at 15, Lucas had five children by the time she was 22, and had seven in all. They, like her, were discouraged by continual harassment from finishing school, though several went back and earned graduate degrees later on. Lucas writes about her work as a farm worker, an advocate for the rights of migrant farm workers, and as a union organizer.

266. Lucky (190?-1958?). *Lucky, the Navajo Singer*. Ed. Joyce J. Griffen. Recorded by Alexander H. and Dorothea C. Leighton. Albuquerque: University of New Mexico Press, 1992. ISBN: 0826313744. 240 pages; photographs; maps; bibliography.

This life history was prepared in the 1940s. Lucky was 40 years old at the time. A sheepherder, Lucky was also a ceremonial singer. He describes the role of singing in everyday life and his own participation in ceremonies as an apprentice or assistant singer, and then achieving independent status. Representative of the Navajo people in transition, Lucky was caught between living a traditional lifestyle and living a more Euro-American lifestyle wrongheadedly encouraged by the federal government. As a result of this anomie, Lucky suffered from addictions to alcohol and gambling which, he himself notes, were significant problems on the Navajo reservation during his lifetime.

267. Lyles, Charlise (1959-). *Do I Dare Disturb the Universe?: From the Projects to Prep School*. Boston: Faber and Faber, 1994. ISBN: 0571198368. 226 pages.

Charlise Lilliane Lyles explores her formative years in her book which describes her childhood from about 1968 through 1974. Influenced by her poetical and thoughtful, but chronically unemployed father, Lyles was also a dreamer. Although an avid reader like her father, Lyles was placed in the slowest class by the time she was in junior high because she was unable to maintain her concentration in class. She describes the events that brought her to this state: her family's financial problems—her mother was no longer able to afford their house after her father left—and their move to the projects; Lyles's friends and their child-hood games turned mean and hard; daily threats of physical abuse; and the reality of murder claiming even the most innocent victims. When Lyles's native intelligence and creative spirit were uncovered by one of her teachers, everything began to change. Lyles writes about the new direction her life took, the build-ing of her self esteem, and the development of a belief in the possibility of having a meaningful future. In her story, Lyles shows the importance of many pro-grams which followed in the wake of the successes of the Civil Rights Movement, including such programs as Head Start, ABC (A Better Chance, Inc. Program), and the school breakfast and lunch programs; pro-grams which made a difference for many children, in-cluding Lyles and her brothers and sisters. She also paints a clear picture of how poverty and lack of oppor-tunity can kill a person's spirit no matter how brilliant or talented. She writes the following about her own rescue: "In those days of opportunity, Mrs. Tierce and others were always on the lookout to salvage any child mistakenly discarded into the pile of academic rejects. And there were many. Mrs. Tierce and others like her found us, the children whose intelligence shone through despite traumas and terrors that kept us silent, numbed dumb" (p. 189).

268. MacDonald, Peter (1928-). *The Last Warrior: Peter Mac-Donald and the Navajo Nation*. Written with Ted Schwarz. The Library of the American Indian. New York: Orion Books, 1993. ISBN: 0517593238:1561290939. 371 pages; photographs.

Peter MacDonald wrote this autobiography from prison. He was convicted by Navajo and Federal Courts of misappropriating tribal funds during his fourth year of tribal chairmanship. He writes exten-sively about the Big Boquillas land purchase that led to his court battles and the investigations and legal events that followed. MacDonald describes his child-hood growing up on the Navajo reservation, his Bu-

reau of Indian Affairs (BIA) schooling, military service, and eventually his successful and lucrative career
as an engineer. He left this career behind to return to
the reservation with his family, where eventually he
became involved with tribal politics to resist the land
and resource grabs constantly being made by state and
federal entities. He defends himself in this work, presenting his side of the story, and he places it in the context of other tribes (e.g. the Crow and the Northern
Cheyenne) living on energy-rich lands who have also
encountered legal problems and interference from the
BIA.

269. Madden, T. O. *We Were Always Free: The Maddens of
Culpepper County, Virginia: A 200-Year Family His-
tory.* Written with Ann L. Miller (1954-). New York:
W. W. Norton, 1992. ISBN: 0393033465:0393033473.
218 pages; photographs; bibliography; documents.
Note: Also published New York: Vintage Books, 1993.
ISBN: 0679745815.

In this family history, Madden begins his story with
his great-great grandmother Sarah, born in Spotsyl-
vania County, Virginia, in 1758. She was the daughter
of a black man and a white woman. Because her
mother was a free woman, Sarah's own freedom was
insured. Sarah and her mother Mary, however, were
destitute and Sarah was taken from her when she was
2 to become an indentured servant, bound until she
was 31. When Madden wrote this book, he had at his
disposal a remarkable amount of information about
his ancestors which he found in a document-filled
trunk that had belonged to Sarah and been passed
down through the generations. Madden goes on to
trace other members of his family and their fortunes
and failures, up through his own siblings. In his final
chapter, he describes his own life, especially his encounters with racism and experiences with segregation.

270. Mam, Teeda Butt. *To Destroy You Is No Loss: The
Odyssey of a Cambodian Family.* Written with Joan D.

Criddle. New York: The Atlantic Monthly Press, 1987.
ISBN: 0871131161. 289 pages.
Note: Also published New York: Anchor Books, 1989.
ISBN: 0385266286.

This is a story of the Khmer Rouge takeover of Cambodia, and the executions, and forced labor (for those who were spared) which followed. It is the story of one family's own experiences, tragic struggles, and losses. Teeda Butt Mam tells of her three lives: first as the child of a well-to-do family, second as a forced laborer under the Khmer Rouge, and finally as an American citizen. This work describes the events leading up to her safe arrival in the United States with the remaining members of her family after two horrifying escapes from Cambodia.

271. Mankiller, Wilma Pearl (1945-). *Mankiller: A Chief and Her People*. Written with Michael Wallis. New York: St. Martin's Press, 1993. ISBN: 0312098685:0312113935. 292 pages; photographs; bibliography.

Mankiller spent her early childhood at Mankiller Flats on the Cherokee Reservation in Oklahoma. Her family decided to take part in the U.S. Government's removal program, which paid Native families to move off the reservation and into urban areas where there would be more employment opportunities. The transition was not easy for Mankiller or the rest of her family. Employment opportunities were not what they had expected, and they missed the closely knit community of the reservation. Mankiller found some comfort at the San Francisco Indian Center, and it was through the associations she made there that she became interested in civil rights activities and Vietnam War protests. She eventually became part of the movement that led to the nineteen-month occupation of Alcatraz in the name of Indians of All Tribes. Through her involvement with this movement, Mankiller became a skillful and dedicated community activist. She eventually returned to Oklahoma, where she became involved in tribal work which led to her election to Deputy Chief, and then Principal Chief of the Cherokee Nation of Oklahoma.

272. Marcere, Norma (1908-). *The Fences Between*. Canton, Ohio: Daring Publishing Group, 1989. ISBN: 0938936875. 455 pages; photographs.

Norma Marcere was determined to be independent and have a career despite her mother's strong desire to have her stay at home and help raise her younger brothers and sisters. She was abused physically and emotionally by both her mother and siblings, and she eventually left them. When she applied for a teaching position, however, the local superintendent told her quite bluntly that he would never hire a "colored teacher as long as I am superintendent of these schools!" (p. 66). Marcere documents her fight against daily encounters with racism to pursue a meaningful career. She also writes of the daunting task of trying to succeed at marriage, motherhood, and a demanding profession all at the same time.

273. Martin, Patricia Preciado. *Images and Conversations: Mexican Americans Recall a Southwestern Past*. Photographs by Louis Carlos Bernal. Tucson: University of Arizona Press, 1983. ISBN: 0816508011:0816508038. 110 pages; photographs; illustrations.

Martin describes her collection as "personal reminiscences, folktales, anecdotes, and traditions . . . an intimate narrative of Tucson's Mexican-American pioneers . . ." (p. 10). Thirteen oral histories depict changes that have taken place over the past century. Those individuals interviewed are Antonio Cordova, "The Tanque Verde & Sabino Canyon"; Herminia Cordova, "Sasabe & El Hoyo"; Leonardo Martinez, "The Rincons & Barrio Anita"; Maria Soto Audelo, "The Sierritas & Barrio Historico"; Alberto S. Urias, "Barrio Libre & Carrillo Gardens"; Elina Laos Sayre, "The Old Pueblo"; Jacinta Carranza, "Fort Lowell & Barrio Anita"; Henry Garcia, "El Hoyo & The Old Pueblo"; Felix Olivas, "Los Reales"; Frank Escalante, "The Far East Side & the Rincons"; Margarita Martinez, "Along the Rio Santa Cruz"; and Miguel Amado, "Amado, Arizona."

274. —. *Songs My Mother Sang To Me: An Oral History of Mexican American Women*. Tucson: University of Arizona Press, 1992. ISBN: 0816512795:0816513295. 224 pages; photographs.

Martin presents ten life histories of Mexican American women from the Tucson area. These women grew up in agricultural communities and have witnessed the transformation from a rural to an urban lifestyle. They describe their daily lives, the structure of their families and communities, and the role of the woman in both. Many include songs and poetry as part of their oral testimonies. The ten women are Livia León Montiel, Julia Yslas Vélez, Paulina Moreno Montoya, Socorro Félix Delgado, Carmen Celia Beltrán, Esperanza Montoya Padella, and Virginia Gastelum.

275. Martinez, Adrian (1932-). *Adrian: An Autobiography*. Written with Felix Garcia. Austin: Morgan Printing and Publishing, 1986. ISBN: none. 140 pages.

276. Maruoka, Emily Franklin. *Success, In Spite of Adversities: An Autobiography*. N.p.: n.p., 1989. ISBN: none. 61 pages.

277. Masaoka, Mike (1915-). *They Call Me Moses Masaoka: An American Saga*. Written with Bill Hosokawa. New York: W. Morrow, 1987. ISBN: 0688062369. 383 pages; photographs.

Japanese immigrants were not allowed to become citizens in the U.S. until 1952, and discriminatory immigration laws were not eliminated until 1965. At the time Masaoka's parents settled in the United States, Japanese Americans were not allowed to own land, so Masaoka's family moved to Utah, which is where Mike and his brothers grew up. Masaoka's political work began in college, where he became a member of the Japanese American Citizens League (JACL) and in following years one of their national leaders, working full time for the organization after graduating from the university. He played a central role in negotiating, though unsuccessfully, on behalf of the rights of Japanese Americans with the U.S. Government after the bombing of Pearl Harbor. Younger generations of Japanese Americans have accused Masaoka of complicity with the internment plans because of JACL's recommendation that all Japanese Americans should cooperate with the government as a symbol of their patriotism. He claims, however, that the organization leaders had no idea that mass relocation and internment was part of the United States' master plan. Although he was not interned because of his responsibilities with JACL, Masaoka volunteered for military service as soon as Japanese Americans were legally allowed to sign up for active duty. Masaoka worked full time on behalf of Japanese American rights, including naturalization for the Issei and restitution for internees, during and after World War II.

278. Mays, Willie (1931-). *Say Hey: The Autobiography of Willie Mays*. Written with Lou Sahadi. New York: Simon & Schuster, 1988. ISBN: 0671632922. 286 pages; photographs.

Family legend has it that Willie Mays began walking at six months, his father using an elusive baseball as incentive. Mays's father, a baseball player with the Birmingham Industrial League, was teaching his son to play baseball before he was a year old. The result was that Mays was playing professionally with the Black Barons of the Negro League by the time he was 16. In that same year, Jackie Robinson broke the color barrier in the major leagues. A few years later, Mays followed Robinson and joined the New York Giants. Mays gives a careful account of his life in baseball, describing the high quality of the players in the Negro League, his work with Leo Durocher, the Giants' move to San Francisco, and his transfer to the Mets in the final years of his career.

279. McCall, Nathan. *Makes Me Wanna Holler: A Young Black Man in America.* New York: Random House, 1994. ISBN: 0679412689. 404 pages.
Note: Also published New York: Vintage Books, 1995. ISBN: 0679740708.

In telling his story, McCall deals with the issue of black-on-black violence: male-to-male, male-to-female, and female-to-male. He sees the prevalence of this violence as a reaction to a lack of self-esteem and to self-hatred developed over three hundred years of white dominance and racism. McCall suggests that the black man may feel powerless to strike out at the real enemy, the white power structure. Consequently, in demanding the respect from his acquaintances denied him by the larger society, he develops a macho posture which manifests itself in violent actions. In undergoing his transformation from a life of violence on the street to a successful journalism career working for the mainstream press within the white power structure, McCall analyzes the influences that shaped his life. He describes the many social and psychological barriers which he had to overcome to leave the street permanently. He considers why he was able to do so and why others have not succeeded:

> But I'd come from a stronger, intact family and a neighborhood where there were lots of hardworking, right-doing black men and women whose lives demonstrated that there were many alternatives to life in the streets. There had always been some older person—a teacher, a neighbor, a relative—to encourage me when I'd faltered or fallen down. Even when I chose the gutter, I'd always had a frame of reference for a better life. That had made all the difference in the world. (p. 395)

280. McCarthy, James (1895-). *A Papago Traveler: The Memories of James McCarthy.* Ed. John Glendower Westover. Sun Tracks 13. Tucson: University of Arizona Press, 1985. ISBN: 0816509336:0816509425. 200 pages; photographs; map.

McCarthy, baptized Macario Antone, was born in Littlefield Village on the Big Papago Reservation of Arizona. His story describes Papago life in the early twentieth century, including details of family life and

Indian boarding schools. McCarthy describes his no-
madic life, telling how he attended several schools in
several states, traveled with the military during and
immediately following World War I, and then covered most of the Western half of the United States as
he sought out various employment opportunities.
The story ends as McCarthy completes his wanderings
in 1957, settling with his wife and children in the Tucson area.

281. McCarty, Billy (1904-). *Billy McCarty, Sr.: Ruby*. Interviews conducted and text prepared by Yvonne Yarber
and Curt Madison. Yukon-Koyukuk Biography Series.
Fairbanks: Spirit Mountain Press, 1983.   ISBN:
0910871035. 72 pages; photographs; maps.
Note: Produced by Yukon-Koyukuk School District of
Alaska.

McCarty was born to an Irish father and an Athapascan
mother. Besides the descriptions of his hunting, fishing, and trapping experiences, McCarty describes the
flu epidemic of 1918. He was herding reindeer during
that time, and when trying to deliver goods to the
town of Unalakleet, he was kept out. The town had
quarantined itself, letting nothing in and no one out
in an effort to keep the residents free of the disease.
Even the mail was fumigated. McCarty describes another town, Egarik, in which nearly everyone died.
Visiting there at the end of the epidemic, McCarty
writes of the complete horror and destruction which
he confronted. The town was later completely abandoned.
For a brief description and list of autobiographies in
this Yukon-Koyukuk School District series, see the entry for Moses Henzie.

282. McCauley, Anna Kim-Lan. *Miles From Home*. Wake-
field, Massachusetts: AKLM Publications, 1984. ISBN:
0961243007. 103 pages.

As a child, Anna Kim-Lan McCauley suffered from an
infection which left her completely blind. Living in
Vietnam at the time of the war, McCauley's parents at-

tempted unsuccessfully to abandon her once and, another time, left her in an orphanage. When the country was split into North and South, McCauley chose to move with the orphanage from Hanoi to Saigon rather than return to her parents. This sequence of events led to an opportunity to attend a high school for blind children in Boston. McCauley writes about her education and social life, her eventual marriage and motherhood, and how she learned to be self-sufficient, caring for herself and for her family.

283. McClane, Kenneth A. *Walls: Essays, 1985-1990*. African American Life Series. Detroit: Wayne State University Press, 1991. ISBN: 0814321348. 120 pages.

These essays describe a variety of different events which McClane, first and foremost a poet, was inspired to write because of his brother's death at the age of 29. In these short works, McClane explores his feelings at the time of his brother's death, gives an account of his visit to a maximum security prison, describes his first meeting with James Baldwin, portrays his first college writing teacher, and writes about his traumatic experiences at a predominately white, rigidly-operated private school in New York City, and about his involvement with students and fellow faculty members at Cornell University during a series of anti-apartheid protests.

284. McCoy, James (1912-). *Rooted in Slavery: Memoirs*. New York: Del Casa Educational Productions, 1981. ISBN: none. 226 pages.

James McCoy provides the reader with a portrait of three generations of his family beginning with his grandparents, all four of whom were born during slavery, and ending with himself. He describes life on his grandparents' farm in Fayetteville, North Carolina and then in Petersburg, Virginia, after the family moved north. McCoy places his own family history in the context of the history of African Americans in this country and the special problems that have arisen out of that history. McCoy ends the book with a series of chapters which provide moral and philosophical guidelines for leading a happy and productive life.

285. McPhatter, Thomas Hayswood. *Caught in the Middle: A Dichotomy of an African American Man: They Called Him Troublemaker: A Historical Autobiography of Leadership*. San Diego: Audacity Books, 1993. ISBN: 0963465805:0963465813. 452 pages; photographs.

McPhatter describes his origins, giving his family's history as it was passed on to him by his parents, aunts, and uncles. His own history includes schooling at Redstone Academy, a private Presbyterian school that provided African American children with an education far superior to the one they were able to receive in South Carolina's segregated school system; attendance at Johnson C. Smith University, where he helped lead a five-day student strike; dropping out of college to join the Marine Corps during the final years of World War II; and becoming a pastor and returning to service in the Marine Corps as a chaplain. This honest account of McPhatter's life includes both his successes and his mistakes and the lessons he learned thereby. McPhatter also documents his willingness to combat injustice as it confronts him and those close to him.

286. Mebane, Mary E. (1933-). *Mary*. New York: Viking Press, 1981. ISBN: 0670459380. 242 pages.
Note: Also published Chapel Hill: University of North Carolina Press, 1994. ISBN: 0807844489.

In this work, Mary Mebane explores the emotional hardships of her childhood in a rural town near Durham, North Carolina and examines the toll on her self-esteem caused by segregation and the accompanying status of second-class citizenship. One of the most debilitating elements of Mebane's childhood was her sense that her mother merely tolerated and made the best use of Mebane's existence, not caring for her or showing her any affection. After the death of Mebane's father, the family suffered, her brothers becoming remote and violent. Along with these personal revelations, Mebane describes in great detail the natural world as she experienced it as a child.

287. —. *Mary, Wayfarer*. New York: Viking Press, 1983. ISBN: 0670459607. 230 pages.
Note: Also published Chapel Hill: University of North Carolina Press, 1994. ISBN: 0807844497.

In this work, Mebane continues the story of her life, focusing on her teaching and writing career. The emotional damage caused by her relationship with her mother continues to haunt her, and that, combined with her sense of ostracism within the black community due to her dark skin color and social class, causes her severe depression, neurosis, and insomnia. Mebane explores the class and color distinctions within the Black community, her struggle with her family, and her own professional ambitions.

288. Meeks, Cathy. *I Want Somebody to Know My Name*. Rev. ed. Macon, Georgia: Smyth and Helwys, 1994. ISBN: 1880837781. 114 pages.
Originally published Nashville: T. Nelson, 1978. ISBN: 0840756429.

289. Meeks, Cordell D. *To Heaven Through Hell: An Autobiography of the First Black District Court Judge of Kansas*. Kansas City: Corcell Publishers, 1986. ISBN: none. 242 pages; photographs.

Meeks' childhood was fairly prosperous, but his father lost his job during the Great Depression. After leaving the family to find work, Meeks' father disappeared and the now-impoverished family never heard from him again. Meeks, nonetheless, followed his dream of pursuing a legal career. While in high school, he was involved in politics and public speaking, steadily preparing himself for his future. To attend the University of Kansas and, later, its law school, Meeks held down a number of jobs to finance his education. He writes about his legal and political career, his many clashes with a racist and still-segregated society, his eventual professional success, and the success of his children in the face of seemingly insurmountable odds.

290. Mendoza, Lydia. *Lydia Mendoza: A Family Autobiography*. Compiled by Chris Strachwitz with James Nicolopulos. Houston: Arte Publico Press, 1993. ISBN: 1558850651:155885066X. 409 pages; photographs; bibliography; discography.

Lydia Mendoza was a star of Mexican American music in the 30s and 40s. She performed with her family, singing the folk songs of Mexico. This book consists of narrative contributions from Lydia, her brothers and sisters. They relate their family history and the course of their musical careers.

291. Meng, Chih. *Chinese American Understanding: A Sixty-Year Search*. New York: China Institute in America, 1981. ISBN: none. 255 pages.

Chih Meng originally intended this work to be a history of the China Institute in America. When the project proved to be immense, he revised the work and turned it into his memoirs, thinking that a "wider audience would perhaps be interested to read how an antiforeign Chinese became an Americanophile and devoted his life to the search for Chinese-American understanding" (p. 13). Chih Meng's memoir accomplishes much more than this. It provides a history of significant events from his own and China's past. Chih Meng summarizes the contents and significance of the traditional Chinese education, and he promotes two-way cultural exchange. He describes the aspects of traditional Chinese values and teachings that he believes could benefit Americans, and the aspects of U.S. culture that might be useful for Chinese society. Chih Meng concludes his memoir with a plea for both China and the United States to learn and absorb what is best from each culture and to work toward world unity, the pursuit of peace, and the realization of Confucius' vision of the Great Commonweal.

292. Miles, Gregory (1953-). *C'mon You Mudhens! Reflection in [sic] the True Story of a Black Santa*. Southfield, Michigan: United Sticks, 1984. ISBN: none. 112 pages; photographs; bibliography.

Gregory Miles describes his youth and formative years during the late 50s and 60s. He relates the events of the Civil Rights Movement, the deaths of Martin Luther King, Jr., John F. Kennedy, and Robert Kennedy as they coincided with the events of his own childhood. Miles writes of his father's triumphs and tragedies, and establishes the many contributions that he made to the family's community. Miles also tells about his own educational difficulties stemming both from the racial tensions of the early years of integration and from his limited eyesight.

293. Minatoya, Lydia Yuriko (1950-). *Talking to High Monks in the Snow: An Asian American Odyssey*. New York: Harper Collins, 1992. ISBN: 0060168099. 269 pages.
Note: Also published New York: Harper Perennial, 1994.

Growing up in a predominantly-white neighborhood, Minatoya struggled with separation and assimilation. Her mother was a Kibei, born in America and educated in Japan, and her father immigrated to the United States as a boy five years after his parents had done so. Their marriage was arranged in a United States internment camp during World War II. Minatoya writes about her education and her brief tenure as a university professor—the termination of which led to her move to Okinawa to teach on the military base. During her stay in Japan, Minatoya made an extended visit to China to teach and took a trip to Nepal. Familiar enough with Japanese culture not to be overwhelmed by it, she was completely comfortable with her position as a Japanese American in Japan. As she prepared to return to the United States, however, she found herself questioning her identity:

> Was I now Asian? Was I still American? Would I have to choose between the two? . . . While I had been living in Asia, Asia had begun living in me. She pulsed through my heart. She traveled through my bloodstream. She changed

> my perceptions, my thoughts, and my dreams. . . . But, O
> America—my stern, beloved fatherland—would I be worthy
> in your eyes? (p. 264)

294. Modesto, Ruby. *Not for Innocent Ears: Spiritual Traditions of a Desert Cahuilla Medicine Woman.* Written with Guy Mount. Arcata, California: Sweetlight Books, 1980. ISBN: 0960446214. 120 pages; photographs; bibliography.
Note: Reissued by Sweetlight Books, 1989. ISBN: 0960446206.

Ruby Modesto was destined to be a *pul*, or shaman, after spontaneously dreaming to the 13th level at the age of 10. She explains that most dreamers seeking to dream beyond the first level take a certain herb, but that she accomplished the feat without this aid. Modesto also explains the different dream levels, the first being ordinary sleep, the second and higher beginning with the dream self lying down and beginning to dream. It is in the second and higher levels that one finds a helper, and it is the helper that gives the *puls* their special healing and spiritual powers. Modesto describes creation as she and other Desert Cahuilla people see it, relates some of her experiences with healing, and narrates several traditional stories.

295. Mohr, Nicholasa (1938-). *Growing Up Inside the Sanctuary of My Imagination.* In My Own Words. New York: J. Messner, 1994. ISBN: 0671741713. 118 pages; photographs.

Mohr is a writer of fiction for children, young adults, and adults. This book is part of a series intended for young readers. She writes in her introduction that this work is a "real story about my emotions, my beliefs, and my search for self-esteem while growing up Puerto Rican and poor in these United States" (p. viii). Mohr was the seventh child born to her parents, and the first girl. Her early years were colored by her father's suspicion that she was not his daughter. The problem seemed to resolve itself enough to enable her to have a normal childhood, if a childhood beset with poverty and discrimination can be considered normal.

Mohr did not begin to write until she was an adult. She describes how her mother encouraged her to draw, having failed to convince her to sew, embroider, or crochet. When Mohr received the praise and encouragement from her mother that she had always craved, she threw herself into her drawings, and her skills developed accordingly. Mohr began writing somewhat by chance. After her initial publishing successes, she exchanged her career as a visual artist for that of a writer.

296. Momaday, N. Scott (1934-). *The Names: A Memoir*. Sun Tracks 16. Tucson: University of Arizona Press, 1987. ISBN: 0816510466. 170 pages.
Originally published New York: Harper & Row, 1976. ISBN: 0060129816.

297. Monroe, Mark (1930-). *An Indian in White America*. Ed. Carolyn Reyer. Philadelphia: Temple University Press, 1994. ISBN: 1566392349:1566392357. 236 pages; photographs.

Mark Monroe was suddenly confronted with violent racism, segregation, and harsh living conditions when his family moved from Wood, South Dakota, to Alliance, Nebraska. Monroe writes of daily fights at school, of Native American children placed in an "Opportunity Room," where they were taught nothing, for their entire elementary-school career, and of local businesses with signs forbidding the entrance of "Indians or dogs." The army afforded Monroe his first opportunity to feel accepted and liked. His time in Korea, however, left him full of regret and self contempt. He writes that he went to Korea, killed men, and destroyed villages as he was trained to do, without knowing where Korea was or why he was there. This regret, together with his childhood years of hardship and humiliation, left Monroe unable to cope with life. He describes years of uncontrolled alcoholism, during which he drank himself to the verge of death. After a year spent in a poorly run, impersonal treatment program where he made no progress, a concerned social worker helped Monroe enter another program where he received round-the-clock care which included the doctor personally helping Monroe to chew and swallow his food. Monroe was able to leave this program several months later, completely sober. His story continues with a description of his work in politics, as a mental health worker, and a community activist.

298. Monroe, Sylvester. *Brothers: Black and Poor — A True Story of Courage and Survival.* Written with Peter Goldman and Vern E. Smith. New York: W. Morrow, 1988. ISBN: 068807622X. 284 pages; photographs.
Note: Also published New York: Ballantine, 1989. ISBN: 0345361563.

This work presents the stories of eleven men, including Sylvester Monroe, who grew up in the Robert Taylor Homes of Chicago. Monroe began the project as a series of interviews with the men, all of whom were his childhood friends. The interviews were published in *Newsweek* in 1986, and then expanded and revised into narrative form for this book.

299. Montero, Juan M. (1942-). *Halfway Through: An Autobiography.* Filipinos in the United States 1. Indianapolis: Philippine Heritage Endowment Publications, 1982. 200 pages; photographs.
Note: "A Historical Preservation Project of the Philippine Heritage Endowment Fund, Indiana University Foundation, Bloomington, Indiana."

Montero, a native of the Philippines, intended from childhood to become a doctor. This book is the story of his education and career. His training and professional career took place in the United States, and Montero describes the rigors of becoming an established surgeon in the U.S. medical system. He relates some of his notable cases in great detail, and concludes with an account of a mission trip by a group of 20 Ohio surgeons, including himself, to the Philippines.

300. Moore, Sadie. *Fred Moore: Narration in the First Person.* Denton, Texas: Terrill Wheeler Printing, 1984. ISBN: none. 69 pages.

301. Mora, Pat. *Nepantla: Essays From the Land in the Middle.* Albuquerque: University of New Mexico Press, 1993. ISBN: 0826314546. 181 pages.

With these essays, Mora covers a wide range of issues which are connected to her interest in what she calls the "culturally endangered." Mora writes about being a writer, being a Chicana writer, being a Latina writer, and being a writer from the United States. She has an immense sense of humility concerning her craft, and a drive to continue because of her responsibility to her "ethnic community" and to the community of all "like-minded souls seeking a more equitable world." Mora writes about her visits to other countries, and what she learned from these visits about herself and about society in the United States. Although she writes as a member of a marginalized group, she also acknowledges her position of social and economic privilege. Two essays discuss the importance of multi-cultural education for all students in the primary and secondary grades and in higher education. In her final essay, Mora discusses the need for the arts to be an accepted part of mainstream culture in the United States.

302. Morgan, Kathryn L. *Children of Strangers: The Stories of a Black Family.* Philadelphia: Temple University Press, 1980. ISBN: 0877222037:0877222401. 122 pages; photographs; bibliography.

Morgan recounts the stories told to her by her mother that have become part of the family's traditional lore. The stories are those of her great grandmother who was born into slavery, her grandmother, and mother. Morgan gives brief accounts of her memories of listening to these stories, and records them as her mother told them to her. The stories served as lessons for moral and spiritual development for Morgan and her siblings and provided a strong sense of family history and self-worth.

303. Morris, Dorothy. *None of Your Black Business.* N.p.: D. Morris, 1989. ISBN: none. 89 pages.

304. Morrow, Curtis. *The Return of the African American.*
Chicago: C. Morrow, 1983. ISBN: none. 177 pages.

Morrow left the United States for Ghana in 1965. He
was not sympathetic with certain aspects of the Civil
Rights Movement, namely the commitment to nonviolence and integration, and decided to forge new ter-
ritory for himself on the African continent. Morrow
describes settling in with both American expatriates
and native Ghanaians. An artist, he incorporated
many Ghanaian elements into his work. He returned
to New York after eleven years of living in Ghana and
Togo. Morrow found it difficult to admit that he
missed anything about the United States: "I would
think about ghettos, the jails, the prisons and the white
man's justice—but in the end, my mind would always
return to my mother and my family . . . and I knew I
would have to return someday—and soon" (p. 154).

305. Morrow, E. Frederic (1909-). *Forty Years a Guinea Pig.*
New York: Pilgrim Press, 1980. ISBN: 0829803998. 235
pages.
Note: Morrow's previous autobiographical works in-
clude: *Black Man in the White House: A Diary of the
Eisenhower Years by the Administrative Officer for
Special Projects, The White House, 1955-1961.* New
York: McFadden-Bartell, 1963. And *Way Down South
Up North.* Philadelphia: United Church Press, 1973.
ISBN: 0829802460.

Morrow graduated from college in 1930 and went on to
be the first African American in almost every position
he held. He describes with painful detail the conditions for African Americans in the segregated army of
World War II: the poor conditions, lack of services, of-
ficers who had failed in their positions with white
troops and so were miserably unqualified to work with
often demoralized black troops, inadequate diet, and
finally, boot camps located in the Jim Crow South,
which meant no services in or out of the camp. Morrow gives an account of his fight to get into Officer
Training School (OTS) after being told that he, the only
college graduate in his group of test takers, had failed

the IQ test. Morrow finally gained admittance to OTS and finished his four years in the army as a major, but faced constant harassment, sabotage, and both direct and subtle racism throughout his tour of duty. The major part of this work is devoted to Morrow's work in two Eisenhower administrations. Here, too, he was the first African American to fill a position—this time in an executive post on a presidential staff—and he was again forced to assert his authority, demanding the same respect and treatment afforded others in similar positions. Because he was an advisor to the president, Morrow was called upon by leaders within the black community to convince Eisenhower to intercede in the growing violence directed at African Americans in the South related to the desegregation of schools, public transportation, and public accommodations. Morrow made repeated efforts in this direction, but the blame for Eisenhower's reluctance to get involved in this issue fell upon Morrow. Morrow spent his final years as a vice president with Bank of America, again the first African American to hold such a position, and had, once more, to fight prejudice, stereotypes, harassment, jealousy, and ignorance to succeed. He writes that he began to tire of the daily battle and found that, for the first time, he did not have the energy to fight back:

> Why have I stayed? Where could one go that would be better at this late day [referring to his age]? Frankly, I remained hopeful that there would be a change. And remaining had a certain nuisance value. Besides, as a pioneer in a field that had just opened to Blacks, I had to remember that pioneers seldom achieve the ultimate, but they do carve a path that marks the way for those who follow. (p. 6-7)

306. Moseley, Margaret (1901-). *Moving Mountains One Stone at a Time: Memoirs of Margaret Moseley*. Written with Berry Shea and Judith Barnet. Massachusetts: M. Moseley, 1993. ISBN: none. 45 pages; photographs.

Margaret Moseley, born in 1901, grew up in Massachusetts. She describes how she learned to cope with the racial discrimination which seemed to intensify as she grew older. Upon finishing high school, she attempted to enter a nurses training program. Despite her good academic record, Moseley was not admitted to any of the programs located in the Boston area, all of which were run by hospitals. She received a similar response from prospective employers in other fields as well, and ran into more discrimination when looking for housing. Shortly after finding a decent house for her family to live in, a new landlord evicted her, and it was weeks before she was able to find alternative accommodations. These years of receiving such treatment based solely on skin color motivated Moseley to dedicate her time to improved housing conditions and equal job opportunities, both locally in Massachusetts and internationally. In this memoir, she describes her work with The Women's International League for Peace and Freedom (WILPF), the NAACP, and the Fair Housing Committee—a group Moseley was partially responsible for forming. Through the WILPF, Moseley worked for the promotion of the UN's Universal Declaration of Human Rights, and went to Selma in 1965 to assist with the voter registration effort.

307. Moses, Mary (1827-1939). *Mary Moses's Statement*. Fairfield, Washington: Ye Galleon Press, 1988. ISBN: none. 70 pages; maps; photographs.

This brief statement was recorded by historian William Compton Brown. It first appeared in the Spokane *Spokesman-Review* in 1939. In this statement, Moses gives an account of her family including brief details of who they were and how they died. She also describes the injustices of a treaty instigated by Governor Stevens in 1855. The treaty affected the lives of thousands of Native Americans and many tribes which acknowledged many different chiefs, yet it contained only 14 signatures, and they were, according to Moses, the signatures of tribal members of "no apparent standing" (p. 11). Mary Moses provides a glimpse into the hostilities that existed among tribes and between tribes and the U.S. Government.

308. Mountain, Simeon (1932-). *Simeon Mountain, Nulato*. Interviews conducted and text prepared by Yvonne Yarber and Curt Madison. Yukon-Koyukuk School

District Biography Series. Fairbanks: Spirit Mountain Press, 1983. ISBN: 0910871051. 80 pages; photographs; maps.
Note: Produced by Yukon-Koyukuk School District of Alaska.

Simeon Mountain writes about his family, hunting and fishing, and the reinstitution of the ceremonial Stickdance. He tells stories of the hostilities that often erupted in war between neighboring villages, as told to him by his grandfather. Mountain describes some of the changes that have taken place which have improved daily life in his small town of Nulato, his struggle with alcoholism which he finally overcame after a serious accident, his work as a Postmaster, his travels to Rome and Japan, and his desire for his children to attend college.
For a brief description and list of autobiographies in this Yukon-Koyukuk School District series, see the entry for Moses Henzie.

309. Mourning Dove.
     See *Hum-ishu-Ma*.

310. Mura, David. *Turning Japanese: Memoirs of a Sansei.* New York: Atlantic Monthly Press, 1991. ISBN: 0871134314. 376 pages.
     Note: Also published New York: Anchor Books, 1992. ISBN: 0385423446.

     Although these memoirs are about his experiences in Japan, Mura devotes significant space to reviewing his childhood and college years, especially with regard to his relationships with his parents, and his wife Susie, who is white. While in Japan, Mura studied traditional and avant-garde Japanese art forms, wrote, took part in political activities, and became a part of a close circle of friends who were artistically and politically active. Mura discovered that, despite the many aspects of life in the United States which disturb him or cause him to feel out of place, and the ethnocentric attitudes of many white Americans, he was American and not Japanese:

Japan helped me balance a conversation which had been taking place before I was born, a conversation in my grandparents' heads, in my parents' heads, which, by my generation, had become very one-sided, so that the Japanese was virtually silenced. My stay helped me realize that a balance, which probably never existed in the first place, could no longer be maintained. . . . I could have lived there a few more years if I had had the money and time, but eventually I would have left. (p. 370)

311. Murray, Pauli (1910-1985). *Proud Shoes: The Story of an American Family*. New York: Harper & Row, 1987. ISBN: 0060131098:0060906170. 280 pages; photographs. Note: Originally published New York: Harper, 1956.

See annotation for *Song in a Weary Throat* below.

312. —. *Song in a Weary Throat: An American Pilgrimage*. New York: Harper & Row, 1987. ISBN: 0060157046. 451 pages; photographs.
Note: Also published as *Pauli Murray: The Autobiography of a Black Activist, Feminist, Lawyer, Priest, and Poet*. Knoxville: University of Tennessee Press, 1987, 1989. ISBN: 0870495968.

Murray's first memoir, *Proud Shoes: The Story of an American Family* (1956, reissued 1978 with a new introduction by the author), was also a family history which she wrote specifically for her nieces and nephews. Her accounts of her predecessors are based on the stories told to her as a child. Her portraits of her immediate family are based on her own childhood memories. *Song in a Weary Throat* was published posthumously. In this work, Murray describes the premature deaths of both her mother and father, and her life from that point on living with her Aunt Pauline. She recounts many painful racial incidents and her personal efforts to confront discrimination, including her unsuccessful attempt to enroll in the graduate school at the University of North Carolina. Murray came of age during the depression, and struggled financially through college and was faced with a bleak employment prospect, along with everyone else, at the time of her graduation. Despite her many emotional and economic hardships, Murray pursued several successful careers: as a lawyer, as a college professor in Ghana and in the United States, as a politician, and as one of the first ordained female Episcopal Priests. Murray was also one of the creative forces behind the founding of NOW (National Organization for Women).

313. Nash, Armelia. *Armelia: How I Crossed the Tracks*. N.p.: n.p., 1989. ISBN: none. 52 pages; photographs.

Armelia Nash credits her father and grandfather for her strong self-esteem and her determination. Confronted with many obstacles throughout her adult life, she describes how she was able to raise her children alone without losing faith or hope, and without relying on public assistance. Nash provides an account of some of the misfortunes she has encountered through her unique life, and how she survived and surmounted them.

314. Neakok, Sadie Brower (1916-). *Sadie Brower Neakok, an Iñupiaq Woman*. Recorded and edited by Margaret Blackman. Seattle: University of Washington Press, 1989. ISBN: 0295971800. 274 pages; photographs.

Sadie Neakok was born to a white father and an Iñupiaq, or Eskimo, mother in Barrow, Alaska. She had some idea of western culture, although raised by her native mother, because of her father's influence and a western-style education. When her father took her to San Francisco to attend high school, however, Neakok was completely overwhelmed. While she quickly developed a taste for candy and other sweets, Neakok found the concept of fashion perplexing. A snowless winter and continual alternation between night and day caused Neakok some disorientation as well. She was homesick her entire four years in San Francisco. Neakok returned to Barrow, where she eventually married an Eskimo who had been raised in the traditional manner and was a subsistence hunter and fisherman. Neakok began to relearn some of what she had forgotten, and much that she had never known. She describes her sense of exhilaration in returning to this more traditional life style. Neakok also had a brief teaching career and was the federal magistrate for her area for many years. She gives an account of her work as magistrate, describes many cases, and demonstrates the unique qualities she brought to this position. Blackman, the editor, intersperses her own commentary with excerpts from previously published ethnographies and from the autobiography of Neakok's father, Charles Brower, throughout this text.

315. Nelson, Jill. *Volunteer Slavery: My Authentic Negro Experience*. Chicago: The Noble Press, Inc., 1993. ISBN: 1879360241. 243 pages.

Nelson, a freelance magazine writer, decides to take a stab at high pay and prestige at the *Washington Post*. Her book chronicles her experiences with the *Post* from her interview with management, through her brush with alcoholism, to her final departure, completely sober, four and one-half years later. Nelson writes about many of her experiences with humorous hindsight, but there are some tragic episodes from her professional and personal life that hindsight cannot soften.

316. Nelson, Rachel West.
See *Webb, Sheyann*.

317. Newby, Elizabeth Loza. *A Migrant With Hope*. Richmond, Indiana: Friends United Press, 1992. ISBN: 0805472185. 140 pages.
Note: Also published Kansas City: Beacon Hill, 1981; Nashville: Broadman Press, 1977.

Newby writes about her life as the daughter of migrant farm workers. The family's home was in the back of a truck until she was 13. Central to her story is her struggle to complete her education against the wishes of her father.

318. Newkirk, Gregory. *Frog Town*. New York: Vantage Press, 1981. ISBN: 0533039444. 30 pages.

Newkirk moved from Newark, New Jersey, to Savannah, Georgia, with his sister after their mother's death. Their stay in Savannah was a time of increased white violence against the African American community, but also a time of change brought about by the Civil Rights Movement. Newkirk describes some of these events in the African American community during these Savannah years, as well as some of the emotional upheavals of his childhood.

319. Niatum, Duane (1938-). "Autobiographical Sketch." *I Tell You Now: Autobiographical Essays by Native American Writers.* Ed. Brian Swann and Arnold Krupat. Lincoln: University of Nebraska Press, 1987. ISBN: 0803227140.

See entry under *Swann, Brian* for a complete list of authors included in this anthology.

320. Nictune, Oscar (1901-). *Oscar Nictune, Sr., Alatna.* Interviews conducted and text prepared by Curt Madison and Yvonne Yarber. Alaska Series. Surrey, British Columbia: Hancock House, 1980. ISBN: 0888390629. 80 pages; photographs; maps.
Note: Produced by Yukon-Koyukuk School District of Alaska.

A storyteller, Nictune tells about his parents, and about hunting, fishing, and trapping in and around the Eskimo village of Alatna on the Arctic Circle. His wife died giving birth to their ninth child, so Nictune raised his family alone, never taking any public relief. He had a bout with tuberculosis, but was lucky enough to recover completely.
For a brief description and list of autobiographies in this Yukon-Koyukuk School District series, see the entry for Moses Henzie.

321. Njeri, Itabari. *Every Good-bye Ain't Gone: Family Portraits and Personal Escapades.* New York: Times Books, 1990. ISBN: 0812918053. 246 pages.
Note: Also published New York: Vintage Books, 1991. ISBN: 067973242X.

Njeri, a journalist, singer, and actress, began writing

this work intending it to be a novel, but instead ended up writing "the literal truth; many might not have believed the portrayals otherwise" (p. 6). She writes about members of her family, her grandparents, mother, father, aunts, and cousins, and of her own life with them and on her own. Njeri writes of their achievements and of their despair and tragedies; she includes the effects of years of both overt and subtle racism. Njeri also describes her coming of age, her work with Amiri Baraka and the Congress of Afrikan Peoples (CAP) and her work as a journalist.

322. Noble, Gil. *Black is the Color of My TV Tube*. Secaucus, New Jersey: Lyle Stuart, Inc., 1981. ISBN: 0818402970. 190 pages; photographs.
Note: Also published New York: Carol Publishing Group, 1990. ISBN: 0818405384.

In this autobiography, Noble relates the story of his entrance into television journalism at WABC in New York via a small radio station which served a predominantly black audience. He provides a summation of the history of African Americans in broadcast journalism, the current state of broadcasting (as of 1980), and a description of his own experiences with radio and television. Beginning as a street reporter, Noble eventually began to host and then produce his own weekly program entitled "Like It Is." This program was dedicated to presenting programs about African Americans and African American culture and issues. Noble developed a number of important documentaries for this program, including the Emmy award-winning documentary on Harry Belafonte. Noble discusses the dangers and virtues of television, and specifically the importance of documentaries to represent under- or misreported issues, events, and people:

> [T]he documentary is a critically important device for informing and shaping minds that have grown flabby through watching entertainment-only television programming. . . . It remains a powerful weapon to change false values, correct historical error, and cure the poison prejudice in the minds of black and white Americans. (p. 107-108)

Noble gives numerous examples of misrepresented, biased, under-reported, or otherwise inaccurate accounts of African American individuals, events in the African American community, or of cultural importance to African Americans (and thus all Americans). He argues for more black journalists and film makers and more air time devoted to documentaries.

323. *Haa Kusteeyi, Our Culture: Tlingit Life Stories.* Ed. Nora and Richard Dauenhauer. Classics of Tlingit Oral Literature 3. Seattle: University of Washington Press, Sealaska Heritage Foundation, 1994. ISBN: 0295974001: 029597401X. 888 pages; English and Tlingit; bibliography; map.

The editors write that they wish to introduce these Tlingit elders to readers outside of their community and to the younger generations within the community, "reminding all audiences, the whole world, how wonderful these subjects were and are, and why they should be remembered" (p. ix). They add, however, that this genre of Tlingit biography or autobiography is "un-Tlingit," and that the elders complied "only with much cajoling on the part of well-meaning folklorists, anthropologists, and oral historians" (p. ix). These life histories discuss personal and group identity, political fights related to land use, hunting and fishing rights, citizenship, the condition of the Tlingit language, the role of western religions and schooling, and other cultural and family issues. An extensive preface and introduction discuss the contents of this work and explain Tlingit social structure and history. The collection is a combination of autobiography and biography.

324. Northway, Walter. *Walter Northway.* Interviewing and editing done by Yvonne Yarber and Curt Madison. Fairbanks: Alaska Native Language Center, College of Liberal Arts, University of Alaska, 1987. ISBN: 1555000304. 53 pages; photographs; maps.

This book presents Northway's own account of some significant events in his life and also recollections about him by his granddaughter and daughter. Aged 111 in 1987 as this book was being completed, Northway talks about his parents, his first encounter with white people, his rite of passage into adulthood, and his marriage and children. He also presents stories of a variety of hunting, fishing, and trapping experiences.

325. Nuñez, Bonita Wa Wa Calachaw (1888-1972). *Spirit Woman: The Diaries and Paintings of Bonita Wa Wa Calachaw Nuñez.* Ed. Stan Steiner. San Francisco: Harper & Row, 1980. ISBN: 0064519759. 243 pages; illustrations; photographs.

This book contains excerpts from Nuñez's diaries and reproductions of her paintings. From early childhood, Nuñez showed signs of remarkable talents, which, together with her upbringing, allowed her to lead an unusual life. Taken from her mother at birth, Nuñez was raised by a white woman, Mary Duggan, and her brother, Dr. Cornelius Duggan. According to her diaries, Nuñez grew up in an extremely loving and socially-enlightened atmosphere, and she, in turn, respected and loved her adoptive parents. However, despite the closeness of her adoptive family, she did feel the great loss of her birth mother and was saddened by the knowledge of the poverty which caused her birth mother to give her away. Nuñez, from an early age, was aware of the plight of Native Americans in the white world and dedicated her life to working for Native rights. She writes, "We no longer will accept laws that say: You are not Human! We know understanding is one of the most powerful Natural laws. The agony of the color of a Man will pass. . . . Our textbooks will no longer ridicule skin color" (p. 229).

326. Oda, Patsy. *Heart's Desire.* Wheaton, Illinois: Living Books, 1987. ISBN: 0842313133. 136 pages.

Patsy Oda was converted from Buddhism to Christianity at the age of 8. Despite her families strong connection to Buddhism, Oda remained a devout Christian. In this book she tells the story of her desire for a Christian Japanese American husband who would come to her through God's power, and how this actually came to pass.

327. Oishi, Gene (1933-). *In Search of Hiroshi.* Rutland, Vermont: E. Tuttle Co., 1988. ISBN: 080481533X. 190 pages.

Gene Oishi writes of the psychological trauma which he and other Nisei suffered because of their experiences of evacuation and internment during World War II. This book is part of an ongoing attempt by Oishi to rediscover the person he was before running up against the virulent anti-Japanese sentiments of the time leading up to and following the bombing of Pearl Harbor.

328. *Oral Histories of African Americans.* Interviews conducted by Kathryn Waddell Takara. Honolulu: The Center, 1990. ISBN: none. 406 pages; photographs.
Note: University of Hawaii at Manoa. Social Science Research Institute. Oral History Program.

Takara, a native of Tuskegee, Alabama, and a resident of Hawaii since 1968, has focused her academic work on African Americans in Hawaii. For this publication, Takara interviewed ten individuals, nine of whom gave their permission for the interviews to be published. Interviewees each edited their own transcripts, making corrections, additions, and deletions. The interviews cover the topics of childhood, family life and parental influences, education and employment, discrimination, segregation, social and cultural life in African American communities, politics, World War II, and life in Hawaii. The ages of the interviewees range from fifty-seven to eighty. All of the subjects were born on the mainland, and most in the South. Several of them have led particularly notable lives: Gladys Crampton was among the first Black models in the United States, William Henry Waddell formed the School of Veterinary Medicine at the Tuskegee Institute, and Howard Eugene Johnson was a dancer at the Cotton Club and an organizer for the Communist Party in its early years. Other individuals interviewed are Walter J. Alexander, Alexander Lewis, Lucille Maloney, Ulysses C. "Mushy" Robinson, Bertha Elliott Dunson, and Ernest LeFaris Golden.

329. Ortiz, Simon J. (1941-). "The Language We Know." *I Tell You Now: Autobiographical Essays by Native American Writers*. Ed. Brian Swann and Arnold Krupat. Lincoln: University of Nebraska Press, 1987. ISBN: 0803227140.

> See entry under *Swann, Brian* for a complete list of authors included in this anthology.

330. Ortiz Cofer, Judith. *Silent Dancing: A Partial Remembrance of a Puerto Rican Childhood*. Houston: Arte Publico Press, 1990. ISBN: 1558850155. 158 pages.
Note: 2nd edition published 1991.

> Ortiz Cofer looks to Virginia Woolf's work *Moments of Being* (New York: Harcourt Brace Jovanovich, c1976) as a model and inspiration for her own autobiographical work. She writes that she "wanted the essays to be, not just family history, but also creative explorations of known territory . . . a meditation on past events" (p. 12). However, in these essays, Ortiz Cofer does describe her family—her grandparents, parents, aunts, and uncles—and compares and contrasts life for a young girl in New York and in Puerto Rico. She has an unusual perspective on life as an immigrant because of her frequent travels, back and forth, between her native land and her adopted country. Her mother never adjusted to life in New York and was always longing to return to her home and family in Puerto Rico. About her father, Ortiz Cofer writes: "He was a sensitive, intellectual man whose energies had to be entirely devoted to survival. And that is how many minds are wasted in the travails of immigrant life" (p. 123).

331. *Our Stories, Our Lives: A Collection of Twenty-three Transcribed Interviews With Elders of the Cook Inlet Region*. Transcribed and edited by A. J. McClanahan. Anchorage: CIRI Foundation, 1986. ISBN: 0938227017. 245 pages; maps.

> Interviews for this collection were taped in sessions ranging from three to five hours in length. The histories were guided by questions asked by the editor, who made the final decisions on what was included in the

book and how each narrative was arranged. The shareholders of the Cook Inlet Region, Inc., have migrated from areas all over Alaska, and the interviewees were selected so that all the major Native groups of Alaska would be represented. Participants had to be at least 55 years old. McClanahan writes that though many of the shareholders were reticent about discussing their private lives, they "agreed to participate because of their desire to communicate a bit of their view of the world to young people" (Preface, p. 7).

332. Padilla, Felix M.
See *Santiago, Lourdes.*

333. Pai, Margaret K. (1914-). *The Dreams of Two Yi-Min.* Honolulu: University of Hawaii Press, 1989. ISBN: 0824811798. 200 pages; photographs.

Pai writes that her book is about the "day-to-day activities of our family and the families we knew—from 1914, when I was born, through the great depression, World War II, and the postwar years, to the middle of this century" (p. x). Pai was born in Hawaii to parents who were recent immigrants, or Yi-Min, from Korea. Pai's father was an inventor/designer. He started up an upholstery and bamboo drapery factory with which the entire family of six was involved. Pai includes generous detail about the food, clothing, and customs of both Koreans and Korean Americans in Hawaii. She portrays the difficulty first generation children had trying to honor and please their parents, while at the same time attempting to realize their own dreams and hopes. The book also includes a depiction of three years Pai and her mother spent in Korea when her mother returned with her to participate in the March 1st, 1919, demonstration staged to protest Japanese Imperialism in Korea (see also *Man Sei!* by Peter Hyun).

334. Pale Moon, Princess. *Pale Moon: The Story of an Indian Princess.* Falls Church, Virginia: American Indian Heritage Foundation, 1982. ISBN: none. 106 pages.

Originally published Wheaton, Illinois: Tyndale House Publishers, 1975. ISBN: 0842348786.

335. Paquin, Ron. *Not First in Nobody's Heart: The Life Story of a Contemporary Chippewa*. Written with Robert Doherty. Ames: Iowa State University Press, 1992. ISBN: 0813818370:0813838362. 259 pages; photographs.

A victim of emotional and physical neglect, and sexual and physical abuse at home and at school, Paquin's life has been a long struggle. Responding to a childhood of abuse, Paquin, who was homeless for most of his teen years, resorted to alcoholism and violence as a means of survival. After spending time in reform school, prison, and a mental institution, he was fortunate in meeting a woman who cared about him and was able to motivate him to give up drinking and renounce his violent tendencies. Although he and this woman, who became his wife, struggled financially, they were supportive of each other and good parents to their son, an only child. As a commercial fisherman in Michigan, Paquin was involved in the fight for Native treaty rights with regard to fishing. This book documents some of the legal battles waged by Native groups in Michigan against the state and sport fishermen, and the suffering caused by the state's gradual closing of lakes to commercial gill net fishing.

336. Park, Lanhei Kim (Mrs. No-Young Park). *Facing Four Ways*. Ed. Chinn Callan. Oceanside, California: Orchid Park Press (Xerox Reproduction Center), 1984. ISBN: none. 358 pages; photographs; maps.

Lanhei Kim Park presents a detailed account of her life from her earliest years in Korea as a member of a politically influential and intellectually accomplished family, to her adult life in the United States married to Korean author and lecturer No-Young Park. She writes of her youth spent in exile in Manchuria because of her parents' involvement in the Korean Independence Movement, her return to Korea and subsequent imprisonment and torture at the hands of the Japanese police, and then, incredibly, two fruitful years of study in Japan. Upon her return to Korea and graduation from Ewha College, Park set sail for the United States to continue her education, becoming a citizen in 1953 after the U.S. immigration laws changed to allow Asians to become naturalized citizens. She writes in her preface,

> I have lived in Korea, China, and Japan, always intimately with the native people, as a student and as a happy youth learning their culture and forming close friendships among them. Now I live with Americans as an American citizen myself. I have written this memoir to remember all the experiences I had with my dear friends of four nations. It is my wish that this book will help young readers find successful lives in their futures.

Park is an accomplished artist and the author of *The Heavenly Pomegranate* (1973), the retelling of a Korean folk tale.

337. Parks, Gordon (1912-). *A Choice of Weapons*. St. Paul: Minnesota Historical Society Press, 1986. ISBN: 0873512022. 274 pages.
New preface by the author.
Originally published New York: Harper & Row, 1966.

338. —. *Voices in the Mirror: An Autobiography*. New York: Doubleday, 1990. ISBN: 0385266987. 351 pages; photographs.
Note: Also published New York: Anchor Books, 1992. ISBN: 0385266995.

A photographer, writer, composer, and film director, Parks writes that the energy he might have channeled into anger he instead put into proving that the racists who viewed him as inferior were wrong. Parks spent his childhood in Fort Scott, Kansas, a strictly segregated community, where he faced "the daily anguish of racism" (p. 5). He describes his struggles to support himself from the time he was in his early teens—trying to work and attend high school simultaneously. After a number of different work experiences, Parks became a successful photographer and was the first black photographer to work for *Vogue, Glamour,* and *Life.* Parks also writes about his marriages, his children, and his grandchildren.

339. Parks, Rosa. *Quiet Strength: The Faith, the Hope, and the Heart of a Woman Who Changed a Nation.* Written with Gregory J. Reed. Grand Rapids, Michigan: Zondervan Publishing House, 1994. ISBN: 0310501504. 93 pages; photographs.

In this short book, Parks presents brief inspirational vignettes using her civil rights work, work with young African Americans, and her Christian faith as a context. Her vignettes address the following themes: fear, defiance, injustice, pain, character, role models, faith, values, quiet strength, determination, youth, and the future.

340. Parks, Rosa (1913-). *Rosa Parks: My Story.* Written with Jim Haskins. New York: Dial Books, 1992. ISBN: 0803706731:0803706758. 192 pages; photographs.
Note: Also published by New York: Scholastic Books, 1994. ISBN: 0590465384.

The popular legend concerning Rosa Parks is that she inadvertently provided the fuel that began the Civil Rights Movement simply because she had had a long day, and thus refused to stand when the Montgomery bus driver ordered her to do so. Although Parks' decision to refuse to relinquish her seat may have been spontaneous and without motive, she knew exactly what the consequences of her action would be:

> People always say that I didn't give up my seat because I was tired, but that isn't true. I was not tired physically, or no more tired than I usually was at the end of a working day. I was not old, although some people have an image of me as being old then. I was forty-two. No, the only tired I was, was tired of giving in. (p. 106)

Parks was brought up in a politically aware family, and married a politically active man, Raymond Parks. Even before her controversial action, she was deeply committed to change and had been working with the NAACP, which had been looking for a test case on bus segregation. She documents the work that had been done by the NAACP and other groups specifically on the issue of busing, and she points out that she was one in a long line of those arrested for refusing to cooperate with the daily humiliation of bus segregation.

Parks provides a summation of the work for civil rights that had begun long before the bus boycott began, including the work of her husband and others around the nation to defend the Scottsboro Boys (nine black men arbitrarily arrested and charged with rape), the fight to increase registration of African American voters, and a variety of issues concerning public transportation and public accommodations. Parks also writes of her acquaintance with several politically active women, Septima Clark, Jo Ann Robinson, and Virginia Durr. She met Clark at the Highlander Folk School, which was originally organized to train labor leaders and union organizers, but by the 1950s had shifted its focus to the issue of voting rights. About her experience at the Highlander Folk School, which was eventually forced to close by the State of Tennessee, Parks writes:

> I was forty-two years old, and it was one of the few times in my life up to that point when I did not feel any hostility from white people. I experienced people of different races and backgrounds meeting together in workshops and living together in peace and harmony. I felt that I could express myself honestly without any repercussions or antagonistic attitudes from other people. (106-107)

341. Patel, Jayant (1936-). *Seeking Home: An Immigrant's Realization.* Ed. Deborah Pappas. Bayside, New York: J. Patel, 1991. ISBN: none. 181 pages.

Patel, a successful businessman in the United States for 18 years, writes of his dream to return to his home country, India, with his wife and children. They, however, were thoroughly Americanized and had no desire to leave the United States. Patel recounts his two failed attempts to return to India and set up a business. The failures were due to his family's refusal to join him, and his own unwillingness to force them to follow his wishes or to live apart from them. Patel also writes about his devotion to the teachings of Dada Bhagwan and includes a transcription of a conversation which illustrates Bhagwan's spiritual beliefs.

342. Peay, Mrs. Sadie F. Nick. *Memoir, Nurse—Midwife: Mrs. Sadie F. Nick Peay.* Columbia, South Carolina: n.p., 1985. ISBN: none. 72 pages.
Note: This booklet was conceptualized and compiled by Jean S. Hopkins.

343. Peery, Nelson (1925-). *Black Fire: The Making of an American Revolutionary.* New York: New Press, 1994. ISBN: 1565841581. 340 pages; photographs.

Peery began this autobiography at the age of 24, just after returning from World War II, but completed it close to 50 years later, in his "old age." He focuses on his conversion to radical politics, beginning with his introduction to the American Communist Party while still in high school, and including his experience as an African American soldier in a segregated army. Peery was strongly motivated to enlist in the armed services because of his affinity for Russia and his fear of Hitler and what he represented, but he writes that the black soldiers "found more and more to fight against and less and less to fight for" (p. 152) as they languished in their southern boot camps, continually experiencing racist attitudes and outright attacks. Peery's wartime duty took him to the Philippines, where he became involved with the Filipino communists. Although he attempted to stay to assist them with their fight, they urged him to return to the U.S. to represent their cause.

344. Pemberton, Gayle. *The Hottest Water in Chicago: On Family, Race, Time, and American Culture.* Boston: Faber & Faber, 1992. ISBN: 0571129366. 266 pages; bibliography.
Note: Also published as *The Hottest Water in Chicago: Notes of a Native Daughter.* New York: Doubleday, 1993. ISBN: 0385468423.

Pemberton, a scholar of American Literature, examines her father's life and motivations while considering various significant periods and events in her own life. She had hoped to write her father's story together with him, but he died prematurely. The impetus for this book, however, was created when she discovered three sheets of paper upon which her father had apparently begun his autobiography. Pemberton writes that her father was a "'race man'—that is, for almost all of his adult life he worked for an organization that promotes racial equality" (p. 3). Pemberton describes her father's work with the Urban League, and her own personal fight to withstand racism and discrimination. As a school girl, she was involved in the early years of public school desegregation following the *Brown vs. Topeka Board of Education* decision, and continued to break the color line as a graduate student and faculty member. Experiencing both racism and sexism, Pemberton explores how she attempted to cope with constant marginalization and stereotyping.

345. Pérez, Ramón (Tianguis). *Diary of an Undocumented Immigrant/Diario de Un Mojado.* Translated by Dick J. Reavis. Houston: Arte Publico Press. ISBN: 1558850325. 237 pages.

Pérez describes the means and perils of getting across the border to El Norté, and the precariousness of existence once the other side is safely reached. He details his efforts to find employment, the variety of jobs he held, the people he associated with, the immigrant culture, and the reasons for his return to Mexico.

346. Peter, Katherine (1918-). *Neets'aii Gwiindaii/Living in the Chandalar Country.* Ed. Mary Jane McGary. Fairbanks: Alaska Native Language Center, University of Alaska, 1992. ISBN: 0933769113. 108 pages; photographs.
Note: Written in English and Gwich'in.

Peter was born into a Koyukon Athapascan-speaking family but was raised speaking the Gwich'in (or Kutchin) Athapascan dialect, which became her first language. Peter has become a leading figure in the teaching of Gwich'in and has been responsible for the transcription of thousands of pages of stories from tape; she has written over fifty schoolbooks in Gwich'in and has been a major contributor to the

Gwich'in dictionary. She has also taught university courses in Gwich'in. This book is the first extended narrative written in Gwich'in. Peter prepared the English translation, which was edited for publication by Mary Jane McGary. The narrative covers the years 1937-1947.

347. Peters, James S. (1917-). *The Epic of a Proud Black Family: An Allegorical History*. San Francisco: International Scholars Publications, 1994. ISBN: 080593474X. Bibliography.

348. —. *The Memoirs of a Black Southern-New Englander*. Pittsburgh: Dorrance Publishing Co., 1994. ISBN: 080593474X. 166 pages.

Born in Ashdown, Arkansas, Peters made his way to Connecticut by way of Louisiana, Chicago, and Massachusetts. In this autobiography, Peters chronicles his education, and related activities. He received degrees from Southern University in Louisiana, Hartford Seminary in Connecticut, the University of Chicago, and Purdue University. Both he and his wife Marie earned doctoral degrees. Peters was a pacifist during World War II, but enlisted in the Navy where he became a Specialist Teacher, First Class. He describes discrimination in the Navy, in university program admissions at the University of Chicago, and in housing opportunities in Massachusetts and Connecticut. He also acknowledges those individuals who countered the trend of racism, helping to open doors both in the South and in the North.

349. Phan, Vinh Trung. *Tren Tam Muoi Nam Tai The Gian/Over Eighty Years on This Earth*. Translated by Clara Phan Knudson. San Jose, California: The Author, 1994. ISBN: none. 234 pages; photographs by James A. Smestad; reproductions of the author's water colors in color and black-and-white.

Trung Vinh Phan gives an account of his life in Vietnam from his birth in 1912 to his departure in 1975, days before the North Vietnamese entered Saigon.

While discussing his education and career as an archi-
tect and engineer, he depicts a beautiful and peaceful
Vietnam, but also describes the many political changes
which he experienced, including life under French
rule, the Japanese occupation and Allied bombing during World War II, the Viet Minh revolution that
erupted with the end of World War II, and the events
leading up to the fall of Saigon. His paintings, many of
which are reproduced in this publication, represent his
memories of a rural Vietnam untouched by war. One
painting has the caption "I am reminiscing about the
region of Central Vietnam, which is formerly a region
of peace and tranquillity" (p. 150).

350. Piper, Aurelius (1916-). *A Quarter-Acre of Heartache*. As
told to Claude Clayton Smith. Blacksburg, Virginia:
Pocahontas Press, 1985. ISBN: 0936015012:0936015004.
168 pages; photographs; maps.

Smith writes "I have chosen to write in the first person, in the voice of Chief Big Eagle as I have come to
know it, to let the Chief speak for himself" (p. xiii).
His text is based on Piper's tape-recorded accounts, and
so this book is apparently something of a cross between
biography and autobiography. How much of the text
is actually in Piper's own words is unclear. In 1976,
Piper, who had attempted to live a traditional lifestyle
in the forests of Maine, returned to his reservation in
Connecticut, the quarter-acre Golden Hill Reservation
of the Paugussett Indians, to help protect the land from
state and private interests. Piper describes the events
of the battle he waged. After the victory, he participated in the creation of a cultural museum built on
the quarter-acre.

351. Pittmon, Woodrow K. (1924-). *To Be a Man*. New York:
Vantage Press, 1992. ISBN: 0533101077. 103 pages.

Pittmon presents this story of his life with the hopes
that he will convince young girls and boys living in
urban or rural poverty that their futures are not hope-
less. He was born, the youngest of a large family, in
rural Georgia, where he picked cotton at the age of

three, chopped wood at six, and was plowing at seven. His opportunities for advancement were limited. Schooling past the seventh grade was hard to come by, and there were no schools for black children in his own or nearby communities. Pittmon's determination, his abilities and intelligence, and the concern others had for his welfare, helped him to surmount the obstacles of location and tuition to continue his education at a private high school 150 miles from his home. Pittmon continued his education at Morehouse College, and the New School for Social Research, and then finally decided to study drafting. He never completed a degree, but obtained an education and found meaningful employment for himself. After moving to New York, Pittmon moved into the "900 block" in Brooklyn. He describes the area, its residents, and his own activities during the time he lived there, including the details of his career as the first black employee at the Liquidometer Corporation. Pittmon discusses his feelings about the Civil Rights Movement, and the turmoil of the decades of the 50s and 60s. Having grown up in a single-parent household, and having himself raised his two daughters alone following his divorce, Pittmon is sensitive to the difficulties created for children who lack adult role models, especially male role models. He concludes his work with an inspirational chapter especially addressed to young boys, encouraging them to keep their goals in sight, and to decide to survive no matter how hostile their environment.

352. Ponce, Mary Helen. *Hoyt Street: An Autobiography*. Albuquerque: University of New Mexico Press, 1993. ISBN: 0826314465. 338 pages.

Ponce refers to her work as both a life history and a communal history. She provides character sketches and a detailed account of the day-to-day lives of her family and neighbors, relying almost entirely upon her memory and some minimal input from her siblings. She also gives a careful description of Pacoima, her home-town, which is to the northeast of Los Angeles. Ponce describes some of the religious holidays and fes-

tivals celebrated in the Mexican Catholic church and
their significance to herself and to the community.
Community members were viewed by outsiders as
poor and lacking in good hygiene. Ponce remembers
being confused by this attitude when confronted by it
at school: "We Mexican Americans . . . had so many
things wrong with us that I wondered why it was we
were happy. I, for one, lived in a loving home, did
well in school, played 'kick the can' in the street, enjoyed the church bazaars, and loved catechism; I lived
what I felt was a good life. We felt content . . ." (p. 122).
In fact, it was this sense of confusion, caused by the dis-
crepancy between how she felt about her life and how
institutional authorities viewed it, which motivated
Ponce to write this book.

353. Pryor, Rayford V. *A Tough Row to Hoe.* Huntington,
West Virginia (59 Oak Lane, Spring Valley 25704):
Aegina Press, 1988. ISBN: 0916383490. 184 pages; pho-
tographs.

In his book, Pryor presents the history of his family,
describing the Great Depression, how his grandparents
managed to survive after losing everything, his parents' courtship and marriage, and his own childhood,
term in the Navy, and career with the United States
Postal Service. Pryor writes that when he joined the
Navy, he began "a lifelong education of segregation,
separation, discrimination, racism, integration, and all
the social and economic barriers that existed in varying
degrees throughout the United States and the military
installations" (p. 60). As a supervisor with the U.S.
Postal Service, Pryor filed discrimination complaints
with the EEOC and attempted to change its practice of
inequitable pay and promotion opportunities for
African Americans.

354. Puckett, Kirby. *I Love This Game: My Life and Baseball.*
New York: Harper Collins, 1993. ISBN: 0060177101.
289 pages; photographs.
Note: Also published New York: Harper Paperbacks,
1994. ISBN: 006109210X.

Puckett writes about his career in baseball, beginning with a full scholarship to Bradley University, signing with the Twins as a minor league player, and joining the Twin's major league team. Puckett's upbeat story includes a description of the events surrounding the arrival of his and his wife's first adopted child, Catherine; an account of the work that he and his wife participate in on behalf of children; and the difficulties involved in making his final decision to accept another five-year contract with the Minnesota Twins.

355. Quintasket, Christine.
    See *Hum-ishu-ma*.

356. Ray, Clarence. *Clarence Ray: Black Politics and Gaming in Las Vegas, 1920's-1980's.* With Helen M. Blue and Jamie Coughtry. Reno: University of Nevada, Oral History Program, 1991. ISBN: 1564750027. 109 pages; photographs.

Clarence Ray, of mixed African American and Creek heritage, grew up in Oklahoma in the Creek Nation. He spent his life as a professional gambler and moved to Las Vegas with the intention of making it his career. Ray describes his profession and other aspects of his life, including his work as a founding member of the local chapter of the NAACP.

357. Redding, J. Saunders (1906-). *A Scholar's Conscience: Selected Writings of J. Saunders Redding, 1942-1977.* Ed. Faith Berry. Lexington: University Press of Kentucky, 1992. ISBN: 0813117704:0813108063. 238 pages; bibliography.

J. Saunders Redding, a novelist, essayist, biographer, historian, and critic, was first published toward the end of the Harlem Renaissance. He was among the first scholars of African American literature, though his scholarship and expertise covered the vast area of English-language literature. This collection of his writings includes four autobiographical reminiscences, two of which are taken from his books *No Day of Triumph*, New York: Harper, 1942, 1968, and *On Being*

Negro in America, Indianapolis: Bobbs-Merrill, 1951; reprinted by Charter Books 1962; Harper and Row, 1969. Two complete selections are also included: "A Writer's Heritage," first published in Stanton Wormley and Lewis Fenderson, eds. *Many Shades of Black*. New York: W. Morrow, 1969; and "My Most Humiliating Jim Crow Experience," which was published in *Negro Digest*, Dec. 1944. In his essay, "A Writer's Heritage," Redding writes about his New England college experience:

> We Negroes were aliens, and we knew it, and the knowledge forced us to assume postures of defense and to take on a sort of double-consciousness. It was not a matter of real ambivalence, or a question of identity: we knew who we were, but we feared to act ourselves, feared to "act the nigger," whatever that meant. . . . It was then that I began to write out of what I have since called my 'Negroness.' It was all I had and all I still have, and all any colored person born and reared and schooled in America has to write out of if he pretends to honesty. . . . To think otherwise is a delusion, to feel otherwise is fakery. (p. 18)

358. Redner, Albina. *Albina Redner, a Shoshone Life: An Oral History*. An oral history conducted by Helen M. Blue. Reno: University of Nevada-Reno, Oral History Program, 1990. ISBN: 1564753468. 150 pages; photographs; maps.

Albina Redner is from the Western Shoshone tribe of Nevada. She writes of life in and around the reservations of Nevada, giving some history and description of the reservations in her general region. Besides providing details of her childhood and adult years, Redner discusses the Shoshone language, explains some of the tribe's traditional foods, and depicts rituals such as those followed for childbirth and for a girl's coming of age. She emphasizes the importance of language in maintaining one's Native identity. Although her mother stressed Redner's mixed ancestry and the misery that her heritage would bring her, Redner writes that she always identified herself as Shoshone: "I spoke my language and my thoughts were Indian thoughts" (p. 6).

359. Reed, Cecil (1913-). *Fly in the Buttermilk: The Life Story of Cecil Reed*. Written with Priscilla Donovan. Singular Lives. Iowa City: University of Iowa Press, 1993. ISBN: 0877454159:0877454167. 184 pages; photographs.

Reed describes growing up in an all-white neighborhood and attending all-white schools in a small town in Iowa, and the difficulties which he and his siblings experienced because of their racially isolated situation. He then watched as his own children suffered through the same experiences. In his youth, Reed learned what was happening among blacks elsewhere in the country from the African American railroad employees who would come through their small town. A successful entrepreneur as an adult, Reed gives an account of his various commercial and political activities, including opening up a motel that served the needs of African Americans, and winning a seat in the Iowa State Legislature in 1966. While in office, Reed introduced an open housing bill which passed unanimously.

360. *Return to Topaz '93: Recollections, Reflections, Remembrances*. Salt Lake City, Utah: Return to Topaz '93 Anthology Committee, 1993. ISBN: none. 52 pages; photographs.
Note: "War Relocation Authority, Central Utah Project, 1942-1945."

This collection contains Nisei and Sansei recollections of life in the Topaz (Central Utah) Internment Camp. Other essays are provided by Sansei and Yonsei (fourth generation Japanese Americans) whose parents or grandparents were in the camps. This younger generation presents their reaction to hearing about the camp experiences and of attending a 1993 reunion held at Topaz.

361. Revard, Carter (1931-). "Walking Among the Stars." *I Tell You Now: Autobiographical Essays by Native American Writers*. Ed. Brian Swann and Arnold Krupat. Lincoln: University of Nebraska Press, 1987. ISBN: 0803227140.

See entry under *Swann, Brian* for a complete list of authors included in this anthology.

362. Rice, Sarah (1909-). *He Included Me: The Autobiography of Sarah Rice.* Transcribed and edited by Louise Hutchings Westling. Athens: University of Georgia Press, 1989. ISBN: 0820311413. 181 pages; photographs.

Sarah Rice grew up in rural Alabama during the early part of the twentieth century. She was the daughter of a school teacher and an American Methodist Episcopal (A.M.E.) minister. The family also operated a small farm. In this oral testimony, Rice provides her family history and describes the members of her immediate family. She gives an account of what life was like for rural children, describes life in a small African American community, and comments on her own teaching career and marriage. Rice describes her town's annual Emancipation Day celebration which was held on May 28, because, according to her mother, that is when the slaves in that area first learned of their freedom. Rice also talks about her work with the Baptist Church and expresses her feelings about the status of women in the church.

363. Rivera, Edward. *Family Installments: Memories of Growing Up Hispanic.* New York: W. Morrow, 1982. ISBN: 0688012310. 300 pages.
Note: Also published New York: Penguin, 1983. ISBN: 0140067264.

Rivera, born in Puerto Rico, writes about his family's history on both his mother's and father's side. Rivera's father became responsible for his livelihood at a young age, and met Rivera's mother when working for her father. The family eventually immigrated to the United States. Rivera gives a humorous account of the rigors of Catholic School and, more seriously, of balancing work and night classes in order to get a college degree. He returned to Puerto Rico to attend a funeral and sadly noted the many changes that had occurred since he was last there.

364. Rivera, Vicente L. *A Glimpse of My Past and a Look at the Future*. Detroit: V. L. Rivera, 1984. ISBN: none. 18 pages.

365. Roberts, Josephine (1922-). *Josephine Roberts, Tanana*. Interviews conducted and text prepared by Curt Madison and Yvonne Yarber. Fairbanks: Spirit Mountain Press, 1983. ISBN: 0910871027. 64 pages; photographs.
Note: Produced by Yukon-Koyukuk School District of Alaska.

Roberts tells of her childhood in Galena and adult years as a nurse's assistant in Tanana. As a child, Roberts helped her parents with the work at their seasonal camps for fishing, trapping, and hunting. She describes various activities participated in by children, who had little time for actual play. As a nurse's assistant at the Tanana Hospital beginning in 1940, Roberts learned on the job. Hunting and fishing continued to be an important part of her life even while working at the hospital. Roberts writes that she is anxious to pass on to her grandchildren her language and the traditional knowledge that she herself received from respected elders and medicine women.
For a brief description and list of autobiographies in this Yukon-Koyukuk School District series, see the entry for Moses Henzie.

366. Robeson, Paul Leroy (1898-1976). *Here I Stand*. Boston: Beacon Press, 1988. ISBN: 0807064386:0807064459. 121 pages.
Originally published New York: Othello Associates, 1958.

367. Robinson, Amelia Boynton (1911-). *Bridge Across Jordan*. Rev. ed. Washington, D.C.: Schiller Institute, 1991. ISBN: 0962109541. 414 pages; photographs.

Amelia Robinson revised this book, originally published in 1979, to reflect her participation in the Schiller Institute founded by Lyndon LaRouche and his wife, Helga Zapp-LaRouche. Robinson documents her lifetime commitment to improve conditions for

African Americans in Selma, Alabama, where her scope of activity broadened after Martin Luther King led the marches for voting rights there. Robinson continued as a leader and active participant in the Civil Rights Movement after King's death. She began her association with LaRouche in 1983, becoming a member of the board of directors of the Schiller Institute in 1984. Among other events, Robinson discusses her trip to East Germany in 1990.

368. Robinson, Barbara A. *And Still I Cry*. Edgewood, Maryland: M. E. Duncan and Co., Inc., 1992. ISBN: 1878647016. 220 pages.

In this account of her life, Robinson recounts her horrific childhood. She was a victim of child abuse, both physical and sexual, poverty, and homelessness. She attended college against tremendous odds, only to become pregnant, drop out and marry a man who had not yet completed his divorce. Although Robinson did complete college and finally bring her life together while still married to her first husband, she became involved in drug and alcohol abuse. Robinson describes how she recovered from incredible hardship, and went on to a life as a successful businesswoman.

369. Robinson, Jo Ann Gibson (1912-). *The Montgomery Bus Boycott and the Women Who Started It: The Memoir of Jo Ann Gibson Robinson*. Ed. David J. Garrow. Knoxville: University of Tennessee Press, 1987. ISBN: 0870495240:0870495275. 190 pages; photographs.

Robinson, as head of the Women's Political Council (WPC) in Montgomery, began making plans for a bus boycott in 1954. When Rosa Parks, one of many who had resisted the discriminatory conventions of Montgomery's transportation systems, was arrested, Robinson and her group were poised to begin the boycott which, after 13 months, achieved its goal. Robinson describes the daily humiliation African Americans faced taking the bus before the strike, and considers the effect of this humiliation on their lives. She also provides an account of the aftermath of the strike. Many of the participants were employed by Alabama State, as was Robinson herself; some were forced to resign and many others left because of political pressure. But despite the danger and personal hardships experienced by the participants, Robinson writes that the boycott will be "the most beautiful memory that all of us who participated will carry to our final resting place" (p. 11).

370. Robinson, Joseph J. *Growing Up in Chi-Town: A Story of the 1960s.* Chicago: The Committee (P. O. Box 1082, Evanston, Illinois 60204), 1980. ISBN: none. 40 pages; photographs; bibliography.

Robinson writes a brief account of his participation in the events of the mid- to late- 1960s. During this time he changed from a casual, only partially informed participant, to an individual dedicated to change. This change came about through his growing interest in and association with the Black Panther Party. Robinson describes the FBI's and the Chicago Police's war on the Panthers, and gives a detailed account of the raid on Fred Hampton's apartment in the middle of the night, which resulted in the death of Fred Hampton and the wounding of several others. Robinson was inspired to finish high school and to attend college through his work with the Panthers and Hampton. At the end of this history, he writes that he is a janitor with a college degree. "The 'gig' keeps me fed, the degree is for serving the people, like Chairman Fred would have wanted us to do" (p. 35).

371. Robinson, Robert (1902-). *Black On Red: My 44 Years Inside the Soviet Union: An Autobiography.* Written with Jonathan Slevin. Washington, D.C.: Acropolis Books, 1988. ISBN: 0874918855. 436 pages; photographs; maps.

Robinson, who was born in Jamaica, spent his childhood and youth in Cuba, and began his adult years in Harlem and Detroit. Educated as a tool and dye maker in Cuba, Robinson found that there was no place for individuals of African descent in the skilled labor pool of the United States. He started out as a floor sweeper at Ford Motor Corporation, and, after three years, finally worked his way into the ranks of the tool and dye makers. Robinson was one of many Americans with special skills who in the early years of the Great Depression were wooed to the Soviet Union on one year contracts to be "American Specialists." He was promised, and received, much higher pay than he was receiving in Detroit. While he was celebrated for his skills and technical contributions, he was also despised and shunned by his new associates. Robinson found himself to be a pawn of the Soviet Union, learned to trust no one, felt unable to form close associations with women, and lived in a state of fear for his entire 44-year stay. He was forced to give up his American citizenship, but was finally given permission to travel to Uganda in 1973. At this point, Robinson planned never to return to the U.S.S.R. He regained his U.S. citizenship in 1986. Robinson describes his 44 years in great detail (his original manuscript was 1,000 pages long). He lived through two of Stalin's purges and watched as many friends, acquaintances, and fellow employees disappeared; he survived the hardships of World War II, nearly dying of malnutrition; he was spied on continuously; and he risked imprisonment, insane asylums, or deportation to stubbornly pursue his exit visa. He writes that he hopes his "years of struggle in the Soviet Union will provide many people with valuable insight on the realities of life in that country, where good and decent people live and die in frustration under a system of government that views freedom as a threat to its existence" (p. 434).

372. Rodriguez, Luis (1954-). *Always Running: La Vida Loca, Gang Days in L.A.* Willimantic, Connecticut: Curbstone Press, 1993. ISBN: 1880684063. 260 pages. Note: New York: Simon & Schuster, 1994. ISBN: 0671882317.

Rodriguez documents his life growing up in the barrios of East Los Angeles. He describes the desperate conditions and pressures that push young men and women into the violent, nihilistic life of the gangs and the difficulty of leaving that life. A number of supportive adults recognized Rodriguez's writing and intellectual capabilities. With their encouragement, he tried many times to leave the gang life behind. But the ties of loyalty were strong and hard to resist. Rodriguez finally did escape and now lives in Chicago, where he is active as a poet, editor, publisher (Tia Chupa Press) and journalist.

373. Rodriguez, Richard. *Days of Obligation: An Argument With My Mexican Father.* New York: Viking, 1992. ISBN: 0670813966. 230 pages.
Note: Also published New York: Penguin, 1993. ISBN: 0140096221.

This second book by Rodriguez was published more than a decade after his still-controversial autobiography *Hunger of Memory.* In these essays, Rodriguez writes about a wide range of subjects, including his trips to Mexico and his impressions of the Mexican people and of Mexico's social and artistic culture; his Indian heritage, and popular conceptions of Native Americans from both sides of the U.S./Mexican border; Victorian architecture; parent-child relationships in immigrant families; California lore, the missions, and Catholicism; and the role of the U.S. public school system in the process of assimilation or "Americanization."

374. —. *Hunger of Memory: The Education of Richard Rodriguez: An Autobiography.* New York: David Godine, 1981. ISBN: 0879234180. 195 pages.
Note: Also published New York: Bantam Books, 1983. ISBN: 0553231936:0553272934.

Writing about the significance of language in his life, Rodriguez describes the move from intimate family life surrounded by spoken Spanish to a solid place in public life surrounded by spoken English. In writing about this transformation, which he describes as grievous but necessary, he debates the utility of bilingual education and affirmative action—taking stands that have stirred controversy. In response, Rodriguez emphasizes more than once that although his life may speak to others, it is indeed just his life, and he is not claiming that it is a representative Hispanic American life.

375. Romano-V., Octavio Ignacio (1923-). *Geriatric Fu: My First Sixty-five Years in the United States.* Berkeley: TQS Publications, 1990. ISBN: 0892290188. 236 pages.

Romano-V. wrote this autobiography upon his retirement from teaching at the University of California, Berkeley. An anthropologist, Romano-V. begins his life story by surveying world events when he was in his seventh month of gestation (deducing that nothing has changed except for the advent of computers), and ends it shortly before his retirement. Romano-V. is selective about what life events he shares with the reader, and we learn as much or more about his world view as about the details of his life. He finds much to criticize and much to praise about this country and the world. He challenges academics and other professionals, especially questioning "the very strange tradition of the social sciences to never consider the poor as capable of intellectual and abstract thought . . ." (p. 68), and providing evidence from his personal experience to refute this view. Romano-V. provokes both tears and laughter as he describes the tragedies experienced by himself and his friends and acquaintances, and pokes fun at society's weaknesses. This book is published by the publishing firm that Romano-V. founded in 1967, Quinto Sol Publications (now called Tomtiuh-Quinto Sol or TQS), which specializes in the works of Chicano writers.

376. Rose, Wendy (1948-). "Neon Scars." *I Tell You Now: Autobiographical Essays by Native American Writers.* Ed. Brian Swann and Arnold Krupat. Lincoln: University of Nebraska Press, 1987. ISBN: 0803227140.

See entry under *Swann, Brian* for a complete list of authors included in this anthology.

377. Ross, Allen C. (1940-). *Ehanamani "Walks Among": An Autobiography*. Rev. ed. Denver: Bear, 1993. ISBN: 0962197726:0962197718. 226 pages; illustrations.

     After discussing his childhood, his family life, education, and years stationed in Germany as a member of the armed forces, Ross describes his growing interest in his cultural heritage. As he learned more about the history of his people, the Santee (Dakota) Indians, Ross also became more interested in Santee spiritual beliefs and practices. He began participating in such ceremonial events as the Sun Dance, and gradually became a spiritual leader and healer. This autobiography is written to accompany his earlier prophetic work, *Mitakuye Oyasin/We Are All Related*, Denver: Bear, 1989.

378. Rowan, Carl T. *Breaking Barriers: A Memoir*. Boston: Little, Brown, 1991. ISBN: 0316759775. 395 pages; photographs.
     Note: Also published New York: Harper Perennial, 1992. ISBN: 0060974478.

     Carl T. Rowan broke a number of racial barriers in his rise from poverty and hopelessness to political prominence. He was among the first black general assignment newspaper reporters, and held prominent positions in the Kennedy and Johnson administrations. Rowan struggled with wanting to present his unique perspective as an African American, but at the same time not wanting to be pigeon-holed into representing any particular point-of-view. He wrote this book after the controversy surrounding his shooting (in the wrist) of an intruder with a gun that was not properly registered. He was acquitted of all charges brought against him.

379. Rust, Art (1927-). *Recollections of a Baseball Junkie*. Written with Edna Rust. New York: W. Morrow, 1985. ISBN: 0688031072. 181 pages; photographs.

     Art Rust grew up playing, watching and talking about baseball. He became hooked for life, however, when, during a month-long quarantine with scarlet fever, he listened to all of the broadcasts of the Newark Bear's games. Rust explains why, although an ardent baseball player, he chose to become a broadcaster and sportswriter instead of a player. He was still a boy when Jackie Robinson signed with the Brooklyn Dodgers, but he and his friends felt there was no future for African Americans in the major leagues because of the racism inherent in the institution. Rust provides an insider's view of baseball, sharing his historical and anecdotal knowledge of the game.

380. Salas, Floyd. *Buffalo Nickel: A Memoir*. Houston: Arte Publico Press, 1992. ISBN: 155885049X. 347 pages.

In this book, Salas writes about his relationship with his older brother Al, who was in and out of reform school, jail, prison, detox, and mental institutions throughout his life. Al had pursued a career as a boxer, and trained Floyd as well, but neither stayed in the sport for the long term. Floyd pursued his boxing activities mainly as a means of pleasing his brother. In *Buffalo Nickel*, Salas writes about his family and the many tragedies they confronted, about his own desire to write, the many obstacles he faced while trying to attend both high school and college, and his love for and the mostly futile efforts he made to help his brother Al and his children.

381. Salisbury, Ralph (1926-). "The Quiet Between Lightning and Thunder." *I Tell You Now: Autobiographical Essays by Native American Writers*. Ed. Brian Swann and Arnold Krupat. Lincoln: University of Nebraska Press, 1987. ISBN: 0803227140.

See entry under *Swann, Brian* for a complete list of authors included in this anthology.

382. Santiago, Esmeralda. *When I Was Puerto Rican*. Reading, Massachusetts: Addison-Wesley, 1993. ISBN: 0201581175. 274 pages; includes glossary of Spanish terms.
Note: Also published New York: Vintage Books, 1994. ISBN: 0679756760.

Esmeralda Santiago writes of her childhood in Puerto

Rico, where she was the oldest child in a family that would soon include seven children. Her parents had a turbulent relationship, and her father often lived away from home. Santiago's mother eventually took the children to New York, leaving their father for good. At the time of the move, Santiago had just turned 13 and spoke very little English. The change from life in a remote rural area in Puerto Rico to the urban complexities of New York was traumatic. Despite this, the family's poverty, and the subsequent birth of four more children, Santiago, encouraged by her mother's ambitions and her own drive to succeed, excelled in school, was admitted to the Performing Arts High School, and eventually attended Harvard.

383. Santiago, Lourdes and Felix M. Padilla. *Outside the Wall: A Puerto Rican Woman's Struggle*. New Brunswick, New Jersey: Rutgers University Press, 1993. ISBN: 0813519861:081351987X. 214 pages; bibliography.

Raised by overly-strict parents, Santiago's marriage at age 15 to a gang leader was as much for love as to assert her independence and take control of her life. Although he never gave up his gang involvement, her husband had regular work and was attending a technical college. This attempt at a stable lifestyle, however, was soon to end when he was arrested on what Santiago claims were fabricated charges, and sentenced to 70 years in prison. Santiago believes that he was targeted by rival gang members and the police, who were anxious to lock up leaders. Santiago writes about how she has learned to cope with her husband's imprisonment, and how she has tried to help the family members of other inmates cope as well—providing support for each other and for the inmates. After nine years, Santiago set up a one-woman organization to run support groups, provide transportation for visitations, and in other ways advance issues of justice for the inmates. She describes the consequences she believes her activism has had for herself and for her husband.

384. Sarasohn, Eileen Sunada (1943-), ed. *The Issei, Portrait of a Pioneer: An Oral History*. Palo Alto, California:

Pacific Books, 1983. ISBN: 087015236X. 296 pages; photographs.

This is a collection of short narratives by Issei, or first-generation Japanese immigrants. Some of the subjects came to the United States on their own, and some followed their parents or spouses. Many arrived in the early part of the century, and all experienced racism and discrimination. The recollections include their reactions upon first hearing about the bombing of Pearl Harbor; feelings of disbelief, fear, and incredulity at what followed for them; and the consequences of the evacuation and internment for the older and younger generations.

385. Savala, Refugio. *The Autobiography of a Yaqui Poet*. With background and interpretations by Kathleen M. Sands. Tucson: University of Arizona Press, 1980. ISBN: 0816506981:0816506280. 228 pages; illustrations; maps; bibliography.
Note: Also published New York: Ballantine Books, 1992. ISBN: 0345376765.

Savala was born in 1904 during the Mexican government's campaign to remove the Yaqui from their homeland in Sonora. Savala moved with his family, along with many other Yaquis, over the Mexican-U.S. border to Arizona, where many found work with the railroads. Savala describes life in Tucson, Arizona, the Yaqui community there, and its social and religious practices. His creative writing abilities were discovered when he was asked to describe a particular dance for an anthropologist. Savala continued to work with anthropologists, producing both word by word translations and paraphrases of Yaqui texts. Although the editor has provided extensive critical apparatus with Savala's autobiography, she has presented the material as it was originally written by him.

386. Scott, Kesho. *The Habit of Surviving: Black Women's Strategies for Life*. New Brunswick, New Jersey: Rutgers University Press, 1991. ISBN: 0813516463. 208 pages; bibliography.

Kesho Scott presents the life stories of four women between the ages of 46 and 52. The women, whose names have been changed, talk about their families and men, feminism, politics, and God. Scott points out that these four women are representative of how black women are "committed to anti-racist, nonsexist human relationships among people of all colors, sexes and classes" (p. 12) even though they may not be active in the mainstream, predominantly white women's movement. Scott includes her own life-history in this volume as well.

387. Scott, Kody.
     See *Shakur, Sanyika.*

388. Seay, S. S. (Solomon Snowden) (1899-1988). *I Was There By the Grace of God.* Montgomery, Alabama: S. S. Seay, Sr. Educational Foundation, 1990. ISBN: 0962861707. 296 pages; photographs; bibliography.

At the age of 88, Seay looks back at his life and career in this chronicle of the Civil Rights Movement. Seay records both positive and negative aspects of his childhood growing up the sixteenth of 21 children on a farm in rural Alabama. His parents worked as field hands and also raised their own crops and livestock on which the family subsisted. Seay writes that his first realization in life was that he was poor, and that it was his second realization to learn that he was black in a world dominated by whites. Because of his large family and its poor financial situation, obtaining an education was difficult, but Seay somehow realized his ambition to become a minister in the A.M.E. Zion Church. His book describes his work as a minister, in Montgomery, Alabama, and how it led him into the Civil Rights Movement. Seay documents the many forerunners and participants in this movement with photographs and biographical sketches.

389. Sellers, Cleveland. *The River of No Return: The Autobiography of a Black Militant and the Life and Death of SNCC.* Written with Robert L. Terrell. Jackson: Uni-

versity Press of Mississippi, 1990. ISBN: 087805474X.
289 pages.
Originally published New York: W. Morrow, 1973.

390. Semaken, Goodwin. *Goodwin Semaken: Kaltag*. Interviews conducted and text prepared by Yvonne Yarber
and Curt Madison. Yukon-Koyukuk School District
Biography Series. Fairbanks: Spirit Mountain Press,
1984. ISBN: 0910871086. 86 pages; photographs; maps.

Born to an Iñupiaq mother and a Koyukon father, Semaken grew up in the small village of Kaltag. His parents were reluctant to send him to school, and instead
wanted him to learn the outdoor life. Semaken tells
stories of hunting, fishing, trapping, and traveling by
dog sleds and by snow mobiles. He gives his view on
the importance of family, and how alcohol often ruins
a family, causing husband and wife to mistreat each
other and their children.
For a brief description and list of autobiographies in
this Yukon-Koyukuk School District series, see the entry for Moses Henzie.

391. Shakur, Assata. *Assata: An Autobiography*. Westport,
Connecticut: L. Hill, 1987.   ISBN: 0882082213:
0882082221. 274 pages.

Shakur, in alternate chapters, documents her brutal arrest and her life from birth through the arrest. Her
nightmarish ordeal at the hands of the New Jersey police force and the FBI includes a hospital stay during
which, though she was near death, she was questioned
and beaten by members of both of these law enforce-
ment agencies; her imprisonment, most of which was
spent in isolation; and the court ("Kourt") trials in
New York and New Jersey on apparently trumped up
charges. Shakur was one of a number of targets or victims of the FBI's notorious COINTELPRO activities,
which were designed to disrupt a variety of Black nationalist and civil rights organizations—two prominent targets were Martin Luther King and the Southern Christian Leadership Conference (SCLC), and the
Black Panther Party. Shakur had been a member of the

latter, but became a target of FBI harassment after leaving the group. Shakur was only convicted of one of
the many charges brought against her. She somehow
escaped from prison and wrote this book during her
exile in Cuba.

392. Shakur, Sanyika (1964-). *Monster: The Autobiography of
an L.A. Gang Member.* New York: Atlantic Monthly
Press, 1993. ISBN: 0871135353. 383 pages.
Note: Also published New York: Penguin, 1994. ISBN:
0140232257.

Shakur went through his gang initiation the night he
graduated from sixth grade. He was, from the start, a
single-mindedly dedicated member—killing two rival
gang members his first night out. Shakur provides a
detailed account of his life and activities as a gangster.
He describes the complex culture that has evolved
over several decades within the gangs, specifically the
Crips, and of the changes that have taken place with
the advent of drug dealing and the availability of large
sums of money. Shakur only occasionally questioned
his gang life, and repeatedly writes of his total dedication to this way of life. He was converted to the New
Afrikan Independence Movement during a four and
one-half year stay in prison and, with his conversion,
gained a new purpose in life. "Gangsterism continues," he writes, "but more importantly, the struggle to
eradicate the causes of gangsterism continues. And it
is this struggle to which I am dedicated" (p. 377). At
the time of the writing of this book, he was back in
prison serving his third year in solitary confinement,
having received a seven-year sentence for beating a
crack dealer who refused to leave his neighborhood:

> I make no excuses for this, and I have no regrets. When the
> police and other government agencies don't seem to care
> about what is going on in our communities, then those of us
> who live in them must take responsibility for their protec-
> tion and maintenance. As it turned out, this specific dealer
> was also a paid police informant. (p. 379)

Shakur writes that he is being held in isolation because
of his "political views and for assertions" that he has
made (p. 380). He also writes in the Epilogue that he
believes the country's

130-year-old experiment of multiculturalism has failed. Perhaps it was never designed to work. My fear is that an atmosphere is developing here similar to that in Bosnia and Herzegovina, due to the failure of positive multicultural existence. My personal belief is that separation is the solution. (p. 382)

Shakur puts out a call to "every thinking person with a stake in life—especially those involved in the fighting—" (p. 382) to make an effort to end the tragedy of gang culture. He argues that "[t]he children deserve to have a decent childhood where they live. They shouldn't have to be uprooted to the suburbs to experience peace. We cannot contaminate them with our feuds of madness, which are predicated on factors over which we have no control" (p. 383).

393. Shaw, Nate (1885-1973). *All God's Dangers: The Life of Nate Shaw*. Ed. Theodore Rosengarten. New York: Vintage, 1989. ISBN: 0394722450. 575 pages; map.
Originally published New York: Knopf, 1974. ISBN: 0394490843.

394. Shimonishi-Lamb, Mili (1913-). *And Then A Rainbow*. Santa Barbara: Fithian Press, 1990. ISBN: 0931832616. 178 pages; photographs.

Shimonishi-Lamb considered herself thoroughly American. Her husband, however, was a Kibei, born in the United States but educated in Japan. His father was still in Japan, and this kept his ties to that country strong. During World War II, while in the internment camp at Heart Mountain, Wyoming, with their four children, Shimonishi-Lamb's husband answered "no" to the two loyalty questions included on a mandatory questionnaire which was to be filled out by all Nisei and Issei in the camps. A "no" answer to these questions by the Nisei meant that they renounced their U.S. citizenship and, thus, faced deportation at war's end. To keep the family together, Shimonishi-Lamb gave the same answers as her husband although they did not reflect her true feelings. She and her family immigrated to Hiroshima Prefecture, her husband's home prefecture, six months after the dropping of the atomic bomb. They took up farming, an occupation foreign to both Shimonishi-Lamb and her husband. The work was difficult, and they had very little to eat, poor shelter, and no amenities. Shimonishi-Lamb was even more unhappy when her husband adopted a domineering attitude. She writes about her unhappiness, the family's difficulties, finally finding employment for herself off the farm, her ultimate success in regaining her U.S. citizenship, and, finally, her and her children's return to the United States without her husband.

395. Silko, Leslie Marmon (1948-). *Storyteller*. New York: Seaver Books, 1981. ISBN: 0394515897:0865790043. 278 pages; photographs.
Note: Also published New York: Arcade Publishing: Little, Brown and Co., 1981. ISBN: 155970005X.

This work combines Silko's memories of her childhood and family with Laguna legends and stories which were told to her by her great aunt, her grandmother, and others. This style, similar to that used by N. Scott Momaday in his autobiographical works, reflects the traditional oral method of passing history on from generation to generation and is a step away from Western-influenced autobiographical presentations.

396. Simon, Edwin (1898-1979). *Edwin Simon: Huslia*. Interviews conducted and text prepared by Yvonne Yarber and Curt Madison. Alaska Series. Blaine, Washington: Hancock House, 1981. ISBN: 0888390688. 120 pages; photographs; maps.
Note: Produced by Yukon-Koyukuk School District of Alaska.

Edwin Simon writes that he considers himself to have had three lives. From the time he was born in 1898 to about 1930 constitutes his first life: living without any generated power, more or less in the manner of his parents and grandparents; his second life took place between 1930 and 1960, during which time he had a gas-powered boat and oil lamps; and his third life began about 1960, during which time he has had the benefit of most modern conveniences. In this book,

Simon and his wife, Lydia Simon, tell many stories of seasonal activities, subsistence hunting, fishing, trapping, food preparation, family relationships, and traditional healing.
For a brief description and list of autobiographies in this Yukon-Koyukuk School District series, see the entry for Moses Henzie.

397. Smith, Ann Odene. *God's Step Chilluns: Poverty—Raw and Evil, Naked and Ugly.* Edwards, Mississippi: Harlo, 1981. ISBN: none. 171 pages.

398. Smith, Claude Clayton.
See *Piper, Aurelius* (1916).

399. Smith, Gloria Fuller. *Hill District Reniassance [sic] of Memories of African Americana in Pittsburgh, Pennsylvania.* Tucson, Arizona: Trailstones Industries, Inc., 1993. ISBN: none. 69 leaves; photographs; maps; bibliography.

Gloria Fuller Smith recalls the details of her old neighborhood, the 2800 block of Breckinridge Street, which was demolished to make a playing field for the University of Pittsburgh. She has created diagrams and maps of the area, and recalls each of her neighbors, her daily activities there, her friends, and schooling. Smith considers the history of the African American in Pennsylvania, and particularly in Pittsburgh.

400. Solomon, Madeline (1905-). *Madeline Solomon: Koyukuk.* Interviews conducted and text prepared by Curt Madison and Yvonne Yarber. Alaska Series. Blaine, Washington: Hancock House, 1981. ISBN: 0888390661. 97 pages; photographs; maps.
Note: Produced by Yukon-Koyukuk School District of Alaska.

Solomon, half Koyukon Athapascan and half Irish, tells about her childhood moving from camp to camp hunting, fishing and trapping. She gives a month-by-month description of the activities of her tribe, including April and May which were devoted to dancing.

Solomon describes the Athapascans' relationship to the Catholic mission, the emergence of wage jobs and the changes that resulted in the shift from subsistence living to the need to hold a wage job, and the threat to the language caused by historical restrictions on speaking it in school. Solomon now participates in a bilingual teaching program, teaching school children the Athapascan language.

For a brief description and list of autobiographies in this Yukon-Koyukuk School District series, see the entry for Moses Henzie.

401. Someth May (1958-). *Cambodian Witness: The Autobiography of Someth May*. Ed. James Fenton. New York: Random House, 1986. ISBN: 0394548043. 287 pages.

Someth May describes the relatively peaceful years of his childhood leading up to the invasion of the Viet Cong and the take over of Cambodia by the Khmer Rouge. He writes about the dissolution of his family after their evacuation, and their subsequent separation into different work camps. The surviving members of his family eventually found their way to a Thai refugee camp and were able to immigrate as a group to Washington, D.C. Some members of the family were killed by the Khmer Rouge; others died due to conditions in the work camps. Out of a family of 14, only four members survived to immigrate to the United States. Someth May provides a detailed account of his experiences in the work camps, the Vietnamese invasion of Cambodia and defeat of the Khmer Rouge, his family's entry into the United States, and the birth three days later of his sister's first child.

402. Soong, Irma Tam. *Chinese-American Refugee: A World War II Memoir*. Honolulu: Hawaii Chinese History Center, 1984. ISBN: none. 131 pages; photographs; maps.

The main body of Irma Tam Soong's memoir covers two years, beginning shortly after the birth of her first child, a son, in 1940. Soong, a native of Hawaii, was trapped in China during the Japanese occupation. She fled from Chunking, where her journalist husband was stationed, to Hong Kong, where she gave birth to her son, and then to her husband's ancestral village in Canton. Here, her differences as an American were most prominent; basically, Soong was not strong enough to contribute much to the family's day-to-day existence. She writes: "I stood on this Asian ground, the soil of my ancestors, at home and yet not at home, a human being much like the inhabitants in skin and eyes and hair, yet consciously Hawaiian-American in walk and talk and outlook . . ." (p. 3). Soong again joined her husband in Chunking and eventually left for the United States with her son in 1943. She describes the hardships and horrors of living in China and Hong Kong during the years of World War II and the Japanese occupation. She writes of her desire and efforts to stay with her husband who was constantly changing locations, often to the most dangerous areas, and of the eventual dissolution of their marriage.

403. Soto, Gary. *Lesser Evils: Ten Quartets*. Houston: Arte Publico Press, 1988. ISBN: 0934770778. 142 pages.

This collection of Soto's autobiographical essays explores childhood and boyhood rivalries, the father-daughter relationship, his career as a teacher, marriage, pets, his dreams and fears about women, sex, and aging. Soto's essays are generally humorous, although there is an underlying tone of pessimism.

404. —. *Living Up the Street: Narrative Recollections*. New York: Dell, 1985. ISBN: 0440211700. 167 pages.
Note: Also published San Francisco: Strawberry Hill Press, 1985. ISBN: 0894070649; reissued by Dell in 1992.

This collection is one of four autobiographical works published by Soto, Chicano poet and short-story writer. In the opening chapters, he portrays himself as a wild, undisciplined boy. As Soto describes his growing years, however, the stories become more painful, depicting his many disappointments: hours training his younger brother for a parks-and-recreation beauty pageant, only to have him lose to the starched, pressed, and curled competition; trying out for and failing to make the neighborhood Little League team; wished-for romances; a brief, unremarkable stint on the wrestling team; and finally, running away from home and his spirit-deadening employment in a tire factory. Other significant events in Soto's life include his burgling of the house of his friend's sister, and, after experiencing horrible guilt, returning everything, followed by his visit to Mexico, where he received a severe beating from local police who hated Americans.

405. —. *Small Faces*. Houston: Arte Publico Press, 1986. ISBN: 0934770492. 126 pages.
Note: Also published New York: Dell, 1993. ISBN: 0440215536.

In the first essay of this collection, Soto remembers the advice of his grandmother to become a barber and marry a Mexican woman. Although he asserts that he spent his youth searching and pining for the right Mexican woman, he fell in love with a Japanese American woman. Consumed with guilt, he reluctantly visited her parents, only to discover that "her people were like Mexicans only different" (p. 14). This collection of essays centers around his adult married life and his relationship with his wife and daughter, with some forays back into his childhood. Soto concludes with a pessimistic note as he expresses his fears for the future.

406. —. *A Summer Life*. Hanover, New Hampshire: University Press of New England, 1990. ISBN: 0874515238. 115 pages.
Note: Also published New York: Dell, 1991. ISBN: 0440210240.

In this collection of autobiographical essays, Soto focuses on his transformation from a young child with childish interests and pursuits, to a young man awkwardly crossing into adulthood. Soto looks back on his boyhood exploration of sin, the role of the confessional in his Catholic upbringing, and, as he grew older, the development of his feelings toward girls, his need to conform, and his fear of the future. Soto remembers both the humorous and terrifying moments of childhood—a returning warrior uncle who took care of Soto and his sister while readjusting to civilian life, and at the opposite pole, the baby-sitter, recently released from juvenile hall, who took them on a death-defying tour of the city in Soto's mother's car (without seat belts!).

407. Staples, Brent A. (1951-). *Parallel Time: Growing Up in Black and White*. New York: Pantheon Books, 1994. ISBN: 0679421548. 274 pages.
Note: Also published New York: Avon Books, 1995. ISBN: 0380724758.

Staple's story takes place within the framework of his visit to the coroner's office to review the details of his brother's murder three years after the fact. His brother, a drug dealer, had been gunned down by one of his clients, and, at the time, Staples could not bring himself to attend either the funeral or the trial. When Staples finally returned to his family home in Roanoke, Virginia, he went to the coroner's office to study his brother's file and attempt to come to some conclusions about the differences in his and his brother's life. Eventually, Staples began to examine his relationships with all of the different members of his family, his experiences in school, teachers who inspired or stultified him, his admission into college through a special program designed to assist "at risk" youth, his winning a prestigious fellowship to attend the University of Chicago where he earned his Ph.D., and finally his work as a teacher and journalist. As Staples grew older and moved away from his family, he found himself in predominantly white environments, and he contemplates the effect that this shift had on him. He describes only a few incidents in which he was overwhelmed by overt racism, although this is not to say that racism was not a constant element of his life. Relevant to Staples' attempt to reconcile the different directions taken by himself and his brother are the questions he was asked at job interviews which he calls "The Real Negro" questions. He interprets these questions as the interviewer's attempt to find out whether or not he was "authentic." Staples writes that "my inquisitor was asking me to explain my existence. Why was I successful, law-abiding, and literate, when others of my kind filled the jails and the morgues of the homeless shelters? A question that asks a lifetime of questions has no easy answer. The only honest answer is the life itself" (p. 259).

408. Stephenson, Genevieve Abel (1920-). *Just Genevieve: An Autobiography*. Baltimore: Gateway Press, 1992. ISBN: none. 59 pages.

409. Stewart, Irene (1907-). *A Voice in Her Tribe: A Navajo Woman's Own Story*. Interviews conducted by Mary Shepardson and Doris Ostrander Dawdy. Ballena Press Anthropological Papers 17. Socorro, New Mexico: Ballena Press, 1980. ISBN: 0879190884. 84 pages; photographs.

Mary Shepardson began working with Irene Stewart in 1955 and, in 1965, asked her to write her life story. Stewart wrote this book over an extended period of time in the form of letters, which have been arranged by the editor into short stories to create something like a narrative. The stories begin with a brief telling of the origins of Stewart's tribe, the Dine'e, which take the reader up to the time of her grandparents. The final chapter is Stewart's father's story of Changing Woman, which is the legend of the beginning of the Dine'e and the revelation of their religion. A striking element of Stewart's stories of her own life is the struggle she had moving back and forth between the white-influenced world of the schools she attended and her Navajo home and community.

410. *Stories of Survival: Conversations with Native North Americans*. Ed. Remmelt and Kathleen Hummelen. New York: Friendship Press, Inc., 1985. ISBN: 0377001503. 76 pages; illustrations; photographs.

This collection consists of 20 narratives by Native

Americans representing various tribes from the United States and Canada.

411. Storm, Hyemeyohsts. *Lightningbolt*. New York: Ballantine Books, 1994. ISBN: 0345367103. 534 pages; illustrations; photographs.

Storm continues to expand on the meaning and importance of medicine wheels in this sequel to *Seven Arrows* (New York: Harper & Row, 1972. ISBN: 0060141344:0345329015). He explains that the character of Lightning Bolt is himself. This book traces Lightning Bolt's life, emphasizing his student-teacher relationship with the medicine woman, Zero Chief, and flower soldier, Estcheemah. Intertwined with the story are Estcheemah's teachings, an explication of the different medicine wheels, and the history of the religious system out of which comes the tradition of Zero Chiefs and flower soldiers.

412. Strawberry, Darryl. *Darryl*. Written with Art Rust. New York: Bantam, 1992. ISBN: 0553075411:0553561383. 342 pages; photographs.

Strawberry writes about the emotional strain of meeting expectations in the major leagues, especially in New York. The combination of professional stress, his youth and inexperience going into the game, and family difficulties caused by his frequent absences led to Strawberry's alcoholism and lack of concentration. In this book, he talks about his problems with the Mets and his road to recovery with the Dodgers.

413. —. *Hard Learnin'*. Written with Don Gold. New York: Berkley Books, 1990. ISBN: 042512651X. 275 pages.

414. Strode, Woody. *Goal Dust: An Autobiography*. Written with Sam Young. Lanham, Maryland: Madison Books, 1990. ISBN: 081917680X. 262 pages; photographs.

Woody Strode was one of the first African American athletes to participate in college athletics at UCLA and, with fellow UCLA star Kenny Washington, to break the color barrier in professional football in 1946, when he was signed to the Los Angeles Rams. He writes that the players were not a problem, but the management who signed him was. After having been one of UCLA's top players, he was given little opportunity to play as a Ram, and was released after a year—possibly due to his employers' reaction to his marriage to a Hawaiian woman. He played several years in Canada before retiring and returning to the Los Angeles area to become a professional wrestler. Strode's wrestling career, a showcase for his exceptional physique, brought him to the attention of the film industry. He was given minor parts, playing African, Native American, and Chinese roles, and, his first high-paying role, the lion in *Androcles and the Lion*. Strode writes about his work in Hollywood, his transformation from a character actor into a star, his work and friendship with John Ford, and his experiences in Italian film.

415. Suleri, Sara. *Meatless Days*. Chicago: University of Chicago Press, 1989. ISBN: 0226779807. 186 pages; photographs.
Note: Reissued University of Chicago Press, 1991. ISBN: 0226779815.

Born to a Pakistani father and a Welsh mother, Sara Suleri grew up in London and Pakistan. As an adult, Sara moved to the United States, where she now teaches English and third world literature. Her story is made up of discrete essays in which she writes about her many brothers and sisters, her politically active father, her mother—a teacher, and her paternal grandmother.

416. Sun Bear (1929-). *Buffalo Hearts: A Native American's View of His Culture, Religion and History*. 8th ed. Spokane: Bear Tribe, 1991. ISBN: 0943404010. 124 pages; bibliography.
Originally published Healdsburg, California: Naturegraph, 1970. ISBN: 0911010866.

417. Sun Bear. *Sun Bear, the Path of Power*. As told to Wabun and to Barry Weinstock. Spokane: Bear Tribe, 1983. ISBN: 094340437. 267 pages; photographs.

Note: Also published New York: Simon & Schuster, 1992. ISBN: 0671765299; New York: Prentice Hall Press, 1988. ISBN: 0136534031.

Sun Bear spent much of his childhood on the White Earth Reservation in Minnesota. Of Chippewa/Ojibwa descent, he formed The Bear Tribe, an intertribal, interethnic group founded on the precepts of love and harmony devoted to closing the gaps between people caused by racism and misuse of technology. He describes growing up during the Great Depression, and his years in Los Angeles working as an actor. While in Los Angeles, Sun Bear first began his work with Native peoples. He organized services for Native Americans who came to the city at the urging of the federal government, which was trying to get them off reservations and into urban areas, and opened a sort of halfway house to help them get settled. He went on to do similar work with tribal people in the Reno-Sparks area in Nevada. Sun Bear explains his philosophical beliefs and practices, and the ceremonies he conducts as leader of the Bear Tribe. He gives specific attention to illustrating and describing the medicine wheel gatherings which he holds in various locations.

418. Sundance, Robert (1927-1993). *Sundance: The Robert Sundance Story.* Written with Marc Gaede. Ed. Marnie Walker Gaede. La Cañada, California: Chaco Press, 1994. ISBN: 0961601981:096160199X. 300 pages.

A chronic alcoholic living in Los Angeles, Sundance found himself spending more time in jail than out of it. When he learned that alcoholism was considered a disease, Sundance began to develop the legal argument that incarceration for public drunkenness is synonymous with incarcerating someone because he or she is ill. He was able to test his argument in court and found himself in battle with a huge, inert bureaucracy. "The Sundance Case focused national attention on the issues of alcoholism and alcohol-related problems, and revealed that the systems weren't doing their duty" (p. 275). This life story chronicles Sundance's exploits under the influence of alcohol leading up to his days on the streets and in the jails of Los Angeles and to his court case, which spurred criminal and public health reform in California.

419. Sutton, Joseph L. (1885-1980). *Praise the Bridge that Carries You Over: The Life of Joseph L. Sutton.* Interviews recorded and prepared by Shepard Krech. Boston: G. K. Hall, 1981. ISBN: 0816190380. 209 pages; photographs; bibliography.
Note: Also published Cambridge: Schenkman Publishing Co., 1981. ISBN: 0870736507.

Sutton was born and lived his life in Talbot County, Maryland, the birthplace of Frederick Douglass. Sutton's life spanned nearly a century, 1885-1980. He describes family life, the complex relationships with whites in neighboring towns, virulent racism, the move to desegregation in the 50's, and his struggle with poverty and illness. Appendices include historical notes on Talbot County.

420. Swan, Madonna (1928-). *Madonna Swan: A Lakota Woman's Story.* As told through Mark St. Pierre. Norman: University of Oklahoma Press, 1991. ISBN: 0806123699. 209 pages; photographs; maps; bibliography.

After spending a warm and sheltered childhood with a large family, Swan was sent to boarding school. Her experiences there were not made easier by her own deteriorating health and the deaths of many of her friends due to "quick consumption." When she herself was diagnosed with tuberculosis, she was sent to the Sioux Sanitorium, where she spent the next six years. Conditions were unsanitary, and no serious efforts were made to improve the health of the self-described inmates. Swan writes that there was no separation of the very sick from the recovering, thus allowing a constant cycle of reinfection. Those with any strength were required to care for the most seriously ill, including bathing, feeding, and changing of bed clothes. Swan escaped during her sixth year, and finally received a court order allowing her to enter the "white" sanitorium, where she received a much higher quality of care. However, it was another four years before she was able to leave this sanitorium after undergoing experimental surgery that required a lengthy recovery and rehabilitation.

421. Swann, Brian and Arnold Krupat, ed. *I Tell You Now: Autobiographical Essays by Native American Writers.* American Indian Lives. Lincoln: University of Nebraska Press, 1987. ISBN: 0803227140. 283 pages; bibliography.
Note: Reissued University of Nebraska Press, 1989. ISBN: 0803277571.

These essays were written by recognized Native American writers specifically for this anthology. General suggestions were given by the editors as to what might be included in the essay, such as memories of childhood, education, or the experiences of being a part of two cultures. Brief biographical information is given for each author. The anthology concludes with a list of small presses which publish the works of many of these writers, and a bibliographic essay with suggestions for further study of topics related to the collection.
The authors and essays included in this collection are the following:
Mary TallMountain, "You *Can* Go Home Again: A Sequence." TallMountain, Koyukon Athapascan, writes about becoming a writer and her struggle with alcoholism.
Ralph Salisbury, "The Quiet Between Lightning and Thunder." Salisbury, Cherokee, uses excerpts from his poetry and prose to illustrate what it is like to be a Native American writer.
Maurice Kenny, "Waiting at the Edge: Words Toward a Life." Kenny, Mohawk, compares his father's love of hunting to his own love for writing, calling himself a "hunter of words" (p. 40).
Elizabeth Cook-Lynn, "'You May Consider Speaking about Your Art. . . .'" Cook-Lynn, Crow-Creek-Sioux, explains her view of the poet's responsibility and what it is that she hopes to accomplish as a writer.

Carter Revard, "Walking Among the Stars." Revard writes about growing up on the Osage reservation in Oklahoma.

Jim Barnes, "On Native Ground." Barnes, Choctaw, writes about the natural and social changes that have occurred during his lifetime in eastern Oklahoma. He expresses a special concern for the preservation of Native languages.

Gerald Vizenor, "Crows Written on the Poplars: Autocritical Autobiographies." Vizenor, Minnesota Chippewa, explores the art of autobiography.

Jack D. Forbes, "Shouting Back to the Geese." Forbes, Powhatan-Delaware-Saponi, uses poetry and prose to describe his philosophy of life.

Duane Niatum, "Autobiographical Sketch." Niatum, Klallam, writes about what has influenced him as an individual and as a poet.

Paula Gunn Allen, "The Autobiography of a Confluence." Allen, Laguna Pueblo, writes about her eclectic heritage.

Jimmie Durham, "Those Dead Guys for a Hundred Years." Durham, Wolf Clan Cherokee, writes about his relatives, living and dead.

Diane Glancy, "Two Dresses." Glancy, Cherokee, writes about the awakening of her awareness of herself as Native American.

Simon J. Ortiz, "The Language We Know." Ortiz, Acoma Pueblo, writes about the importance of language.

Joseph Bruchac, "Notes of a Translator's Son." Bruchac, Abenaki, writes about his love for the Adirondack Mountains, where he was raised.

Barney Bush, "The Personal Statement of Barney Bush." Bush, Shawnee, writes about being a writer and an activist for Native American Rights.

Linda Hogan, "The Two Lives." Hogan, Chickasaw, writes about being poor in a land of privilege.

Wendy Rose, "Neon Scars." Rose, Hopi-Miwok, discusses writing and autobiography.

Joy Harjo, "Ordinary Spirit." Harjo, Creek, writes about being a poet.

422. Takekoshi, Takewo. *Reminiscences of My 60 Years in the United States*. Los Angeles: Takewo Takekoshi, 1990. ISBN: none. 223 pages; photographs; maps.

Takekoshi was born in the United States while his parents were traveling on business in Washington. After their business was concluded, however, they returned to Japan. This chance occurrence aided Takekoshi later when seeking United States citizenship. Raised in the northern area of the Japanese island of Hokkaido, Takekoshi decided to go to the United States to seek education and fortune. He came over on his own and had no one to meet him when he arrived. Takekoshi writes about his studies and teaching experience both in California and in New York. He became a valuable member of the Southern California Japanese business community because of his fluency in both English and Japanese. This fluency also worked in his favor during the mass relocation of West Coast ethnic Japanese. Many Issei were arrested on the day of the bombing of Pearl Harbor, but Takekoshi's relative youth, fluent English, and his American business habits apparently kept him from suffering the same fate. In fact, Takekoshi and his wife and children avoided internment altogether by moving to Denver. Takekoshi describes the war years, his military experience, and his adjustment to the post war world.

423. TallMountain, Mary (1918-). "You *Can* Go Home Again: A Sequence." *I Tell You Now: Autobiographical Essays by Native American Writers*. Ed. Brian Swann and Arnold Krupat. Lincoln: University of Nebraska Press, 1987. ISBN: 0803227140.

See entry under *Swann, Brian* for a complete list of authors included in this anthology.

424. Tanaka, Michiko Sato (pseud.) (1904-). *Through Harsh Winters: The Life of a Japanese Immigrant Woman*. As told to Akemi Kikumura. Novato, California: Chandler and Sharp, 1981. ISBN: 0883165449: 0883165430. 157 pages; photographs; bibliography.

This oral history was recorded and transcribed by Akemi Kikumura, Tanaka's daughter, over a five-year period. Tanaka came to the United States with her husband in 1923. He had already been to the United States, and she was curious to see what it was like. Unfortunately, Tanaka's husband was a compulsive gambler, and they were never able to hold onto enough money to return to Japan. Tanaka emphasizes the suffering that she endured throughout her life in the United States. She opens her story with this statement: "I didn't know you had to suffer before you could understand life. When I was a young girl in Japan, suffering was unknown to me" (p. 15). Tanaka had thirteen children, eight of whom were born before she was 31. She worked as a migrant farm worker, cook, laundress, and mother. The only times that she felt she had enough money to support her family were when her husband was in prison, when they were in the internment camps of World War II, and finally, when her husband died. Tanaka became a U.S. citizen in 1980, 57 years after coming to the United States. When asked by her daughter why she decided to become a citizen, Tanaka tells her:

> I have to protect myself. . . . America will be facing hard times. They won't be helping foreigners. I've been here since 1923—57 years! I have 11 children . . . 22 grandchildren. All American citizens! I should be entitled to citizenship, but I'm still considered a foreigner. (p. 108)

425. Tanimoto, Charles Katsumu. *Return to Mahaulepu: Personal Sketches*. Honolulu: C. K. Tanimoto, 1982. ISBN: none. 180 pages; photographs; maps.

Tanimoto explains that being a Nisei means looking Japanese and being raised Japanese by Japanese parents. The conflict arises, then, when the Nisei, adapting to their new culture, do not meet with the expectations of their parents. Tanimoto faced this dilemma when he chose to attend school rather than to follow the wishes of his parents and stay at home to help with the farm. His family had moved to a one-acre farm which they cultivated intensely to produce food to sell and to feed the family. Originally they were plantation workers, and Tanimoto provides a colorful description of life on the plantations, the variety of cultures represented, and how the various groups adopted each others' cultures, especially food and celebratory traditions. Tanimoto briefly describes the internment of Japanese Americans after the bombing of Pearl Harbor, and in retrospect is quite bitter over the emotional burden brought upon himself and others. He writes: "When war broke out, why did I burn or destroy books, pictures, and artifacts simply because they carried memories of the old country? Why did I have to go through physical pain and frequent humiliation to prove my loyalty to my country. . . ?" (p. 136).

426. Tarry, Ellen. *The Third Door: The Autobiography of an American Negro Woman*. The Library of Alabama Classics. Tuscaloosa: University of Alabama Press, 1992. ISBN: 0817305793. 319 pages.
Originally published New York: D. McKay Co., 1955.

427. Taulbert, Clifton L. *The Last Train North*. Tulsa, Oklahoma: Council Oaks Books, 1992. ISBN: 0933031629. 205 pages; photographs.
Note: Also published New York: Penguin, 1995. ISBN: 0140244786.

Taulbert writes about his youthful dream of traveling north in style: namely, as a passenger on the train. Taulbert took one of the last trains to St. Louis before passenger service was discontinued at his local stop in Greenville, Mississippi. Upon his arrival in St. Louis, Taulbert found that the reality of the material and social conditions for African Americans in the north was vastly different from his dream of equality, freedom, and economic plenty. Housing and employment possibilities were scarce for Taulbert despite the lack of official Jim Crow. Taulbert arrived in St. Louis in the early 1960s just as the war in Vietnam was escalating, and social unrest related to racial tensions and the war was fomenting. To avoid being drafted, he enlisted in the Air Force. Taulbert describes his time in the military, which provided him with his first experience with integration.

428. —. *Once Upon a Time When We Were Colored*. Tulsa, Oklahoma: Council Oak Books, 1989.   ISBN: 093303119X. 153 pages; photographs.
Note: Also published as *When We Were Colored*. New York: Penguin, 1995. ISBN: 0140244778.

Although Taulbert is descended from black landowners, his family's land was lost, and this story is about the "mostly landless people, the coloreds, who lived in Glen Allan and other small southern towns during the last years of segregation" (p. 6). Taulbert writes that for him the everyday joys and sorrows of childhood were enough to shield him from awareness of segregation and its implications. As he grew older, however, reality was harder and harder to ignore or accept. He began high school in 1959, five years after the *Brown v. Topeka Board of Education* decision, but segregation was still the law in his community. Taulbert commuted over 100 miles a day in order to attend a black high school even though the all-white high school was just blocks from his house. He went north to attend college, but even there he ran into difficulty with the limited employment opportunities open to African Americans, and it took him eight years to graduate, working all day and attending classes at night. Taulbert also describes his community, and daily activities. Politics were considered "white folks' business," and were not discussed, at least within the hearing of children. But Taulbert has a vivid memory of a large church meeting which was held to send off a representative from the community to an NAACP national meeting in Baltimore. Taulbert emphasizes the security provided to children and all members of the community by the closeness and sense of shared responsibility in the African American communities of the rural South.

429. Taylor, Prince Albert (1907-). *The Life of My Years*. Nashville: Abingdon, 1983. ISBN: 0687218543. 152 pages; photographs; bibliography.

In relating the recent history of the Methodist Episcopal Church and the issues of race which it reacted and responded to over the years, Taylor presents his own contributions and experiences within the institution, and the circumstances which led to his ordination, election to the position of Bishop, and work in Liberia. The Methodist Episcopal Church had a strong mission program at home and abroad, and Taylor discusses its successes and failures in pursuing this mission specifically in Liberia, and among African Americans in the United States. Taylor concludes his work with a summary of the progress made by both African Americans and women within the existing United Methodist Church. (The Methodist Episcopal Church is a distinct organization from the African Methodist Episcopal Church, and one of many Methodist church bodies which through various mergers became part of the United Methodist Church in 1968.)

430. Te Ata. *As I Remember It.* Written with Jane Werner Watson. Ranchos de Taos, New Mexico: Assembled by D. A. Bennett, 1989. ISBN: none. 205 leaves; photographs.

Te Ata was born in Oklahoma, a member of the Chickasaw Nation and a descendant of both the Choctaw and Chickasaw tribes. She stopped using her "school name" and began using only her tribal name, Te Ata, after joining a touring Chautauqua tent show as one of three Native American girls of different tribes who would present their traditional culture. Te Ata describes her experiences on the Chautauqua circuit and her progression to world-wide tours as a solo performer.

431. Teamoh, George (1818-1883?). *God Made Man, Man Made the Slave: The Autobiography of George Teamoh.* Ed. Nash Boney, Rafia Zafar and Richard L. Hume. Macon: Mercer, 1990. ISBN: 0865543682. 219 pages; illustrations; photographs; bibliography.
Note: Historical and critical commentary provided by the editors.

This autobiography was written as the era of Reconstruction came to an end. In it, Teamoh looks back on

his years as a slave, the period of his life after he escaped to the North, and then, finally, after Emancipation, returning to Virginia and taking part in radical
politics during a time when there was hope that conditions would improve for newly freed African Americans. As a slave, Teamoh believed his mistress to be a
generous and good person. He had a certain amount
of freedom of movement and was able to teach himself reading, writing, and arithmetic in secret (he
writes that the master of the slave was deemed as
guilty as the slave under the law which forbade slaves
to learn to read and write). Teamoh was married, but
his wife and three children belonged to another family, who sold them. The two oldest children were
taken and sold separately. The wife and youngest child
were sold together. Teamoh describes the heartbreak
of this separation, and his attempts to provide his wife
some comfort. "I now leave S[ally] at Fortress Monroe
where, on the most trifling pretense she is clubbed to
the earth by her young Master, then only about thirteen years of age. His father, however, chastised him
for thus maiming a valuable piece of 'property'" (p.
91). Virginia law made it difficult for owners to man-
umit their slaves, and Teamoh believes that his mistress made it clear that she intended to aid him in es-
caping to the North when she hired him out to a ship
which was bound for Germany and that would dock in
New York before returning to Virginia. Teamoh did
go back to Virginia toward the end of the Civil War to
attempt to locate his wife and to visit his former
mistress. After Emancipation, he was elected to several terms as a State Senator. He writes in detail about
his political activities and other activists, and of his argument with organized religion and its practice of segregation and generally inhumane treatment of African
Americans, particularly in the South.

432. Terry, Wallace, ed. *Bloods, an Oral History of the Vietnam War*. New York: Random House, 1984. ISBN:
0394530284. 311 pages; photographs; glossary.

Note: Also published with title *Bloods, An Oral History of the Vietnam War By Black Veterans*. New York: Ballantine Books, 1992. ISBN: 0345376668.

Terry describes the term "Bloods" which he uses to identify his subjects in this collection of oral histories.

> [M]any [were] just steps removed from marching in the Civil Rights Movement or rioting in the rebellions that swept the urban ghettos from Harlem to Watts. All were filled with a sense of black pride and purpose. They spoke loudest against the discrimination they encountered on the battlefield. . . . They chose not to overlook the racial insults . . . of their white com-rades. . . . They called for unity among black brothers on the battlefield. . . . (p. xvi)

Terry collected these oral histories to provide historical documentation of the African American presence in Vietnam. The 20 individuals represent a cross section of military branches and positions, and economic and social backgrounds. These veterans write about how they came to be in the military, their experiences in training and in Vietnam, their reactions to what was required and expected of them there, how their experience may have been determined by their race, and their homecoming, whether as a civilian or in an extended career with the military. They describe how, if necessary, they've reconciled their actions in Vietnam with their personal values and sense of morality. The absolute horror of war is made all too clear through these narratives.

433. Thomas, Piri (1928-). *Down These Mean Streets*. New York: Vintage Books, 1991. ISBN: 0679732381. 334 pages.
Originally published New York: Knopf, 1967.

434. Thompson, Era Bell (1907-). *American Daughter*. St. Paul: Minnesota Historical Society Press, 1986. ISBN: 0873512014. 296 pages.
Originally published Chicago: University of Chicago Press, 1946; Chicago: Follet Publishing, 1967; Chicago: University of Chicago Press, 1974.

435. Thompson, Gerald (1956-). *Reflections of an Oreo-Cookie: Growing Up Black in the 1960's*. Monroe, New York:

Library Research Associates, Inc., 1991.   ISBN:
091252653X. 125 pages.

As his father lies dying from cancer, Thompson looks
back on his life, and the work of his mother and father
raising and sustaining the family. He emphasizes that
he was raised by two loving and caring parents, that
neither he nor his siblings were involved in crime or
drugs, and that none of his parents' many siblings
were divorced or involved in any type of criminal
activity. This, however, did not mean that he and the
members of his family were not subject to judgments
based on negative stereotypes. When they moved into
a predominantly white area, the neighbors assumed
that Thompsons' father was the gardener, and the
police stopped by to see what they were doing in the
neighborhood. As the neighbors realized that the
Thompsons were indeed neighbors and not the hired
help, the family became the victims of vandalism,
threatening phone calls, and other abuse. School was
also difficult for Thompson. After adjusting to a
predominantly white elementary school, he began
attending a racially mixed high school and found
himself unacceptable to both the white and black
students. He writes that he tried to walk a middle line,
but that this was not a solution for him. In writing
this book, Thompson is attempting to free himself of
the bitterness that he developed after years of being
pre-judged, discriminated against, and verbally and
physically abused.

436. Tiulana, Paul (1921-). *A Place for Winter: Paul Tiulana's
Story*. Written with Vivian Senungetuk. Anchorage:
CIRI Foundation, 1987. ISBN: 0938227025. 125 pages;
photographs.

Tiulana, considered to be a representative of his people, has played a major role in assisting his own people
and other Alaska Natives with adjustment to urban
life. Tiulana narrates this story with a strong sense of
regret for the loss of native culture and ways of life.
He provides the reader with a description of what life
was like before the American government stepped in

and a glimpse of what life is like now that everything has changed. Tiulana tells the reader, "I do not know what the government is trying to do for Native people. A lot of times, I just reject the idea of the BIA [Bureau of Indian Affairs]" (p. 39). And he concludes his work with these words:

> When the government first came into the villages, Native people did not have any lawyers, state troopers, policemen, jails or correctional centers. The government started to influence us, telling us we required these agencies which were not required before, because we had our own system. I did not see any child abuse in our village when I was young. We did not have any alcohol or drug problems when I was young. We did not have divorces. We could integrate both systems if the government sat down with us and made plans to educate our children the modern way and the village way, to satisfy both sides. . . . We can teach them the Eskimo ways because they are the best ways for our people. And we can make a contribution to modern American society. (p. 42)

437. Tobuk, Frank. *Frank Tobuk, Evansville.* Interviews conducted and text prepared by Curt Madison and Yvonne Yarber. Alaska Series. British Columbia: Hancock House, 1980. ISBN: 0888390645. 64 pages; photographs; maps.

Tobuk describes the traditional Eskimo ways and the changes that have occurred since contact with Europeans. He recounts stories told to him by his grandmother about the very first white men to arrive. He also recalls the lost tradition of the medicine men and women. He writes: "I don't know if it would do young people much good to learn all of the Eskimo ways. They should know a little bit about the old ways of living. Like hunting. . . . Young Native people might need to know some of this to help them in the future" (p. 62).

For a brief description and list of autobiographies in this Yukon-Koyukuk School District series, see the entry for Moses Henzie.

438. Torrence, Jackie. *The Importance of Pot Liquor.* Little Rock, Arkansas: August House Publishers, Inc., 1994. ISBN: 0874833388. 135 pages; photographs; map.

Jackie Torrence writes about growing up in North
Carolina with her grandmother and grandfather.
Through her own story, she provides a background
for the Uncle Remus stories she grew up with and for
which she has become well known. Each of the three
autobiographical chapters is followed by a selection of
the stories as they were told to her when she was a
child.

439. Trask, Haunani-Kay. *From a Native Daughter: Colonialism and Sovereignty in Hawai'i.* Monroe, Maine:
Common Courage Press, 1993. ISBN: 1567510094:
1567510086. 301 pages; photographs; illustrations.

These essays are, as the subtitle suggests, political in
nature. Several, however, deal with specific events in
Trask's life, her personal responses to U.S. colonialism
in Hawaii, and the white historian's interpretation of
Hawaii. Trask notes that there is only one history of
the islands written by a native Hawaiian, Lilikala
Kame'eleihiwa, *Native Land and Foreign Desires.*
Honolulu: Bishop Museum Press, 1992. The essays
which have significant autobiographical content are
the following: "From a Native Daughter"; "What Do
You Mean 'We,' White Man?"; "Racism Against
Native Hawaiians at the University of Hawaii"; and
"The Politics of Academic Freedom as the Politics of
White Racism."

440. Travis, Dempsey J. (1920-). *An Autobiography of Black
Chicago.* Chicago: Urban Research Institute, 1981.
ISBN: 0941484009. 378 pages; photographs; bibliogra-
phy.

Travis writes about his own life within the context of
the history of his family and the history of African
Americans in Chicago from about 1840. With the aid
of census statistics and interviews, Travis discusses the
conditions of African Americans in Chicago from a
time when there were just a few black families,
through the growth of the population as African
Americans migrated from the South. He traces the
evolution of legislation which first restricted the rights

and opportunities of the black citizens, and then the slow changes that took place between the repeal of the Illinois "Black Laws" in 1865 and open-housing legislation in the 1960s and 1970s. Travis focuses on the issue of property for African Americans, a natural interest stemming from his work in real estate and banking. He concludes his book with sixteen brief narratives by prominent African American men and women of Chicago, providing their personal perspective of the city.

441. Travis, Dempsey J. (1920-). *I Refuse to Learn to Fail: The Autobiography of Dempsey J. Travis.* Chicago: Urban Research Press, 1992. ISBN: 0941484122. 198 pages; photographs; illustrations; bibliography.

Travis, at the age of 6, announced to his parents that he planned to be wealthy, and he began, with limited success, his entrepreneurial career that same year. This autobiography is about Travis's determination to succeed despite the many barriers he faced as an African American. His first occupation out of school was as a jazz pianist. This lasted until he was drafted into the army during World War II. He was transferred to Camp Shenango, where Jim Crow was the rule and conditions for African American soldiers were far below acceptable standards. Upon his discharge, Travis was still determined to make it in the business world, but found himself undereducated and under skilled. He decided to attend Roosevelt College, a rare institution in the largely-segregated Chicago of the 1940s.

> In 1948, the spirit of brotherhood that permeated [Roosevelt] University was unlike anything I had experienced. Every morning when I stepped inside the university I was enveloped with a feeling of hope for Black Americans. But, each afternoon when I stepped outside onto Michigan Avenue, I was jarred back to the realization that Roosevelt University did not mirror the real world. (p. 108)

Travis began his real estate career after graduating from Roosevelt. He describes conditions for African Americans looking for housing and loans throughout the 1950s and 60s and into the 70s. He relates his own role in bettering conditions in Chicago in particular, but also nationally. He was part of the National Association of Real Estate Brokers (NAREB), a black real estate organization of "realtists," so called to distinguish themselves from "realtors" who were members of a comparable national organization which at that time did not admit African Americans into their membership. He served as president of the Dearborn Real Estate Board, and had personal contact, either through appointment to committees or as a spokesperson on housing issues, with every President from Kennedy to Reagan. Travis emphasizes his belief that potential African American role models should stay visible in traditionally African American communities.

442. Travis, Nancy (1962-). *Me and Rosemary, Revolutionary Teens: A Memoir of Third World Girls.* N.p.: N. Travis, 1986. ISBN: none. 29 pages.

443. Tsuchida, John Nobuya, ed. *Reflections: Memoirs of Japanese American Women in Minnesota.* Covina, California: Pacific Asia Press: Distributed by Multicultural Distributing Center, 1994. ISBN: 1879600226. 434 pages; illustrations; photographs; bibliography.

These narratives are written by fourteen women who were evacuated from the West Coast. Some chose to relocate to Minnesota immediately (and by doing so, bypassed the internment camps altogether), others were released to attend college there, and chose to stay after finishing their studies. The women give some family history, and describe their experiences after Pearl Harbor and their subsequent lives in Minnesota.

444. Tsukamoto, Mary. *We the People: A Story of Internment in America.* Written with Elizabeth Pinkerton. Elk Grove, California: Laguna Publishers, 1987. ISBN: 0944665411:094466542X. 295 pages; photographs; bibliography.

Tsukamoto writes of growing up with racism that intensified as the Japanese community in Florin, California, grew and prospered. This racism, which was

encouraged by the yellow journalism of the mainstream press, set the stage for the war-time hysteria
that resulted first in curfews and restricted travel, and
ended with mass evacuation and internment in ten
camps scattered throughout the interior of the United
States. Tsukamoto describes the days leading up to relocation, the Japanese traditions that were partly responsible for the lack of protest within the community, and her camp life and the years following her
family's release from the camp. Tsukamoto discusses
the emotional toll the humiliation of discrimination,
segregation, and incarceration had on the Japanese
community. Her own sister committed suicide shortly
after the war's end. Tsukamoto documents how the
Japanese American community recovered both spiritually and economically from the many losses they
suffered during the war.

445. Tubbee, Okah (b. 1810 or 11-). *The Life of Okah Tubbee.*
Written with Daniel F. Littlefield. Lincoln: University
of Nebraska Press, 1988. ISBN: 0803228708. 159 pages;
bibliography.

Okah Tubbee, originally named Warner McCary, was a
slave in Natchez, Mississippi. His mother and brothers were given their freedom at the death of their master, but Tubbee, who may have had a different parentage from his brothers, was willed to his "family" and
he remained enslaved. He escaped this miserable situation by becoming an itinerant musician and doctor
and creating an identity for himself as the long-lost
son of a Choctaw Indian Chief. This autobiography
was originally published to promote Tubbee's musi-
cal/healing tours, and to establish his Native American identity. Tubbee's narrative paints a picture of the
conditions for both blacks and native peoples in the
Old South during the Nineteenth Century. He also
describes his travels performing on musical instru-
ments of his own design and working as a medical
man.

446. Turki, Fawaz (1940-). *Exile's Return: The Making of a Palestinian American*. New York: The Free Press, 1994. ISBN: 0029327253. 274 pages.
Note: Turki's previous autobiographical work is entitled *The Disinherited: Journal of a Palestinian Exile. With an Epilogue 1974*. New York: Monthly Review Press, 1974. 2nd ed. (1st edition, 1972). ISBN: 0853452482.

As the title of this book suggests, Turki writes of the emotional implications of living as an exile, an individual without a home. He explores his changing feelings toward his identity as a Palestinian, his changing view of, and fluctuating involvement in the Palestine Liberation Organization (PLO), and the significance of the peace agreement between Israel and the PLO to the 4,000,000 exiled Palestinians living around the world. Turki provides glimpses into his childhood in the area now called Palestine before the mass exodus of refugees in 1948, his travels throughout the world, his writing and political career, and the feelings of futility and anomie which resulted in his long bout with alcohol and cocaine abuse.

447. Turner, B. Alfred (1908-). *From a Plow to a Doctorate, So What?* Houston: B. A. Turner: Wheeler Avenue Baptist Church, 1985. ISBN: none. 116 pages.
Originally published Hampton, Virginia: B. A. Turner, Burke and Gregory, 1945.

448. Twofeathers, Manny. *My Road to the Sundance [sic]*. Phoenix: Wo-Pila Publishing, 1994. ISBN: 1886340048. 204 pages; photographs.

Twofeathers, born in Arizona and of Aztec descent, describes his work as a craftsmen and itinerant merchant of traditional Native American objects. While traveling in Utah to attend a Native American festival, he observed a Shoshone Sun Dance. Overwhelmed with a sense of energy and spirituality, Twofeathers later experienced a vision which haunted him until he was able to become a participant in this sacred event. In this book, Twofeathers describes his participation in both the Shoshone Sun Dances in Utah, and in the Lakota Sun Dances held in South Dakota. He explains the significance of his commitment to take part in the ritual and its impact on his life.

449. Uchida, Yoshiko. *Desert Exile: The Uprooting of a Japanese Family.* Seattle: University of Washington Press, 1982. ISBN: 0295958987. 154 pages; photographs. Note: Reissued University of Washington Press, 1989. ISBN: 0295961902.

Uchida begins her story with a detailed description of her family and life in Berkeley, California, during her childhood and youth. Her parents were Issei, born and educated in Japan. Uchida and her sister were anxious to blend in with their predominantly white neighborhood, but found as they grew older that they were more comfortable and secure with Japanese friends. Uchida's experience at the University of California at Berkeley was one of almost complete social segregation. The family, however, did have close white friends, including the neighbors on either side of them, and these friends continued to offer support and affection while the Uchidas were incarcerated by the U.S. government during World War II. The first half of the book, focusing on family and daily life, contrasts dramatically with the description of life after the bombing of Pearl Harbor. Changes for the family were immediate. In less than 24 hours, Uchida's father was arrested and imprisoned; Japanese Americans were confronted with hatred and violence; rumors were enlarged and spread by the media; and soon all Japanese Americans in California were evacuated and incarcerated. Uchida writes that she tells her story "for the young Japanese Americans who seek a sense of continuity with their past," and "for all Americans, with the hope that through knowledge of the past, they will never allow another group of people in America to be sent into a desert exile ever again" (p. 154).

450. Uchida, Yoshiko (1921-1992). *The Invisible Thread.* Needham, Massachusetts: Silver Burdett Gin, 1987. ISBN: 0663585651. 136 pages; photographs.

Note: Also Published Englewood Cliffs, New Jersey: J. Messner, 1991. In My Own Words. ISBN: 0671741632: 0671741640.

This is Uchida's young-reader version of her life in Berkeley, California, and her experiences with her family in the internment camps of World War II. See annotation for *Desert Exile*, above.

451. Valencia, Heather.   *Queen of Dreams: The Story of a Yaqui Dreaming Woman*.   With Rolly Kent.   New York: Simon & Schuster, 1991.   ISBN: 0671694472.   271 pages.
Note: Also published New York: Fireside Books/ Simon & Schuster, 1993. ISBN: 0671797239.

Part Cherokee on her father's side, a fact denied by the rest of her family, Valencia describes a childhood of sexual abuse and then an adulthood of troubled relationships with men.   She provides examples of her psychic powers and the prophetic dreams which she has experienced since early childhood.   She is led by her dreams to a Yaqui reservation in Arizona, where she becomes the lover and student of the Yaqui spiritual leader.

452. Vega, Bernardo (1885-).   *Memoirs of Bernardo Vega: A Contribution to the History of the Puerto Rican Community in New York*.   Ed. César Andreu Iglesia. Translated by Juan Flores.   New York: Monthly Review Press, 1984.   ISBN: 0853456550:0853456569.   243 pages; photographs.
Note: Originally published in Spanish as *Memorias de Bernardo Vega*. Ediciones Hurácan, 1977.

Vega arrived in New York from colonized Puerto Rico on the eve of World War I, a committed Socialist.   He described himself as a white peasant from the highlands and a cigar-roller by profession.   Many of the Cubans and Puerto Ricans coming to New York were tabaqueros looking for work in cigar factories.   However, work was hard to find, and Vega started working in the burgeoning munitions industry.   Later in life he operated his own small cigar factory.   As the title suggests, Vega's book tells not only his own story, but the history of his family, and of the Puerto Rican community in New York. He recounts their role in the Antillean Revolution against Spain in the late 19th century, and their ongoing activism in the cause of Puerto Rican citizenship and sovereignty. Vega was, himself, a leader in the fight against Puerto Rico's colonial status. He was also active in the Socialist Party, supporting the cause of Republican Spain during the Spanish Civil War, supporting local Socialist candidates, fighting for labor rights, and against the media war waged against the Puerto Rican community in the United States.

453. Vera Cruz, Philip. *Philip Vera Cruz: A Personal History of Filipino Immigrants and the Farmworkers [sic] Movement.* Ed. Glenn Omatsu and Augusto Espiritu. Los Angeles: UCLA Labor Center, Institute of Industrial Relations and UCLA Asian American Studies Center, 1992. ISBN: 0934052166. 155 pages; photographs; bibliography.

Philip Vera Cruz left for the United States in 1926 intending to study, raise money, and return to the Philippines in a few years. He returned 60 years later. Although his American teachers in the Philippines had taught him about the opportunities in the United States, Vera Cruz found that these were not available to him as a Filipino and a member of a racial minority. Unable to complete school because of the difficulty of earning enough money for himself and his family in the Philippines, Vera Cruz eventually worked his way to California and the grape fields: "My life here was always just a matter of survival. It was always an emergency and I was never ready to go back. That's the way it has been for most of us Filipino old-timers" (p. 24). His story documents the little-known role of the Filipino workers in the development and success of the United Farm Workers Union (UFW). Vera Cruz served as Second Vice-President on the UFW board for 12 years. He resigned that position because of his disagreements with the way the union was operated. Vera Cruz's story provides a new dimension to the history of the UFW and to the history of the Filipinos in the United States. This work includes a bibliography of books on Filipino immigrant labor history prepared by Augusto Espiritu.

454. Verghese, Abraham. *My Own Country: A Doctor's Story of a Town and Its People in the Age of AIDS.* New York: Simon & Schuster, 1994. ISBN: 0671785141. 347 pages.
Note: Also published New York: Vintage Books, 1995. ISBN: 0679752927.

Verghese was born in Ethiopia to parents from Kerala, India. He received his medical education in India and his residency in internal medicine through East Tennessee State University. Verghese specialized in infectious diseases at Boston City University, where, in 1983, he worked with his first AIDS patient. This experience was prior to the discovery of HIV or standard methods of diagnosis. By the time he had completed his training in Boston and decided to return to East Tennessee, the HIV connection with AIDS had been discovered. Verghese writes about the steady growth of AIDS cases during his five years in East Tennessee, and his coinciding educational efforts in the gay community. He tells the stories of some of his patients, his own professional and emotional involvement with them, and the effect of his work on his family. In 1989, Verghese left behind 80 patients at East Tennessee to be part of an outpatient AIDS clinic at the University of Iowa Hospitals.

455. Villa, Louis Arthur (1932-). *The Sexuality of a Black American: One Man's Sexual Biography.* Oakland, California: Ashford Press Publication, 1981. ISBN: 0931290538. 220 pages; photographs.

Villa, after describing his childhood and school age years, goes on to discuss his attraction to white women and to sex in general. He writes:

> If you're wondering just what I've gained by this activity besides a busy sex life, the best answer I can give is I have achieved a knowledge and developed a confidence that I can use in a white controlled society, knowing that this majority

is not to be awed or feared and its vulnerability is fully exposed. (Introduction)

456. Villar Ruiz, David. *A Soul in Exile: A Chicano Lost in Occupied Land.* New York: Vantage Press, 1981. ISBN: 053304720X. 83 pages.

Villar Ruiz took part in La Marcha de la Reconquista, a series of marches and demonstrations in California that began May 27, 1971, in Calexico and continued until August 13, 1971, in Sacramento. These demonstrations, sponsored by the Brown Berets and the National Chicano Moratorium, were held to protest police brutality and overrepresentation of Chicanos and African Americans in the prisons and on the Vietnam War casualty lists. Villar Ruiz had returned from active duty in Vietnam the year before and begun undergraduate studies when he became involved with MECHA (Movimento Estudiani Chicano Aztlán). He provides some insight into the reality of violence as a way of life for many Chicano youth because of the ongoing barrio rivalries and the never-ending chain of defense and revenge. Villar Ruiz gives numerous examples of deaths caused by overzealous policemen, problems of discrimination in the schools and in the job market, and the limited opportunities that lead to alcohol and drug abuse as a panacea. Taking part in the nearly three-month-long march from Calexico on the U.S./Mexican border to the state capitol in Sacramento gave Villar Ruiz time to contemplate Chicano people from his past and present, as well as those he met through chance encounter during the march; his own place within the Chicano culture and the larger "European-American" culture in the U.S.; his motivation for marching and the sense of confidence that participation in the movement afforded him; and what the future holds for him and for all Chicanos.

457. Villasénor, Victor. *Walking Stars: Stories of Magic and Power.* Houston: Piñata Books, 1994. ISBN: 1558851186. 202 pages.

These stories about Villasénor's childhood from his family's past are about overcoming odds, and miraculous and unexplainable occurrences. Villasénor wants to show that there is a "magic power" in life that is waiting below the surface to come out when you most need it. He tells his sons that these stories are not just stories of fantasy, but of "great-awful pain and heart-break, confusion and self-hate and doubt" (p. 10-11) and what it takes to get beyond those pains. Some of these stories are included in Villasénor's historical work about his mother and father and their families: *Rain of Gold*. Houston: Arte Publico Press, 1991. ISBN: 1558850309.

458. Villegas de Magnon, Leonor. *The Rebel*. Ed. Clara Lomas. Houston: Arte Publico Press, 1994. ISBN: 1558850562. 297 pages; photographs; bibliographies; glossary; index of names.

In *Rebel*, Villegas de Magnon covers the events of her life, and the changes which took place in Mexico from her birth in 1876 to the death of Venustiano Carranza in 1920. She was born in Mexico and educated in Texas and New York. She subsequently taught elementary school in the border area of Texas, and it was during this time that she began her participation in the Mexi-can Revolution, which is the focus of her narrative (the title, "Rebel," refers to herself). One of Villegas de Magnon's accomplishments was the establishment of La Cruz Blanca, a medical organization that served the forces of Carranza. She also tells about the largely un-sung heroines who worked with her in the Revolu-tion, many of whom were writers active in alternative newspapers and journals published north of the U.S. border with Mexico.

459. Viloria, Jose B. (1942-). *The Rugged Terrain: A True Story of Life Survival*. San Dimas, California: SGV Publish-ers, 1994. ISBN: none. 485 pages; photographs.

In this rags to riches story, Viloria takes the reader from his birth in a besieged village in the Philippines in 1942, through his sickly childhood and youth, medi-cal studies pursued at the insistence of his father, and then medical practice in the United States. His progression to success was not without detours, however. He had to redo some of his medical education to be licensed in California, ran into various legal problems with partners in two different hospital operations, raised a daughter who, born prematurely, suffered from several physical and psychological problems, and saw both himself and his wife through serious illnesses. He describes all of the challenges and rewards of his life in this autobiography. Professionally, Viloria is a practicing internist, health care management executive, president and CEO of ten different corporations which together are called the SGV Group of Companies, the publisher of, and writer for *The Los Angeles Free Press* (a Filipino American newspaper), and the chairman of various charitable organizations.

460. Vizenor, Gerald (1934-). "Crows Written on the Poplars: Autocritical Autobiographies." *I Tell You Now: Autobiographical Essays by Native American Writers.* Ed. Brian Swann and Arnold Krupat. Lincoln: University of Nebraska Press, 1987. ISBN: 0803227140.

See entry under *Swann, Brian* for a complete list of authors included in this anthology. This essay is also included in Krupat's *Native American Autobiography*. Madison: University of Wisconsin Press, 1994 (see separate entry).

461. Vizenor, Gerald Robert (1934-). *Interior Landscapes: Autobiographical Myths and Metaphors.* Minneapolis: University of Minnesota Press, 1990. ISBN: 0816618488. 279 pages; photographs.

In this highly imagistic work, Vizenor describes his childhood growing up in a series of foster homes and with his unstable mother in Minnesota. His father, a Chippewa Indian from the White Earth Reservation, was murdered at the age of 26. After two years in the National Guard (beginning at age 16), Vizenor joined the army and traveled to Japan, where he was part of the occupational forces during the early fifties. He was heavily influenced by Japanese culture, and began writing haiku. Vizenor's first published book was a collection of haiku. After his return to the United States and the completion of his formal studies, Vizenor worked as a journalist and a university professor. He describes his experiences in these professions, and how his work in both fields has affected his understanding of his Native American heritage and his absorption of Japanese culture.

462. Wade-Gayles, Gloria Jean. *Pushed Back to Strength: A Black Woman's Journey Home*. Boston: Beacon Press, 1993. ISBN: 0807009229. 276 pages; photographs.
Note: Also published New York: Avon Books, 1995. ISBN: 038072426X.

Wade-Gayles, a professor at Spelman College, counters accepted stereotypes of "life in the projects" by describing her own happy and secure childhood growing up in a carefully-maintained housing project in the Jim Crow-era South amidst a closely-knit family and a wide circle of caring and involved neighbors. She credits her family and neighborhood, along with her black church and teachers, with instilling in her a strong self-concept and a sense of dignity. Most importantly, Wade-Gayles focuses on the importance of the transmission of a rich culture from one generation to the next; she believes that the knowledge of being part of a wider culture—specifically a black culture with African roots—is essential for developing self-esteem. Wade-Gayles also describes her participation in the Civil Rights Movement and discusses the complications presented by black-white friendships and alliances. Johnetta Cole, President of Spelman, writes in the forward to this work that "the recollections of one black woman become the mirror into which each of us can see how alike and how different we are. We can encounter the exquisite diversity and amazing similarity in the human condition" (p. viii).

463. Walker, Margaret (1915-). *How I Wrote Jubilee and Other Essays on Life and Literature*. Ed. Maryemma Graham. New York: Feminist Press at The City University of New York, 1990. ISBN: 1558610030:1558610049.   157 pages; portrait; bibliography.

This is a collection of speeches and essays selected and edited by Maryemma Graham. The works in Part I: "Growing Out of Shadow" provide the most autobiographical information. They are entitled "Growing Out of Shadow," "How I Told My Child About Race," "Willing to Pay the Price," "Black Women in Academia," "Richard Wright," and "How I Wrote *Jubilee*." These essays portray Walker's encounter with racism from her earliest childhood experiences through adulthood, her struggles to support her family and complete her education, her friendship with Richard Wright, and the lifetime of work and experience that led up to her writing the noted civil war novel, *Jubilee*.

464. Walking Bull, Gilbert C. and Montana H. R. Walking Bull. *E-ha-ni Wo-e: In This Powerful Manner They Expressed Themselves Long Ago*. Monmouth, Oregon: Walking Bull, 1980. ISBN: none. 91 pages; photographs.

This book is divided between the stories and poems of Gilbert and Montana Walking Bull. Gilbert tells traditional Lakota stories as they were passed on to him, as well as stories from his own life. Montana presents fiction and poetry.

465. Walking Bull, Montana H. R.
See *Walking Bull, Gilbert C.*

466. Walters, Anna Lee (1946-). *Talking Indian: Reflections on Survival and Writing*. Ithaca, New York: Firebrand Books, 1992. ISBN: 1563410222:1563410214. 222 pages; photographs; bibliography.

This book, which was published by Walters to coincide with the Quincentennial of Columbus's arrival in the "new world," combines autobiography, fiction, traditional stories, and tribal history. Walters is both Pawnee and Otoe, and she lives with her Navajo husband and children on the Navajo Reservation in Arizona. She presents the tribal histories of each of these tribes and examines their separate oral-history traditions. Walters considers, in particular, the traditions of the Pawnee and Otoe and their influence on her subject matter and her presentation of material as a writer. The autobiographical segments relate her experiences as a very young child living with her grandparents, her early impression of the world being peopled only by Native Americans, the effect of realizing that the make-up of the larger world was not the warm comfortable community she had imagined it to be, and, then, how she learned to adjust to this realization while keeping a strong sense of her identity as an Otoe/Pawnee woman.

467. Ward, Alvin E. *Daze of My Life: From Darkness to the Marvelous Light*. Cleveland, Ohio: KAT Publication, 1993. ISBN: none. 106 pages; photographs.

Alvin Ward wrote this autobiography over a period of years while working two jobs and taking night classes. Raised by his deeply religious mother, Ward spent his childhood attending church meetings and street-corner revivals with her. He dropped out of school while in junior high and became a husband and father at an early age. His sense of responsibility and the difficulty in finding or keeping any kind of decent employment convinced him to return to school. Through a combination of formal and independent study, Ward eventually worked his way to both a high school and a college diploma. He writes of his work as a journalist, a founder and minister of the Anatholic Church of Christ, and a Congress of Racial Equality (CORE) activist in Cleveland, Ohio. While describing his own life, Ward also addresses the difficulties faced by African Americans in general and African American males in particular, especially in the areas of preparation for employment and the difficulty in finding work that can support a family, availability of decent affordable housing, and appropriate education and role models.

468. Washington, Jerome (1939-). *Beanfields*. Brooklyn: Wee D'People Unlimited, 1990. ISBN: none. 43 pages.

469. Washington, Paul M. *"Other Sheep I Have": The Autobiography of Father Paul M. Washington.* Written with David Gracie. Philadelphia: Temple University Press, 1994. ISBN: 1566391776:1566391784. 248 pages; photographs; bibliography.

Father Washington was dedicated to the ministry by his mother. He accepted this calling at the age of 10 and joined the Episcopal Church while in college, destined for priesthood. He arrived at the Church of the Advocate in North Philadelphia, following mission service in Liberia and prison ministry in Philadelphia. Father Washington presents an account of his work at Church of the Advocate, which became a meeting place for the Black Power Movement under his rectorship. Father Washington worked alongside of the Black Panthers, met with members of MOVE, and worked as an advocate for the residents of North Philadelphia. His dedication to nonviolence and the respect given him by the church establishment, with which he was often at odds, left him immune to FBI investigations. The Church of the Advocate under Father Washington was also instrumental in bringing to fruition the first ordinations of women in the Episcopal Church.

470. Watson, George. *Memorable Memoirs.* New York: Carlton Press, 1987. ISBN: none. 104 pages; photographs; documents.
Note: Reissued in 1993 and 1995.

George Watson, after a brief account of his childhood, describes the daily activities of the 96th Service Group, an all-Black regiment, during World War II. He provides details of daily life throughout their training period at the Tuskegee Air Force Base and the Oscoda Army Air Base, Oscoda, Michigan, and action in Italy from 1942 through 1945.

471. Weary, Dolphus (1946-). *I Ain't Comin Back.* Written with William Hendricks. Wheaton, Illinois: Tyndale House Publishers, 1990. ISBN: 0842316094. 166 pages.

Dolphus Weary grew up in Simpson County, Mississippi, during the 50s and 60s. He was anxious to escape the segregation and violent racism of Mississippi and so he along with a friend, accepted a scholarship to Los Angeles Baptist College. It was not until their arrival that they realized they were the first and only African Americans to attend the school. Weary describes how they learned first to tolerate stereotyping and racism, and then later to constructively confront it. After his ministerial training, Weary returned to Mississippi, although that had never been his intention, to work for change in his home county. He describes the work of Mendenhall Ministries to improve the conditions in the African American community and the organizational and personal struggles he encountered over the years.

472. Webb, Sheyann and Rachel West Nelson. *Selma, Lord, Selma: Girlhood Memories of the Civil-Rights Days.* As told to Frank Sikora. University, Alabama: University of Alabama Press, 1980. ISBN: 0817300317. 146 pages; photographs.
Note: Also published New York: W. Morrow, 1980. ISBN: 0688087442.

Sheyann Webb was eight and Rachel West nine when they became involved in the Selma voting rights marches led by Martin Luther King, Jr., and the Southern Christian Leadership Conference (SCLC). Rachel's parents were already committed to the cause and to participation in the marches and sit-ins, but Sheyann's were not deeply involved. Her parents, however, did allow her to participate as long as she didn't miss school and completed her homework. The demonstrations went on for several months throughout a rainy winter, and the girls got to know King as well as a number of visitors, white and black, who stayed in the homes of participants. The murders of two of these visitors made them aware of the fact that what they were doing could endanger their own lives. Sheyann's parents eventually joined the marchers and demonstrators, inspired by their young daughter's dedication.

473. Welcome, Verda F. *My Life and Times*. As told to James M. Abraham. Englewood Cliffs, New Jersey: Henry House Publishers, Inc., 1991. ISBN: none. 308 pages; photographs; bibliography.

Verda Welcome documents her political career in Maryland, which she began after her retirement from teaching and work as a community activist. She was part of the Colored Women's Democratic Club and helped to form the Fourth District Democratic Organization, which successfully set out to break the local political machine. Welcome was first elected to office in 1959 at the age of 52. She served through the turmoil of the Civil Rights Movement, surviving an assassination attempt in 1964. Welcome describes her political successes and failures and provides a broad picture of the times during which she was politically active, from the Civil Rights Movement, to Black Nationalism, to the Reagan Revolution.

474. Westmoreland, Tony (1915-). *In All Things I Am Not Alone: The True Life Story of a Sharecropper's Son*. Nashville: Winston-Derek Publishers, 1987. ISBN: 1555230598. 140 pages.

In this autobiography, Westmoreland relates the tragedies and successes of his family. Westmoreland grew up in Georgia with his father and mother who farmed and raised fourteen children. Among the several tragedies of his childhood were the shooting deaths of his mother and oldest brother by night-riding Klansmen. This tragedy was immediately followed by the unprecedented generosity of a white landowner who, after reading about the shootings, offered Westmoreland's father the opportunity to farm and harvest timber on his land. Westmoreland's father, who had always been a sharecropper, was also told to keep all of his crops and any profits which he gleaned from crops or timber. Westmoreland's life continued to follow this general pattern of alternate tragedy and good fortune. Some of the events which he writes about are his family's move to Chicago, his marriage, children, and his successful business career.

475. Whitewolf, Jim. *The Autobiography of a Kiowa Apache Indian*. Written with Charles S. Brant. New York: Dover Publications, 1991. ISBN: 0486268624. 144 pages; map; bibliography.
Originally published *Jim Whitewolf: The Life of a Kiowa Apache Indian*. New York: Dover Publications, 1969. 144 pages; bibliography; map. ISBN: 048622015X.

476. Wideman, John Edgar. *Brothers and Keepers*. New York: Holt, Rinehart and Winston, 1984. ISBN: 0030617545. 243 pages.
Note: Also published New York: Penguin, 1985. ISBN: 0140082670; New York: Vintage Books, 1995. ISBN: 0679756949.

This work touches on many issues—life in the ghetto, family relationships, prisons, crime, and the varying definitions of success. In this book, John Wideman's brother, Robby, is serving a life-sentence in prison for his part in a robbery which resulted in murder. Wideman, a successful novelist and college professor, seeks to uncover where his and his youngest brother's paths diverged from each other. Thus, *Brothers and Keepers* is both an autobiography—the reflections of John Wideman about who he is in relation to his family and particularly his brother Robby—and a biography of Robby. Much of what the reader learns about Robby is presented in the first person, with Robby as narrator. Wideman worked with his brother on this auto/biography during visiting sessions at Western Penitentiary. Drafts were mailed back and forth between them, and Robby sent letters and poems to John trying to clarify what passed between them in conversation. In telling his story to John, Robby not only describes the events leading up to his crime, but explains to his brother his motivation for choosing a life of "gangsterism," and debates whether or not his prison sentence was an inevitable result of all that went before.

477. —. *Fatheralong: A Meditation on Fathers and Sons, Race and Society*. New York: Pantheon, 1994. ISBN: 0679407200. 197 pages.

Wideman writes about his relationship with his father, about himself as a son, and about his own two sons. A Pennsylvanian by birth, Wideman's roots are in South Carolina, where he and his father return to do research and to look up family and others who might remember members of their family. Wideman places his father-son relationship within the broader context of society and discusses the obstacles that prevent fathers from fulfilling their role in a meaningful way. Wideman does not remember spending much time with his father, and their trip to South Carolina is their first time alone together. Wideman concludes with an essay about one son's wedding, and another about learning to live with the disappearance and probable kidnapping of his older son seven years earlier. About this book Wideman writes "[t]he pieces that follow on fathers, color, roots, time, language are about me, not my 'race.' They are an attempt, among other things, to break out, displace, replace, the paradigm of race. Teach me who I might be, who you might be—without it" (p. xxv).

478. Wier, Sadye H. (1905-). *Sadye H. Wier: Her Life and Work*. Written with George R. Lewis. Starkville, Mississippi (321 S. Lafayette St. 39759): S. H. Wier, 1993. ISBN: none. 128 pages; photographs; documents.
Note: Wier has also written about her husband in *A Black Businessman in White Mississippi 1886-1974*. Jackson, Mississippi: University Press of Mississippi, 1977. ISBN: 0878050426.

Wier describes her family, childhood, and education in Mississippi. Her father, a Methodist minister, established Noxubee Industrial School in 1898, which provided a much needed educational opportunity to African American children in Mississippi. Her mother taught home economics at the institution for over 40 years. Wier, like her mother, became a home economist and taught in elementary and secondary schools. In 1943 she became the first African American home demonstration agent for Newton County. Wier describes her work, the traveling it entailed, and the details of the skills she sought to teach her clients:

sewing, food preparation, hygiene, and budgeting. She also discusses her community activities, including the restoration and preservation of the Odd Fellows Cemetery in Starkville, Mississippi.

479. Wilbur-Cruce, Eva Antonia. *A Beautiful, Cruel Country.* Wood engravings by Michael McCurdy. Tucson: University of Arizona Press, 1987. ISBN: 0816510296. 318 pages.

Wilbur-Cruce began this book as a fifty-page letter to her nephews and nieces to provide them with an account of her life on the family ranch in Arizona along the Mexican border. She enjoyed writing the letter so much that she decided to continue writing. This book describes her childhood and ranch life at the turn-of-the-century. The ranch, which she inherited and where she lived throughout her life, was situated in a mountainous, arid region which was also the homeland of the Tohono O'odham Indians (Papago) until they were forcibly relocated to a reservation. Wilbur-Cruce recalls the many adventures, events, scenes, and celebrations of her childhood. She roamed freely around the country side and assisted her father with the herding of goats, horses, and cattle. She closes the story of her childhood with a description of the Tohono O'odham exodus and the coinciding rise of "Anglo" intolerance toward the "Hispanics" living in the region.

480. Wilkins, Roger W. (1932-). *A Man's Life: An Autobiography.* New York: Simon & Schuster, 1982. ISBN: 0671226738:0671492683. 384 pages; photographs.
Note: Also published Woodbridge Connecticut: Ox Bow Press, 1991. ISBN: 0918024838.

Wilkins, a journalist and the nephew of NAACP executive Roy Wilkins, began his career of political and social activism as a law clerk under Thurgood Marshall with the NAACP just after the *Brown v. Topeka Board of Education* decision was handed down by the U.S. Supreme Court. Following a brief stint with a commercial law firm in the suburbs, Wilkins decided to pursue, instead, work which would have more of a direct impact on the welfare of society and African Americans in particular. In his book, Wilkins focuses on his work with the Kennedy and Johnson administrations. In these administrations, he worked with AID (Agency for International Development), the Department of Justice, and as director of the Community Action division of the Community Relations Service throughout the Civil Rights and Vietnam War eras. He describes the details of his work in these departments, including his responsibilities during especially tense times, such as the Watts and Detroit riots of 1967, and the hours and days following the assassination of Martin Luther King, Jr. Wilkins also writes about his personal life during his political career, and the toll the demands of his job took on his roles as father and husband. He relates the events of the dissolution of his marriage, and his personal life following the breakup and his subsequent remarriage.

481. Wilkins, Roy (1901-). *Standing Fast: The Autobiography of Roy Wilkins*. Written with Tom Mathews. New York: Viking Press, 1982. ISBN: 0670142298. 361 pages; photographs.
Note: Also published New York: Penguin, 1984. ISBN: 0140073736; New York: Da Capo Press, 1994. ISBN: 0306805669.

Wilkins writes about his family's slave origins in Mississippi, and how the joy of emancipation was overshadowed almost immediately by the Mississippi legislature's passage of the Black Code. These and other southern laws which circumscribed the movements of the African Americans, both newly freed and historically free, were to be supported by test cases in the Supreme Court, leading Wilkins to write that "[i]f the Civil War liberated Grandfather Wilkins, the Supreme Court had circumscribed his possibilities" (p. 2). It was within the Supreme Court, however, that Wilkins would pursue an end to these laws as a member and participant, and later as Executive Director of the NAACP. Wilkins's work on behalf of African Americans began with his career in journalism. Then, at a certain point, he wanted to begin fighting crimes against African Americans, rather than just passively reporting them.   Thus began his work with the NAACP. Wilkins discusses some of his major battles, including unsuccessful attempts to persuade Franklin D. Roosevelt to support anti-lynching legislation, work with the War Department to include African Americans in a meaningful way during World War II, and, of course, the Civil Rights Movement. Wilkins defends the NAACP's use of the court system against the attacks brought against him and others by the younger Black Nationalist movement. He points out that the NAACP had been involved in pursuing the rights of African Americans since the first decades of the century, and that this work should not be dismissed or ignored. He writes that "we realized in the summer of 1966, as we had in the winter of 1909, that racial discrimination corrupts every area of American life" (p. 321).

482. Williams, Patricia J. (1951-). *The Alchemy of Race and Rights*. Cambridge: Harvard University Press, 1991. ISBN: 0674014707. 263 pages; bibliography.
Note: Also published London: Virago, 1993. ISBN: 1853816744.

This collection of essays is both autobiographical and theoretical, about both contemporary and historical conditions and events. Williams' essays reflect her experiences with and observations of racism, discrimination and ignorance within a legal and feminist perspective. She suggests that "Autobiography," "fiction," "Gender Studies," and "Medieval Medicine," would make good subject headings for this work. Williams writes that her book is not just about race, but about boundaries: "While being black has been the most powerful social attribution in my life, it is only one of a number of governing narratives or presiding fictions by which I am constantly reconfiguring myself in the world" (p. 257). Williams also lists gender, ecology, pacifism, "my peculiar brand of colloquial English, and Roxbury, Massachusetts" (p. 257) as defining, boundary-creating factors in her life.

483. Wilson, Woodrow. *Woodrow Wilson: Race, Community and Politics in Las Vegas, 1940's-1980's: An Oral History*. An oral history conducted by Jamie Coughtry. Edited by Jamie Coughtry and R. T. King. Reno: Oral History Program, University of Nevada-Reno, 1990. ISBN: none. 147 pages; photographs.

Born in Mississippi in 1915, Wilson found himself, almost by accident, residing in Las Vegas, Nevada. "I was passing through . . . I'd stay for a year maybe . . . but I got involved with the total community—religiously, politically, helping to bring about change. There was a tremendous challenge here for anybody black who had something to give" (p. 53). Wilson was active in union activities: fighting promotion restrictions and segregated conditions. He continued his fight for increased civil rights for African Americans through leadership in the local NAACP and, in 1966, by being the first African American to be elected to the Nevada legislature.

484. Wolf, Helen Pease (1906-). *Reaching Both Ways*. Written with Barbara Ketcham. Laramie, Wyoming: Jelm Mountain Publications, 1989. ISBN: 0936204664. 125 pages; photographs.

Helen Pease Wolf grew up in the area of Lodge Grass, Montana, on the Crow Indian Reservation. Her parents were half Crow and half European American—Hidatsa through Wolf's mother and Absaroka through her father: both grew up in Crow villages. Wolf gives a brief history of the Crow Indians, describing Crow customs and relating several Crow legends. She also writes about the history of Lodge Grass, her own life, and her Crow and European family. Wolf, raised in a strong Baptist tradition, writes about traditional Crow religious practices and concludes that "[t]he Crows know in their own hearts that their prayers are heard by the same Great Spirit that hears your prayers, whether you are Protestant, Jewish, Catholic, or any other religious faith!" (p. 85). Wolf is proud of both parts of her heritage and ends her narrative by writing: "And so even in my eighties, I am part of the outdoor world of the Indian and the modern lifestyle of a white woman. I am still reaching both ways" (p. 118).

485. Wright, Al. *Al Wright: Minto*. Interviews conducted and text prepared by Yvonne Yarber and Curt Madison. Yukon-Koyukuk Biography Series. Fairbanks: Spirit Mountain Press, 1986. ISBN: 0910871140.

Wright discusses his life as a pilot, wilderness guide, hunter and fisherman. He emphasizes the effect of fish and game regulations on the Native subsistence hunters and fishermen and the conflicting interest of sports and commercial fisherman with those of the subsistence fishermen. Wright also touches on the damage done to lakes and streams because of the silt build-up which is a result of mining activities. Wright and his wife, who live during the winters in Kona, Hawaii, and the rest of the year in the Fairbanks area, hunt, fish, and grow and gather all of their own food. According to Wright "[t]he future looks like steady motoring back and forth between Fairbanks and Kona and trying to grow, catch and hunt as much of our own food as possible. That's important to us no matter where we're living" (Epilogue, p. 71).

486. Wright, Richard (1908-1960). "Black Boy (American Hunger)." *Later Works: Black Boy (American Hunger), the Outsider*. Ed. Arnold Rampersad. The Library of America 56. New York: Library of America, 1991. ISBN: 0940450674. 365 pages.
Note: Also published by New York: Harper Perennial, 1993. ISBN: 0060812508.

Originally published as two separate books, Wright's initial intention was that his autobiography be published as a single volume divided into two parts: "Southern Night" and "The Horror and the Glory." Because of negotiations with the Book-of-the-Month Club, only "Southern Night" was published, with the title *Black Boy: A Record of Childhood and Youth* (New York: Harper & Bros., 1945). "The Horror and the Glory" was not published until 1977 (New York: Harper & Row, 1977, New York: Perennial Library/Harper & Row, 1979) as *American Hunger*. This classic work describes Wright's childhood in the South and his move to Chicago at the age of 19. A significant portion of Part Two is devoted to his experiences with the Communist Party and his development as a writer.

487. Wu, Blanche Ching-Yi. *East Meets West*. Baltimore: R. C. Huang, 1985. ISBN: none. 153 pages; photographs; illustrations.

Wu's first trip to the United States was a leave-of-absence from China's Ginling College to further her education at the University of Michigan in Ann Arbor. She was in Nanking for the Japanese invasion of 1932 and after the bombing of Pearl Harbor. In 1948, she came once more to the U.S., again planning to study and then return to China, but became a U.S. citizen instead. Wu worked in the poultry laboratory at Virginia Polytechnic at Blacksburg, and discusses her research both at Virginia and at Ginling College. Wu describes her research, her studies in Kentucky and elsewhere, her teaching career, and her retirement.

488. Wyman, Russell E. (1950-). *The Stumpin Grounds: A Memoir of New Orleans' Ninth Ward*. Monograph (Southern University in New Orleans. Center for African and African American Studies) 1. New Orleans: Southern University at New Orleans, Center for African and African American Studies, 1993. ISBN: none. 36 pages; map; bibliography.

Russell Wyman writes about his life during the years 1961, when he was 11, to 1965. He describes his interests and motivations, and his family life and friends. Wyman gives a vivid account of the destruction of his neighborhood, in the lower Ninth Ward of New Orleans, by Hurricane Betsy. In a postscript, Wyman chronicles the later years in his life, which included enlistment in the army during the Vietnam War, involvement with the Black Panther Party in Oceanside California, drug abuse, and armed robbery, for which he served 17 years in prison.

489. Yasui, Robert S. *The Yasui Family of Hood River, Oregon*. N.p.: Holly Yasui Desktop Publishing, 1987. ISBN: none. 148 pages.

In this family history, Yasui devotes a chapter each to his mother, father, six brothers and sisters, and himself. In his chapter, Yasui describes the manner in which he was raised, his parents' business and work ethic, and his schooling and participation in sports. Yasui was in college when the evacuations began, and he chose to "escape" to Denver to avoid internment. Yasui recounts the problems he encountered because of race. Temple University accepted him after he wrote to the dean describing the difficulties he was having with the other schools to which he had applied. Yasui finishes his chapter with an account of his medical training and career. About the emotional impact of the war, Yasui writes:

> For many years after the war, many of us were subconsciously ashamed of the fact that our own government had so mistrusted us that it accused us of constituting a serious subversive danger, removed us from our homes and placed us in internment camps. We felt guilt and shame that remained with us for years. We did not tell our children about this dreadful experience. (p. x)

490. Yates, James. *Mississippi to Madrid: Memoir of a Black American in the Abraham Lincoln Brigade*. Seattle: Open Hand, 1989. ISBN: 0940880199:0940880202. 183 pages; photographs; maps.
Note: Also published as *Mississippi to Madrid: Memoirs of a Black American in the Spanish Civil War, 1936-1938*. New York: Shamal Books, 1986. ISBN: 0917886127.

Yates wrote this book as one of just a handful of surviving black soldiers who served in the Abraham Lincoln Brigade during the Spanish Civil War. He presents not only his own story, but documents the participation of nearly 100 African Americans who risked their lives to defend the democratically-elected government of Spain even though American participation had been prohibited by the federal government. Struggling to work and support his family during the

Great Depression, Yates left Chicago for New York in hopes of better employment opportunities. He found none, and was discovered on a park bench in a wine-induced stupor by Communist organizers. Having noticed him reading Du Bois on a previous day, they felt that he might be a candidate for their organization. He thus became a full-time participant and organizer in the Communist Party. This association led to his decision to join the fight against Fascism in Spain. Yates describes his experiences in Spain, his associates—both black and white, American and European, and years free of discrimination and segregation. The Abraham Lincoln Brigade was integrated, and African Americans had the same opportunities and responsibilities as white Americans. Coming back to the United States was shocking for Yates as well as the other African American soldiers when they were once again confronted with discrimination, lack of opportunity, segregation and accompanying humiliation and degradation. Yates realized, upon his return, that his part in the war in Spain might be over, but there was another war still to fight in the United States.

491. Yee, Albert H. *A Search for Meaning: Essays of a Chinese American*. San Francisco: Chinese Historical Society of America, 1984. ISBN: none. 311 pages; photographs; bibliography.

This book is a series of essays describing the author's experiences, lessons learned, and reflections. Yee was born during the Great Depression and was a fourth generation American. He writes of the economic hardships which his family faced during that time, coupled with the racism they faced in school and in seeking employment. In this collection of essays, Yee explores Chinese history and thought, his own reassessment of China, and of himself as a Chinese American, and the issue of race in the United States.

492. Yellowtail, Thomas. *Yellowtail, Crow Medicine Man and Sun Dance Chief: An Autobiography*. As told to Michael Oren Fitzgerald. Norman: University of Ok-

lahoma Press, 1991. ISBN: 0806123338:0806126027. 241 pages; photographs; map; bibliography.

Yellowtail sees this book as a partial fulfillment of his "responsibility to pass on [his] sacred knowledge" (p. 10). In the first part of this book, Yellowtail describes his childhood within the context of the traditions and ceremonies which were still a central part of the daily life of his tribe. The tribe became divided with the introduction of Christianity. Younger generations became less inclined to learn traditional ways and, if they did, tended not to understand the significance of what they were doing. By 1943, traditional dancing had all but died out. Yellowtail, with some others, began a revival within his own tribe and believes this effort may have sparked a nationwide revival. Yellowtail describes the difference between the Peyote way and the Sun Dance way. He has found that the Sun Dance way provides the opportunity for unlimited spiritual growth. Yellowtail became a Sun Dance chief and has now passed that position on to a younger follower. In the second part of this book Yellowtail provides a detailed description and explanation of the Sun Dance ceremony, and in the third section draws conclusions about the conditions and future of tribal life in the United States.

493. Yep, Lawrence. *The Lost Garden*. In My Own Words. Englewood Cliffs, New Jersey: J. Messner, 1991. ISBN: 0671741594:0671741608. 117 pages; photographs.
Note: Also published New York: Macmillan/McGraw Hill School Publishing Co., 1993. ISBN: 0021795495.

Yep describes growing up believing himself to be an American. In school, however, he faced racism from classmates and teachers alike. It wasn't until he began making regular visits to his grandmother in San Francisco's Chinatown that he began not only to accept, but to appreciate his "Chineseness." Yep tells how elements of his life, and people he has known have provided material for his books.

494. Yoneda, Karl G. (1906-). *Ganbatte: Sixty-Year Struggle of a Kibei Worker.* Los Angeles: Resource Development and Publications, Asian American Studies Center, University of California, Los Angeles, 1983. ISBN: 0934052077. 244 pages; photographs.

Yoneda was one the first children born in the continental United States to Japanese immigrant parents. He embraced Communism at an early age and has continued to fight for the rights of working people throughout his life. Yoneda's autobiography documents his and his wife's struggle "for political, economic, [and] social justice and for racial equality as a Communist, trade-unionist, longshoreman, antifascist fighter, writer, and Japanese American" (Introduction, p. XI). Yoneda's strength of character is clearly illustrated by the fact that he was active in trade unionism at a time when Asians were not permitted to be members of most trade unions. Yoneda closes his acknowledgments with the following explanation:

> One of the reasons for writing my story is to let [my son and two granddaughters] and others, especially Asian Pacific youth, know about the many years of struggle that innumerable working people of all races have participated in to find the path to establish ultimately a society in a world of peace and human dignity.

495. Yoshitsu, Masao. *My Moments in the Twentieth Century: An Immigrant's Story.* New York: Vantage Press, 1987. ISBN: 0533072646. 83 pages; photographs.

Masao Yoshitsu was raised in Japan and joined his father in Modesto, California, in 1921, making the 5,000 mile ocean voyage to the United States at the age of 13. The weeks spent on board the ocean liner provided Yoshitsu with his first contact with the West. Starting out in the first grade, Yoshitsu quickly caught up with his own age group, went on to high school, and attended Stanford. Yoshitsu writes that his Stanford economics degree was of no use to him as a Japanese American. It was not until after the war, when legislation was passed to allow Asian immigrants to become naturalized citizens, that Yoshitsu found employment in the field of his choice. Yoshitsu describes his years struggling to support his family with the limited employment opportunities available to Japanese Americans before finally being admitted into the civil service, where he worked with the Navy, the aerospace program, and the United States Department of Health, Education and Welfare.

496. Young, Andrew (1932-). *A Way Out of No Way: The Spiritual Memoirs of Andrew Young*. Nashville: T. Nelson Publishers, 1994. ISBN: 0840769989. 172 pages; bibliography.

Andrew Young presents the significant milestones, decisions, and events in his life in the context of his religious convictions. He describes the individuals, institutions, and situations responsible for his choosing his particular path in life, beginning with his entrance into college at the age of 15, through his attaining the position of consultant with an international law firm. Young, a member of the Congregational Church, attended Hartford Seminary and became a minister. He joined the Civil Rights Movement and worked closely with Martin Luther King. After King's death, Young continued to work with the Southern Christian Leadership Conference (SCLC), and later became a United States Congressman, the United Nations Ambassador under President Jimmy Carter, and then Mayor of Atlanta.

497. Young, Coleman A. *Hard Stuff: The Autobiography of Coleman Young*. Written with Lonnie Wheeler. New York: Viking, 1994. ISBN: 0670845515. 344 pages; photographs; bibliography.

Coleman Young, the five-term mayor of Detroit, looks back on his life and career as he decides not to run for reelection. Young describes his experiences in the segregated armed services of World War II and the rebellious spirit of many of the African American soldiers faced with continual indignities. He writes about his participation in radical politics, for which he was blacklisted from employment in Michigan's automotive industry and questioned before the infamous House

Un-American Activities Committee. Young addresses the many controversial aspects of his long tenure as Mayor of Detroit and his reasons for retirement from office.

498. Young Bear, Ray A. (1950-). *Black Eagle Child: The Face-paint Narratives*. Singular Lives Series. Iowa City: University of Iowa Press, 1992. ISBN: 08774536X: 087745378. 261 pages; photographs.
Note: Also published New York: Grove Press, 1996. ISBN: 0802134289.

This book is a coming-of-age story, an epic mixture of poetry and prose based on Young Bear's own life during the 1950s, 60s, and 70s. Edgar Bearchild represents Young Bear as he struggles through adolescence and develops into a poet. The Black Eagle Child Settlement is the Mesquaki Settlement where Young Bear grew up, located in Tama County in central Iowa. Young Bear writes that the characters and events in this work are taken both from his own experience and from his imagination. What he presents here to the reader is not so much personal revelation as "an exercise in creative detachment . . . there are considerations of visions, traditional healing, supernaturalism, and hallucinogen-based sacraments interposed with centuries-old philosophies and customs." Young Bear's youthful odyssey begins when he is in eighth grade, continues through a variety of relationships, a number of drug-inspired visions in Southern California, and then brings him back to the settlement in Iowa, where he wraps himself in a "paper cocoon," from which he recalls his childhood and develops his writer's voice. He writes: "Childhood was a precious epoch./How I even ever came to be confounded me./It was incredible to think back and see faces/of people who were no longer. I saw these/as warm, windy days when families were strong/and united. My survival was more than a miracle./And I was in a rage for my inability to find/ways to say thank you" (p. 149).

499. Young Bear, Severt (1934-1993). *Standing in the Light: A Lakota Way of Seeing*. Written with R. D. Theisz.

American Indian Lives. Lincoln: University of Nebraska Press, 1994. ISBN: 080324911X. 191 pages; photographs; bibliography; maps.

Young Bear provides a history of the Lakota as well as a treatise of their rituals, traditions, and cultural practices. He discusses the significance of names, explaining the history of names in his own family; relates stories from Lakota oral tradition; and explains the importance of singing, including a history of the Porcupine Singers, of which he was a member. Young Bear writes about his development as a singer and the positive changes that occurred in his life because of his dedication to this art form. He encouraged the resurrection of many Sun Dance songs and began incorporating them into the ceremonies. In discussing the dances, songs, and the ceremonies in which these traditional arts are practiced, Young Bear also tells the history of the U.S. Government's interference with sacred practices, which caused dedicated practitioners to go underground and discouraged others from participating in and passing on these traditions. Young Bear also had connections to the American Indian Movement (AIM) and was present at the 1973 Wounded Knee occupation.

Index

Abenaki Indians 69
Abraham Lincoln Brigade, Spanish Civil War 490
Absaroka Indians 96, 484, 492
Acoma Pueblo Indians 329
actors 88, 201, 414, 430
adoption 111
affirmative action 76
African American 1, 2, 3, 4, 8, 10, 12, 13, 15, 16, 17, 18, 19, 20, 21,
22, 23, 24, 25, 26, 27, 31, 32, 34, 35, 39, 40, 41, 42, 43, 44,
45, 46, 47, 51, 52, 53, 56, 60, 61, 64, 65, 66, 67, 68, 70, 72,
73, 74, 76, 77, 80, 81, 85, 86, 87, 89, 93, 95, 97, 102, 103,
104, 106, 107, 108, 110, 114, 115, 117, 123, 124, 125, 126,
127, 128, 133, 134, 135, 137, 141, 145, 146, 147, 149, 150,
151, 153, 154, 158, 159, 160, 162, 163, 164, 165, 167, 169,
171, 173, 174, 177, 178, 185, 186, 187, 188, 192, 194, 195,
196, 200, 201, 202, 203, 205, 206, 207, 213, 214, 215, 216,
217, 218, 221, 222, 223, 224, 225, 226, 232, 235, 236, 242,
243, 245, 247, 252, 253, 254, 258, 263, 264, 267, 269, 272,
276, 278, 279, 283, 284, 285, 286, 287, 288, 289, 292, 298,
300, 302, 303, 304, 305, 306, 311, 312, 313, 315, 318, 321,
322, 328, 337, 338, 339, 340, 342, 343, 344, 347, 348, 351,
353, 354, 356, 357, 359, 362, 366, 367, 368, 369, 370, 371,
378, 379, 386, 388, 389, 391, 392, 393, 397, 399, 407, 408,
412, 413, 414, 419, 426, 427, 428, 429, 431, 432, 434, 435,
438, 440, 441, 442, 445, 447, 455, 462, 463, 467, 468, 469,
470, 471, 472, 473, 474, 476, 477, 478, 480, 481, 482, 483,
486, 488, 490, 496, 497
African American literature 357
African Methodist Episcopal (A.M.E.) Church 178, 247
African Methodist Episcopal (A.M.E.) Zion Church 247, 388
AIDS 26, 454